DRAGONS TEETH

By Michael Wilding

Milton's Paradise Lost (1969)
Marvell: Modern Judgements (ed.) (1969)
Cultural Policy in Great Britain (with Michael Green)
    (1970)
The Portable Marcus Clarke (ed.) (1976)
Marcus Clarke (1977)
William Lane: The Workingman's Paradise (ed.)
    (1980)
Political Fictions (1980)

DRAGONS TEETH

*Literature in the
English Revolution*

MICHAEL WILDING

CLARENDON PRESS · OXFORD
1987

Oxford University Press, Walton Street, Oxford OX2 6DP
Oxford New York Toronto
Delhi Bombay Calcutta Madras Karachi
Petaling Jaya Singapore Hong Kong Tokyo
Nairobi Dar es Salaam Cape Town
Melbourne Auckland
and associated companies in
Beirut Berlin Ibadan Nicosia

Oxford is a trade mark of Oxford University Press

Published in the United States
by Oxford University Press, New York

British Library Cataloguing in Publication Data
Wilding, Michael, 1942-
Dragons teeth: literature in the English
Revolution.
1. English literature—Early modern,
1500–1700—History and criticism
I. Title
820.9′ 004 PR431
ISBN 0-19-812881-9

Library of Congress Cataloging in Publication Data
Wilding, Michael.
Dragons teeth: literature in the English Revolution.
1. English literature—Early modern, 1500–1700—
History and criticism. 2. Great Britain—History—
Puritan Revolution, 1642–1660—Literature and the
revolution. 3. Puritans in literature. 4. Politics
in literature. 5. Revolutionary literature, English—
History and criticism. I. Title.
PR435.W5 1987 820′.9′358 86-33159
ISBN 0-19-812881-9

Phototypeset by Dobbie Typesetting Service,
Plymouth, Devon
Printed in Great Britain
at the University Printing House, Oxford
by David Stanford
Printer to the University

To H. Neville Davies

For Books are not absolutely dead things, but doe contain a potencie of life in them to be as active as that soule was whose progeny they are; nay they do preserve as in a violl the purest efficacie and extraction of that living intellect that bred them. I know they are as lively, and as vigorously productive, as those fabulous Dragons teeth; and being sown up and down, may chance to spring up armed men.

Milton, *Areopagitica* (*CPW* ii. 492)

CONTENTS

ABBREVIATIONS

CPW   *Complete Prose Works of John Milton*, ed. Don M. Wolfe; i (New Haven and London, 1953); iii (New Haven, 1962); iv (New Haven and London, 1966); v (New Haven, 1971); vii (rev. edn, New Haven and London, 1980)

ELH   *Journal of English Literary History*

ELN   *English Language Notes*

JEGP   *Journal of English and Germanic Philology*

JWCI   *Journal of the Warburg and Courtauld Institutes*

MLN   *Modern Language Notes*

N & Q   *Notes and Queries*

PBA   *Proceedings of the British Academy*

PMLA   *Publications of the Modern Language Association of America*

RES   *Review of English Studies*

1

Introduction

I remember from when I was a child a neighbour's gatestop, a cannon ball from the battle of Worcester. They were often enough ploughed up, solid memorials of the historical. When Cromwell's 'crowning victory' was commemorated after three hundred years with a plaque on the canal bridge, the faithful city divided again with a fierce intensity.[1] The English Civil War and Revolution have been the focus of class, political, and religious tensions not only at their historical moment, but in their ensuing cultural transmissions. T. S. Eliot wrote in 1947:

The fact is simply that the Civil War of the seventeenth century, in which Milton is a symbolic figure, has never been concluded. The Civil War is not ended: I question whether any serious civil war does end. Throughout that period English society was so convulsed and divided that the effects are still felt.[2]

Yet it was Eliot in his essays on Marvell and Milton who did so much to depoliticize the work of those writers who were actively involved in the revolution.[3] The depoliticizing approach followed by Eliot was adopted as a pervasive model for modern literary studies. The way in which this depoliticization was perpetuated by F. R. Leavis and the *Scrutiny* group in Britain and the Commonwealth, and by the New Criticism of Cleanth Brooks and others in the United States of America, and in succession to them by the varieties of structuralists and post-structuralists, has been well documented and does not need to be rehearsed again here.[4] Nor does it need to be

[1] See further J. W. Willis Bund, *The Civil War in Worcestershire, 1642–1646; and The Scotch Invasion of 1651* (1905) (Gloucester, 1979).
[2] T. S. Eliot, *On Poetry and Poets* (London, 1957), p. 178.
[3] John Gross, *Rise and Fall of the Man of Letters* (Harmondsworth, 1973), pp. 137–8. T. S. Eliot, *Selected Essays* (London, 1961), pp. 292–304 (Marvell); id., *On Poetry and Poets*, pp. 138–61 (Milton).
[4] Francis Mulhern, *The Moment of Scrutiny* (London, 1979); Frank Lentricchia, *After the New Criticism* (London, 1980); Terry Eagleton, *Literary Theory* (Oxford, 1983).

demonstrated again that these formalist, ostensibly purely literary, apolitical critical readings have often been the expression of a deeply reactionary politics, an ideology of the apolitical to attempt the suppression of a politically radical literary tradition.

Dragons Teeth: Literature in the English Revolution is an attempt to retrieve the repressed context, historical and political, of some of the major texts of the English Revolution, and to offer an enriched critical reading. I have attempted to politicize and historicize, but I have not offered a political or historical study of the writing of the revolutionary period. The essays are critical readings. It seemed possible to begin with accepted critical methods, with a close reading designed to elicit rather than prevent political and social meanings. With the political, my assumption was that certain political issues persist, that a reading of literary texts which brought out issues of the English Revolution would have a relevance for contemporary political issues. The issues raised by war, the critiques of militarism that can be found in both Milton's and Samuel Butler's writings, have an enduring relevance. But a fuller political reading requires the detail of historical specificity. And an increasing immersion in the historical and social detail raises the issue of 'background', ultimately questioning that whole positioning of history and politics as 'background'; the background becomes foreground, the repressed issues emerge. The traditional reading can soon become overlaid with supporting citation, lengthy commentary can be assembled on lines omitted from the text; but such absurdities and inelegancies break through methodological taboos and allow the repressed to emerge. In order to defamiliarize, in order to circumvent the consensus of non-political readings, new points of entry and departure can be taken: the printing error, the head-note to the poem, the marginal can often open up obscured meanings. The significant absence can illuminate the enigmatic.[5] Rather than looking for overall political allegory or structure at a time of censorship, repression, and ready reprisal, it can sometimes be more profitable to assemble a network of allusions, to establish a field of potentially political reference, a texture of allusion, than to try to discover a sustained political critique.

My methods have been eclectic. The relationships of literature and politics in the English revolutionary period are still actively under

---

[5] Pierre Macherey, *A Theory of Literary Production* (London, 1978), pp. 82 ff.

inquiry. To follow too schematic an approach would be to produce too schematic an account. And political commitments are not always schematic in the individual writer. There are contradictory positions, sedimented layers of past attitudes, some still held, some held no longer, some problematic and in process of transformation.[6] In repressive times, indeed in most times, writers have found it not always wise to be politically unambiguous in print. We need to be aware of tactical concessions, obscurities, ambiguities. It should not be necessary to add that to be concerned with political and historical issues is not to be unconcerned with formal issues. On the contrary, it is that very interest in the pleasure of the language of the poem that directs the serious reader to the political and historical, to the defining and shaping context, social and literary, to the constraints and taboos, within which the text is formed.

The effect of the attacks on Milton by Eliot and Leavis was to suggest his isolation, his literariness.[7] Arguing that he wrote from literary conventions, that he never observed the world around him, that he did not have Shakespeare's or Keats's or Donne's immediate reaction to sense-experience, they presented an image of Milton as a literary, classics-oriented, insensitive figure, utterly isolated from the world by choice and blindness. On the contrary, he was someone who spent twenty years of his life in political pamphleteering and controversy, went blind in part as a result of his work for the republican administration, had some of his writings burnt publicly by the hangman at the Restoration. It is important to remember that Milton was a deeply involved political figure; and, remembering this, we can then find aspects of his political commitment in his poetry.

To use Milton's polemical tracts of the 1640s to illuminate his poems of the pre-revolutionary 1630s is not an illegitimate approach; it is the approach that would have been taken by his contemporaries when his early poems were published with *A Maske* in 1645. To see his mature political tracts echoed in *Paradise Lost* and *Paradise Regained* is a similarly enriching procedure, illumining the great poems as the unchanged revolutionary values are reasserted. We can

[6] Frederic Jameson, *Fables of Aggression: Wyndham Lewis, The Modernist as Fascist* (Berkeley, 1979), p. 140.

[7] F. R. Leavis, *Revaluation* (London, 1936); id., *The Common Pursuit*, (London, 1952). T. S. Eliot, *On Poetry and Poets*.

find that *Paradise Lost* has immediately relevant and urgent things to communicate to us today about war, about militarism, about political manipulation, about authority, about equality. Rather than seeing Milton's years of writing propaganda for the Commonwealth as an impediment between his aim and the achievement of his great poetic work, let us rather look at the poetry in the context of that period of political engagement. When Milton refers to 'my unpremeditated verse' in *Paradise Lost* (ix. 24) we might remember the demand for extempore prayers from the radical Puritans;[8] when he asserts the doctrine of the inner light, we might remember that this is 'the essence of radical individualism';[9] when he chooses the name 'oracle of God' for the temple of Jerusalem, we might note how 'he emphasises prophetic rather than institutional Christianity'.[10] His very decision to write *Paradise Lost* in English 'was a radically political act—an assertion of bourgeois Protestant nationalism over classical and aristocratic culture, or rather an assertive appropriation of those classical modes for historically progressive ends.'[11]

For his contemporaries and for the eighteenth century, Andrew Marvell was almost exclusively known as a politician of probity, a defender of liberty, and a satirist—qualities neglected by twentieth century admirers of his lyrics. There is a prevalent assumption of an incompatibility between politics and poetry, and Marvell is adduced as a representative example. 'Political commitment coincided with the end of Marvell's greatest poetic achievements. Politics, the art of the possible, compelled him to surrender much of the subtlety and complexity that had characterized his lyrics.'[12] Yet there is no surrender of subtlety and complexity in the political 'An Horation Ode on Cromwell's Return from Ireland', even if the political component has often been played down. 'Upon Appleton House', a poem of extraordinary richness and complexity, contains rich and

---

[8] Izaak Walton, 'Life of Sanderson' (1678) in *Lives of John Donne, Sir Henry Wotton, Richard Hooker, George Herbert and Robert Sanderson* (London, 1973), p. 382; cf. ibid., pp. 393–4.

[9] Christopher Hill, *The World Turned Upside Down* (Harmondsworth, 1975), p. 409.

[10] William Kerrigan, *The Prophetic Milton* (Charlottesville, 1974), p. 127.

[11] Terry Eagleton, *Criticism and Ideology* (London, 1976), p. 56.

[12] G. de F. Lord, ed., *Andrew Marvell: Complete Poetry* (New York, 1968; London, 1984), p. xii.

complex political themes. To rehistoricize, to repoliticize Marvell's poetry is to see how extraordinarily skilled and complex and subtle his work is.

Not only the revolutionary Milton and Marvell, but also the conservatives Browne and Butler have been reduced and misrepresented through this prevalent exclusion of the political and the historical in critical readings. Browne's ideological position has been misrepresented, his political commitment underemphasized. Butler, once so popular a poet, has now been elided from the syllabuses. It is as if his uncomfortable politics could not be denied, so he was simply dropped from discussion.

I have discussed texts covering some fifty years from before, during, and after the Civil War and revolutionary period. Not only do the literary productions of the Restoration show a reflection on the events of the Revolution and Civil War, but the concerns and grievances that issued in revolution are to be found in the writings of the years before the Revolution. I begin with looking at Milton's early poems from the 1620s and 1630s, and follow chronologically with readings of Browne's *Religio Medici*, Marvell, and *Hudibras* and *Paradise Lost*, to conclude with *Paradise Regained* and *Samson Agonistes* of 1671. The texts chosen are the recurrent and accepted ones of the educational syllabus. Unfolding their political implications, their historical context, and their contemporary relevance is a necessary and inevitable result of an engagement in literary studies. Earlier versions of some of this material have appeared in *Approaches to Sir Thomas Browne*, ed. C. A. Patrides; *Restoration Literature*, ed. Harold Love; *Modern Language Review*; *Trivium* (Essays in Honour of Peter Davidson); *The Radical Reader*; and *The Teaching of English*.

This volume is but part of a wider movement of ideas, a rereading of the classic literary texts with a renewed awareness of their historical situation and their political implications. I have drawn on the continuing critical tradition of such an approach, a tradition sometimes as obscured and repressed as the politics with which it deals, but always retrievable and continuing. In such a collaborative enterprise to name names would be at the least invidious. My specific debts to published work are recorded in the notes, though my indebtedness to the work of my colleagues and predecessors in this area is obviously greater than to specific points. The great debt is to the spirit of the writers themselves. As Wordsworth wrote in 'London, 1802'

> Milton! thou should'st be living at this hour:
> England hath need of thee.

2

Milton's Early Radicalism

How radical was the young Milton? Can we find evidence of a political commitment in the poetry associated with his Cambridge years? Is there anything in the early work that looks forward to the revolutionary?

Milton's *Poems* of 1645 has generally been seen as an unpolitical or apolitical volume, as embodying Milton's youthful poems of the age before the revolution. For those who find the image of Milton the revolutionary politically embarrassing, it is still possible to preserve Milton in the pantheon of great literary figures, by focusing on this allegedly prepolitical gathering of the 'minor poems'. The 'New Critical' reading of the 1645 volume offered in the commentary by Cleanth Brooks and John E. Hardy, presented a poet shorn of the political.[1] The New Critical, depoliticizing approach to Milton was never as critically exciting as the application of the approach to the metaphysical poets. Milton never became a central figure in new critical practice, despite the earlier essay on 'L'Allegro' and 'Il Penseroso' in Brooks's *The Well Wrought Urn*.[2] But the negative aspects of the approach, the removal of the socio-political context, had their effect and the Brooks and Hardy readings achieved a pervasive influence.

Louis Martz developed the approach in his elegant essay, 'The Rising Poet, 1645'.

Here is the picture of a youthful poet, free from adult cares, sometimes wandering alone, amusing himself, sometimes making music for his friends or acquaintances, sometimes writing in his native vein, sometimes evoking a strain from idealized antiquity—but with a light and dancing posture that we do not usually associate with John Milton: *et humum vix tetigit pede*. It is clear, from many indications, that Milton has designed his book with great care to create this impression.

---

[1] Cleanth Brooks and John E. Hardy, eds, *Poems of Mr. John Milton: The 1645 Edition with Essays in Analysis* (New York, 1951).

[2] Cleanth Brooks, *The Well Wrought Urn: Studies in the Structure of Poetry* (1947) (London, 1968).

The entire volume strives to create a tribute to a youthful era now past—not only the poet's own youth, but a state of mind, a point of view, ways of writing, ways of living, an old culture and outlook now shattered by the pressures of maturity and by the actions of political man.[3]

But whereas Brooks and Hardy had essentially ignored the political, Martz presents a political motive behind the nonpolitical impression. He argues that the volume is contrived to present an unpolitical impression, a commitment to 'the transcendent values of art' rather than 'the political situation'.

Meanwhile, the facing title page prepares us for a volume that will contain songs of unlabored elegance, in the recent courtly style: 'The Songs were set in Music by Mr. Henry Lawes Gentleman of the Kings Chappel, and one of His Maiesties Private Musick'—a notice quite in line with Moseley's preface, which associates Milton's volume with the poems of Waller that Moseley had published a year before. Waller, as everyone knew, had been exiled for his plot against Parliament on the King's behalf; nevertheless Moseley insists on saying: 'that incouragement I have already received from the most ingenious men in their clear and courtious entertainment of Mr. Waller's late choice Peeces, hath once more made me adventure into the World, presenting it with these ever-green, and not to be blasted Laurels'. This bland ignoring, or bold confronting, of the political situation, with its emphasis upon the transcendent values of art, is maintained by reprinting here from the 1637 edition, Henry Lawes's eloquent dedication of Milton's *Mask* to a young nobleman with strong Royalist associations; by the Latin poems in memory of the bishops of Winchester and Ely; by the complimentary writings prefixed to the Latin poems, showing the high regard that Milton had won in Catholic Italy; by Milton's admiration for Manso, the fine old Catholic patron of Tasso; and by other aspects of the volume, notably the sonnet beginning: 'Captain or Colonel, or Knight in Arms, / Whose chance on these defenceless dores may sease'. This is not a poem of presumptuous naïveté but of mature awareness, in which the poet, as Brooks and Hardy say, with a 'wry humor . . . contemplates a little ruefully but still with a fine inner confidence, the place of the poet in a jostling world of men at arms'.[4]

Immediately certain separations need to be made in Martz's account between Milton's activities and those of his publisher. Martz stresses the Waller connection. Milton may not have known of Moseley's intention, may not have agreed with it, may have gone

[3] Louis Martz, 'The Rising Poet, 1645' in Joseph H. Summers, ed., *The Lyric and Dramatic Milton* (New York, 1965), p. 5.

[4] Ibid., pp. 6–7; Brooks and Hardy, *Poems of Milton*, p. 157.

along with it as many an author has gone along with a publisher's promotional strategy that he or she was not in agreement with. Milton may have tacitly accepted the image Moseley was creating. At the same time, the head-notes to the poems themselves and the arrangement of the volume allow a radical theme to be perceived in the volume. Both Moseley as publisher and Milton as writer would have been aware of the advantages of appealing both to Protestant radicals and to royalist aesthetes: a larger audience than appealing to only one sectarian group. Moseley may have endured Milton's radicalism as Milton may have endured Moseley's conservatism. The permutations are multiple. My point is to stress the multifaceted nature of the 1645 volume. Thomas Corns has argued[5] that the 1645 *Poems* show Milton engaged in 'a further attempt to dissociate himself from the archetypal sectary', an image with which his polemical writings had identified him. 'It contains a number of poems which in no way square with his ideological position by 1645, but which serve to restate his social status and aspirations.' And Corns concludes

Milton's volume of poetry indicates clearly enough in its maturer items the Puritanism of the poet. Milton draws attention to it. *Lycidas* is introduced as foretelling 'the ruine of our corrupted Clergy then in their height' . . . The abiding impression, however, of any browser selecting this volume in Moseley's bookshop early in 1646 must surely have been of the eminent respectability of its author. Over and over again the volume declares his wealth, his establishment connexions, his contact with European culture, and his scholarship.

Dr Corns is surely right in pointing to the contradictions within the 1645 volume between Milton's gestures at respectability and his gestures at radicalism. In part the contradictions may have been tactical, in part they may have expressed contradictions within Milton's own political thinking. But in exploring these contradictions it is necessary that both the conservative and the radical impulses should be explored. And though the apolitical, conservative, and respectable reference of the 1645 volume has been established, the radical impetus has been comparatively little examined. Christopher Hill has stressed that

---

[5] Thomas N. Corns, 'Milton's Quest for Respectability', *Modern Language Review*, 77 (1982), 778.

Although at the age of seventeen Milton wrote conventional Latin elegies on two bishops, the Vice-Chancellor and the university bedel, he never composed poems to royalty. Edward King, his junior contemporary, between 1631 and 1637 contributed to six collections of Latin verse celebrating royal births, marriages, etc.[6]

But apart from such important negative, contextual evidence, what signs of radicalism can be read in the poems themselves?

When 'Lycidas' was reprinted as the culminating item in the English poems in the 1645 volume, it was prefaced by an introductory five lines not present on its first appearance in the memorial volume for Edward King:

In this monody the author bewails a learned friend, unfortunately drowned in his passage from Chester on the Irish Seas, 1637. And by occasion foretells the ruin of our corrupted clergy then in their height.[7]

The first sentence exists in the Trinity manuscript. But the reference to 'our corrupted clergy' appears only in the 1645 volume. It is a sentence that draws attention to the radical attack from the Pilot of the Galilean lake:

> How well could I have spared for thee, young swain,
> Enow of such as for their bellies' sake,
> Creep and intrude, and climb into the fold?
>
> (113–15)

If the reader of 1638 missed decoding the pastoral, the reader of 1645 could not avoid the denunciation, could not avoid seeing the poet as placed unambiguously with the forces of reform. And the poet's gifts of political prophecy are likewise made unavoidable:

> But that two-handed engine at the door,
> Stands ready to smite once, and smite no more.
>
> (130–1)

The attack and the promise of doom were written when the clergy were 'then in their height'. It is not a convenient piece of hindsight, but a committed exercise of radical foresight. As Haller remarked in *The Rise of Puritanism*,

---

[6] Christopher Hill, *Milton and the English Revolution* (London, 1977) p. 35.
[7] John Carey and Alastair Fowler, eds, *The Poems of John Milton* (London, 1968), p. 239. All quotations from this edition.

The blazing distinction of its author's genius and character has made it difficult for later generations to understand clearly how intimately and completely he was related to his own time. Milton's poem, with its extra-ordinary denunciation of the prelatical church, has become one of the most admired poems in literature. Yet, it was an expression of the same spirit which had been long making itself heard in the Puritan pulpit and which was at the moment clamoring in the reckless pamphlets of Prynne and Lilburne.[8]

The 1645 superscription draws attention to the apocalyptic political note in 'Lycidas'. But the careful reader in 1638 as well as in 1645 would have detected a threatening gesture to established order in the poem's opening phrase, 'Yet once more . . . '. Brooks and Hardy remark that 'Evidently this is not the first time he has come forward with an immature performance',[9] and this is the usual gloss. But, as a number of commentators[10] have remarked, there is a heavy resonance to 'Yet once more', for all its seeming innocuousness. The allusion is to the Epistle to the Hebrews 12: 25–7:

See that ye refuse not him that speaketh. For if they escaped not who refused him that spake on earth, much more shall not we escape, if we turn away from him that speaketh from heaven: whose voice then shook the earth: but now he hath promised, saying, Yet once more I shake not the earth only, but also heaven. And this word, Yet once more, signifieth the removing of those things that are shaken, as of things that are made, that those things which cannot be shaken may remain.

Both the King James and the Geneva Bibles make cross-reference to Haggai 2: 6–7:

For thus saith the Lord of hosts; Yet once, it is a little while, and I will shake the heavens, and the earth, and the sea, and the dry land; And I will shake all nations, and the desire of all nations shall come: and I will fill this house with glory, saith the Lord of hosts.

The opening phrase, then, establishes the note of doom, of the judgement of the Lord, of the Second Coming. The earth and the heavens will be shaken, and those things that do not stand firm

---

[8] William Haller, *The Rise of Puritanism* (1938) (Philadelphia, 1972), p. 288.
[9] Brooks and Hardy, *Poems of Milton*, p. 170.
[10] David S. Berkeley, 'A Possible Biblical Allusion in "Lycidas" ', *N & Q*, NS 8 (1961), 178; Mother M. Christopher Pecheux, 'The Dread Voice in "Lycidas" ', *Milton Studies*, 9 (1976) 222–3; Edward W. Tayler, *Milton's Poetry: Its Development in Time* (Pittsburgh, 1979) pp. 48–50.

will be removed. And the conclusion of the poem, with Lycidas entertained by

> all the saints above,
> In solemn troops, and sweet societies
> That sing, and singing in their glory move,
> And wipe the tears for ever from his eyes
>
> (178–81)

makes an allusion to Revelation 7: 17, 'wipe away all tears from their eyes'. The references are inescapably apocalyptic. The political pressures about to erupt in the revolution are sensed by the poet-prophet. Doom is spelled out for the corrupt clergy. And the vision of renewal, of the New Jerusalem, is caught in the final line:

> Tomorrow to fresh woods, and pastures new.
>
> (193)[11]

The two indisputable points of emphasis in any collection of poems are the opening and closing positions. If we would argue that Milton deliberately used the concluding position to make a radical political assertion with 'Lycidas', then it is likely that he would make similar use of the opening position. And we notice there is a brief, situating gloss attached to the title of the first poem of the 1645 volume: 'On the Morning of CHRISTS / Nativity. Compos'd 1629'. Typographically 'Compos'd 1629' is presented as part of the title. It does not have the explicit political proclamation of the head-note to 'Lycidas', but it clearly makes some proclamation; why else is it there?

The frequent assumption that Milton was somehow apologizing for early work, distancing himself from juvenilia by attaching dates in this volume has never seemed to me persuasive. Milton does not seem the sort of writer to be apologetic. There were a few poems from the Cambridge years not included in the 1645 volume; if he

---

[11] The political meanings of 'Lycidas' have been explored in Haller, *The Rise of Puritanism*, pp. 288–323; Hill, *Milton and the English Revolution*, pp. 49–53; Mary Ann Radzinowicz, *Toward 'Samson Agonistes': The Growth of Milton's Mind* (Princeton, 1978), pp. 125–6. They have not always been recognized; cf. Louis Kampf, 'The Scandal of Literary Scholarship', in Theodore Roszak, ed., *The Dissenting Academy* (Harmondsworth, 1969), p. 58: 'Dangerous as it is, we may have to accept some student's honest feeling that, for example, Milton's use of pastoral in 'Lycidas' is a foolish irrelevance. To appeal to the tradition of pastoral for the poem's justification is merely to lull the student into a bland acceptance of authority . . .'

did not feel the poems were adequate to stand alone, then why not leave them with the uncollected?[12] Rather than see the attached date as an apology, we might better see it as a political hint. The date worked into the 'Lycidas' head-note, 1637, serves to establish that the poem denounced the clergy at the time of their height and foretold their ruin. The date 1629 puts 'On the Morning of Christ's Nativity' way back in the pre-revolutionary days. And in those days the poet is shown as looking forward to better times to come. We are offered a glimpse of the apocalypse, delayed but promised.

> For if such holy song
> Enwrap our fancy long,
>   Time will run back, and fetch the age of gold,
> And speckled vanity
> Will sicken soon and die,
>   And lep'rous sin will melt from earthly mould
> And hell itself will pass away,
> And leave her dolorous mansions to the peering day.
>
> (133–40)

The process has begun. And even though 'The babe lies yet in smiling infancy' (151), Milton looks forward to the Crucifixion, and from the Crucifixion forward again to the Second Coming:

> When at the world's last session,
> The dreadful judge in middle air shall spread his throne.
>
> XVIII
>
> And then at last our bliss
> Full and perfect is,
>   But now begins; for from this happy day
> The old dragon under ground
> In straiter limits bound,
>   Not half so far casts his usurped sway . . .
>
> (163–70)

Commentators have remarked how Milton moves from his ostensible theme of the nativity to a vision of apocalypse.[13] What I would

---

[12] The uncollected early poems included 'On the Death of a Fair Infant Dying of a Cough', 'At a Vacation Exercise . . . ', and 'Apologus de Rustico et Hero'. Gordon Campbell in 'Milton and the Lives of the Ancients', *JWCI* 47 (1984) 236 suggests that Milton was comparing his literary progress at the age of 21 with that of Virgil, by noting 'Compos'd 1629'.

[13] Haller, *The Rise of Puritanism*, pp. 312–13. Balachandra Rajan, *The Lofty Rhyme: A Study of Milton's Major Poetry* (London, 1970), pp. 12–13.

stress here are the political uses of apocalypse. Although millenarian beliefs were not confined to the radicals, their expression increasingly implied a revolutionary component. At the time the poem was composed, millenarian speculations were suppressed. Joseph Mede's *Key to Revelation* had appeared in Latin two years earlier, but no English translation appeared until 1643 when a committee of the House of Commons ordered one. Hill points out that 'no vernacular translation of the seminal works on Revelation and Daniel by Brightman, Mede, Pareus or Alsted was published in England until after the meeting of the Long Parliament.'[14]

'On the Morning of Christ's Nativity', then, introduces a vernacular glimpse of apocalypse at a historical moment when such visions were suppressed because of their radical Utopian political implications. The poet reminds us of the date. And it is reissued as the opening proclamation to a collection of poems at an historical moment when apocalyptic pronouncements were part of the vanguard of revolutionary ideology. Between composing and publishing the poem Milton had written that powerful apocalyptic vision concluding *Of Reformation Touching Church-Discipline in England* (1641), looking forward to:

> that day when thou the Eternall and shortly-expected King shalt open the Clouds to judge the severall Kingdomes of the World, and distributing *Nationall Honours* and *Rewards* to Religious and just *Common-wealths*, shalt put an end to all Earthly *Tyrannies*, proclaiming thy universal and milde *Monarchy* through Heaven and Earth.[15]

It is a vision that reminds us that apocalyptic imagery was not a 'purely literary' matter, not a matter of pure aesthetics. In the context of the 1640s, a vision of apocalypse was a revolutionary vision. And in 1645 the parade of defeated pagan gods invited a reading that allowed an analogy with the parade of defeated bishops, clergy, and courtiers—Strafford, Laud, and the rest of that crew.

---

[14] Christopher Hill, *The World Turned Upside Down* (Harmondsworth, 1975), pp. 95–6; id., *Antichrist in Seventeenth Century England* (London, 1971), p. 37. See also David Norbrook, *Poetry and Politics in the English Renaissance* (London, 1984), pp. 242–5.

[15] *CPW* i. 616. As Bob Hodge comments on the 1641 passage: 'Christ's coming is imminent, as the Millenarians believed, and will be a political event, not just a spiritual one. Christ's kingdom does not re-inforce the principle of Monarchy on earth; "Just commonwealths" are rewarded, but "all earthly tyrannies" are destroyed.' 'Satan and the Revolution of the Saints', *Literature and History*, 7 (1978), 26.

The oracles are dumb,
No voice or hideous hum
  Runs through the arched roof in words deceiving.
Apollo from his shrine
Can no more divine,
  With hollow shriek the steep of Delphos leaving.
No nightly trance, or breathed spell,
Inspires the pale-eyed priest from the prophetic cell.

                            (173–80)

That 'arched roof' invites a Gothic image. Here we can see the English unpurged church as much as any remote Hellenic ritual, the priest and the cell allowing a ready impression of Roman Catholic leanings.

                           XXI

In consecrated earth,
And on the holy hearth,
  The lars, and lemures moan with midnight plaint,
In urns, and altars round,
A drear and dying sound
  Affrights the flamens at their service quaint . . .

                            (189–94)

We are accustomed to the critical procedure that glosses 'all-judging Jove' in 'Lycidas' (82) as the Christian God. Classical references can be decoded for a contemporary, Christian meaning. It is no remote or illegitimate reading that would see in 'consecrated earth', 'altars', and 'service quaint' a reference to established Anglican ceremonial, the resented altar rather than the table, the quaint idolatrous rituals. As Milton was to write in *Of Reformation*:

the Table of Communion now become a Table of separation stands like an exalted platforme upon the brow of the quire, fortifi'd with bulwark, and barricado, to keep off the profane touch of the Laicks, whilst the obscene and surfeted Priest scruples not to paw, and mammock the sacramentall bread, as familiarly as his Tavern Bisket.[16]

                    Peor, and Baalim,
                    Forsake their temples dim . . .

                          (197–8)

English churches are readily referred to as temples, particularly if the fetishism of church buildings is being denounced. 'O Spirit, that

            [16] *CPW* i. 547–8.

dost prefer / Before all temples the upright heart and pure' Milton
was to write in *Paradise Lost* (i. 17–18):

> And mooned Ashtaroth,
> Heaven's queen and mother both,
>   Now sits not girt with tapers' holy shine . . .
>
>   (200–2)

Once the pursuit of correspondence is begun, it is hard not to read
this as a dismissal of the Roman Catholic cult of Mary.[17]

> In vain with timbrelled anthems dark
> The sable-stoled sorcerers bear his worshipped ark.
>
>   (219–20)

What are these but black surpliced clergy promenading to church
music—music so denounced by radical Puritans who held it was the
work of Antichrist, introduced by the Pope in 666 AD.[18] And to see
this whole 'damned crew' (228) 'troop to the infernal jail' (233) had
an undoubted prophetic touch when the twelve bishops did indeed
troop off to jail in the Tower in 1641/2.

   This is a contextual reading. The events of the early 1640s draw
out a reading that was only prophetically implicit in the Cambridge
of 1629. But the arrangement of the 1645 volume encourages the
emergence of this reading, not only with the opening poem balancing
the explicitly radical attack on the clergy of the concluding poem,
but with the two psalms immediately following 'On the Morning
of Christ's Nativity'. Again they are prefaced with a temporal head-
note: 'This and the following Psalm were done by the Author at
fifteen years old'. There is no need to read in this any apology for
immaturity.[19] Psalm 136 has endured more widely than any of
Milton's verses through its incorporation and happy popular

---

[17] Brooks and Hardy, *Poems of Milton*, p. 101, ask: 'Did Milton, by describing
a notorious heathen goddess in terms which seem to apply to the Virgin, mean to
suggest a thrust at the "Mary-worship" of the Roman Catholics? Perhaps.'

[18] Hill, *Antichrist*, p. 75.

[19] James Holly Hanford expressed the view of the psalms that has been generally
adopted. 'They were preserved and printed in the 1645 edition of the *Poems* not,
presumably, for their own sakes but as evidence of the poet's early devotion to the
Muse of his native land . . .', *University of Michigan Studies in Shakespeare, Milton
and Donne* (New York, 1925), reprinted in James Holly Hanford, *John Milton, Poet
and Humanist* (Cleveland, 1966), p. 6. But Christopher Hill has remarked on their
'political stance' in *Milton and the English Revolution*, p. 35.

acceptance in the English hymn book. If any implication of immaturity remains, it is in the context of truth spoken out of the mouths of babes and sucklings, of powerful, irrefutable, prophetic, Christian utterance from the young poet.

> Our babe to show his Godhead true,
> Can in his swaddling bands control the damned crew.
>
> (227–8)

Not a blasphemous assumption of Godhead; but none the less a clear indication of prophetic possession in youth, the year preceding his matriculation at Cambridge. For what is the subject of these two psalms? We tend too readily to pass them by, see them as part of that psalm-versifying of Protestant tradition, and disregard their quite specific content.

> When the blest seed of Terah's faithful son,
> After long toil their liberty had won
>
> (Psalm 114, 1–2)

> In bloody battle he brought down
> Kings of prowess and renown.
>
> (Psalm 136, 62–3)

In 1634 Milton turned to Psalm 114 again, translating it into Greek hexameters and sending a copy to Alexander Gill. With the victories of the Parliamentary army of 1645, these versions take on a prophetic significance.

To bring out the full political implications of the young Milton's prophetic vision, we need to look at that recurrent image of the Cambridge poems, the music of the spheres. As Arthur Barker remarked, 'The force with which this idea struck Milton's imagination is indicated by the fact that from the [Nativity] "Ode" to "Lycidas" he was almost incapable of writing on a serious subject without introducing the music'.[20] In the context of the image of the music of the spheres, the prophetic note takes on an unavoidable

---

[20] Arthur Barker, 'The Pattern of Milton's "Nativity Ode" ', *University of Toronto Quarterly*, 10 (1940); reprinted in Alan Rudrum, ed., *Milton: Modern Judgements* (London, 1968), p. 54.

millenarian political edge.[21] The lost music can be regained; there
can be a new golden age.

XIII

Ring out, ye crystal spheres,
Once bless our human ears.

(125–6)

And the poet begs the music to ring out for a quite specific social
purpose:

XIV

For if such holy song
Enwrap our fancy long
   Time will run back, and fetch the age of gold.

(133–5)

The age of gold is glossed in political terms, not only in moral terms.
'Lep'rous sin will melt from earthly mould' (138), but also

XV

Yea Truth, and Justice then
Will down return to men,
   Orb'd in a rainbow; and like glories wearing
Mercy will sit between . . .

(141–4)

Truth, Justice, and Mercy have their undeniable reference to earthly
administrations as well as to any larger spiritual context. As

---

[21] David Norbrook remarks on the 'directly millenial associations' of music in the
ode in David Lindley, ed., *The Court Masque* (Manchester, 1984), p. 105. In stark
contrast is Michael Fixler who noted the prophetic poet here, but denied any political
implications: 'The central prophetic vision of the poem, quickened into life by the
Pseudo-Dionysian angelic harmonies and the Pythagorean music of the spheres is that
of the restoration through Christ of the Golden Age. Millenial consummation is
deferred by 'Wisest Fate', but at his birth Christ's slow conquest of "th'old Dragon"
begins and would in centuries to come be completed. No Utopian image is suggested
here by the Golden Age' (Michael Fixler, *Milton and the Kingdoms of God* (London,
1964).) But Professor Fixler offers no argument for his assertion that 'no apocalyptic
urgency disturbs his contemplation of the pattern of the great cosmic drama' (ibid.,
p. 49) in the 'Nativity Ode', *Ad Patrem*, and 'At a Solemn Music'. With the images
of apocalypse and the age of gold so firmly and recurrently present in these early
poems, why are they then evacuated of their customary apocalyptic and political
meanings? The natural reading would take the reassertions of the poet's prophetic
role, the apocalyptic reference, and the vision of the regainable experience of the music
of the spheres and the age of gold as a characteristic Protestant, activist, Utopian
proclamation.

J. B. Broadbent remarked, 'The second descent, of Mercy, Truth and Justice, has only the abstract effect of a reference to eschatology, because Milton is thinking of political rather than spiritual qualities'.[22] And the conclusion of 'At a Solemn Music' suggests the achievement of that music on earth prior to the transcending of the material realm:

> O may we soon again renew that song,
> And keep in tune with Heav'n, till God ere long
> To his celestial consort us unite,
> To live with him, and sing in endless morn of light.
>
> (25–8)

It might be argued that truth, justice, and mercy are easy abstractions. Is there any social specificity in Milton's vision that would entitle us to see a more fleshed-out incipient radicalism? The description of 'the Heav'n-born-child / All meanly wrapp'd in the rude manger' ('On the Nativity', 30–1) certainly allows a sympathy for the poor.

> Nature in awe to him
> Had doff'd her gaudy trim,
>   With her great master so to sympathize.
>
> (32–4)

Milton was later to use the circumstances of Christ's humble birth to make a radical point. 'For notwithstanding the gaudy superstition of som devoted still ignorantly to temples, we may be well assur'd that he who disdaind not to be laid in a manger, disdains not to be preachd in a barn' (*Considerations touching the likeliest means to remove hirelings out of the church*, 1659).[23] And the vision of the shepherds 'Sat simply chatting in a rustic row' (87) again asserts a lowly simplicity. It serves to contrast Christ's heavenly majesty with the humility of his descent to earth, but it serves too to elevate the humble and to devalue the earthly proud; the first shall be last and the last shall be first. Hugh Richmond has remarked on the aesthetic consequences of this note of humility, this rejection of an élitist standpoint.

The theme of a saviour 'All meanly wrapt in the rude manger' encourages in Milton a quaint particularity more characteristic of the humble craftsman than the sophisticated academic . . . the virtues admired in 'On the Nativity' derive from this modest recognition of the Christian rhythm: its acceptance of

---

[22] J. B. Broadbent, 'The Nativity Ode' in Frank Kermode, ed., *The Living Milton* (London, 1960), pp. 23–4.

[23] *CPW* vii, 304. On Christianity's appeal to the poor, see ibid., p. 302.

the humble, quaint, discontinuous nature of experience, which gave the art of anonymous medieval craftsmen a vivid particularity denied to the arid theorizing of the pretentious Schoolmen. Few but scholars and specialists now regularly read even an Aquinas, while millions still delight in the statuary and paintings of the forgotten artisans who were his contemporaries.[24]

Although, as Milton wrote in the vacation exercise of 1628, 'my hand has never grown horny with driving the plough . . . I was never a farm hand at seven or laid myself down full length in the midday sun',[25] he did not fail to remind himself in *The Reason of Church-government Urg'd against Prelaty* (1641) that 'ease and leasure was given thee for thy retired thoughts out of the sweat of other men'.[26] Against the often-presented image of the élitist Milton, we need to reassert his stress on Christ's humble birth, on the simplicity of the shepherds, on the simple manual labour of Adam and Eve, contrasted with the tyrannical pomp of Satan's authoritarian regime in *Paradise Lost*.

So far we have stressed the threatening aspect of the apocalyptic note, the warnings of doom on the ungodly. But the vision of the Second Coming was a vision of universal peace. And so in 'On the Morning of Christ's Nativity'

III

> But he her fears to cease,
> Sent down the meek-eyed Peace,
>   She crowned with olive green, came softly sliding
> Down through the turning sphere
> His ready harbinger,
>   With turtle wing the amorous clouds dividing,
> And waving wide her myrtle wand,
> She strikes a universal peace through sea and land.

IV

> No war, or battle's sound
> Was heard the world around . . .

(45–54)

Rosemond Tuve has stressed the theme of peace in the poem:

---

[24] Hugh Richmond, *The Christian Revolutionary: John Milton* (Berkeley, 1974), pp. 56–7.
[25] Phyllis B. Tillyard and E. M. W. Tillyard, trans. and ed., *Milton: Private Correspondence and Academic Exercises* (Cambridge, 1932), p. 99.
[26] *CPW* i. 804.

Encouraged to do so by Milton's own unifying use of great ancient images towards one thematic end, we could make shift to indicate the theme of this nativity hymn in two symbolic words: *our peace*. Only, however, if they are understood to carry all those wide and deep meanings he has gathered in, touching the redemption of all nature from guilty error, reconciliation and restored participation in the divine harmony, and final union with the divine light; traditional in poetry and liturgy of the season, these were to Milton most familiarly accepted and most natural in the form given them in the New Testament epistles.[27]

But in noting 'all those wide and deep meanings' gathered around peace, Miss Tuve ignores the political. Yet a vision of peace is of course a political vision. It cuts across those vested power-interests that need and create and maintain war. The political context is presented clearly enough by Milton; the implements of warfare — the products of organized political societies — are stressed:

> The idle spear and shield were high up hung,
> The hooked chariot stood
> Unstained with hostile blood,
> The trumpet spake not to the armed throng . . .
>
> (55–8)

It is organized warfare that is alluded to; not just spear and shield but the chariot, product of a technological state; not something that can be dismissed as a small brawl, but 'the armed throng'. And the political organization behind the warfare now brought to a halt is spelled out as monarchy:

> And kings sat still with awful eye,
> As if they surely knew their sovran Lord was by.
>
> (59–60)

They sit there still before the wand of peace. Their reactions are not shown; the blankness of their portrayal is indication enough that Milton could not spell out what had happened to them, a lack of comment that indicates the inexpressible anti-monarchical feeling. In times of press censorship and severe repression, it is the negative evidence that we need to turn to. When monarchy appears again in the poem it is in connection with the Satanic reaction to the beginning of the new age:

[27] Rosemond Tuve, *Images and Themes in Five Poems by Milton* (Cambridge, Mass., 1957), p. 38.

                              for from this happy day
                    The old dragon under ground
                    In straiter limits bound,
                        Not half so far casts his usurped sway,
                    And wroth to see his kingdom fail,
                    Swinges the scaly horror of his folded tail.

                                        (167–72)

It is a kingdom; and the phrase 'usurped sway' evokes the idea of other usurping kings; the Norman Yoke, that imposition of tyranny on the English people by the usurping power of William the Conqueror, one of the most powerful radical images of the revolutionary and pre-revolutionary period.[28]

    To find political radicalism in the non-prophetic early poems as well as in the prophetic ones would strengthen our case. 'L'Allegro' seems an initially unlikely locus for the political: but the force with which the political has been denied here suggests a significant repression.

                    Come, and trip it as you go
                    On the light fantastic toe,
                    And in thy right hand lead with thee,
                    The mountain nymph, sweet Liberty;
                    And if I give thee honour due,
                    Mirth, admit me of thy crew
                    To live with her, and live with thee,
                    In unreproved pleasures free . . .

                                        (33–40)

It is hard to see how 'sweet Liberty' could be construed as anything other than liberty. It is not luxury or licence or anything pejorative. It is a positive value that has an unavoidable political meaning. Switzerland, that Protestant mountainous stronghold of religious freedom, may be implied. Yet Cleanth Brooks in his influential essay in *The Well Wrought Urn* dismisses this natural reading:

If, under the influence of Milton's later political career, we tend to give Liberty any political significance, we find her in 'L'Allegro' in very strange company, consorting with

    [28] 'The Norman Yoke', in Christopher Hill, *Puritanism and Revolution* (London, 1958), pp. 50–122.

> Jest and youthful Jollity
> Quips and Cranks, and wanton Wiles
> Nods, and Becks, and Wreathed smiles . . .
> Sport that wrincled Care derides
> And Laughter holding both his sides.[29]

But the passage Brooks quotes precedes the introduction of 'Liberty'; jest, jollity, quips, and cranks are presented as the qualities or companions of Mirth. Liberty is a more serious quality that Milton distinguishes from Mirth. Brooks offers no argument for his rejection of the political reading of liberty here. He implies that a knowledge of Milton's later career pollutes the reading, but liberty would have meant liberty whatever Milton's later career. And the introduction of Dr Johnson does not clinch Brooks's case. 'Dr Johnson, always on the alert to ruffle up at the presence of Milton's somewhat aggressively republican goddess, does not betray any irritation at the presence of Liberty here.'[30] That Dr Johnson made no political interpretation here does not preclude such an interpretation. Brooks went on to make another distortion that has proved remarkably influential in later readings:

The first scene is a dawn scene—sunrise and people going to work: the ploughman, the milkmaid, the mower, and the shepherd. But though we see people going to work, we never see them *at* their work.[31]

But when we turn to that first scene, Brooks's case simply falls down:

> While the ploughman near at hand,
> Whistles o'er the furrowed land,
> And the milkmaid singeth blithe,
> And the mower whets his scythe,
> And every shepherd tells his tale
> Under the hawthorn in the dale.

> (63–8)

---

[29] Brooks, *The Well Wrought Urn*, p. 43.

[30] Ibid., p. 44. Somewhat rephrased in Brooks and Hardy, *Poems of Milton*, p. 135.

[31] Brooks, *The Well Wrought Urn*, p. 48. Brooks and Hardy, *Poems of Milton* rephrased, p. 140: 'But though we see people going out to work, and whistling or singing as they go, or coming in from their work, we never see them *at* their work . . . '

Stanley Fish has pointed to the pervasive ambiguity of syntax and image and reference in 'L'Allegro' and 'Il Penseroso'.[32] What Brooks did was to accentuate one aspect of the ambiguous and repress the other. The phrases in the poem that can be read as indicating people going to work can as readily be interpreted as accounts of their being engaged in work. The ploughman who 'whistles o'er the furrowed land' may be whistling across a ploughed field on his way to work; or the whistles may express the song of his labour and the speed with which he is ploughing. The milkmaid who 'singeth blithe' may as readily be singing while she works as not. The shepherd who 'tells his tale' can be telling a tale while keeping an eye on the sheep; or he may be counting them, telling his sheep, keeping tally. The clinching case is the mower who 'whets his scythe'. Cleanth Brooks writes as if the sharpening of the scythe was not work, but some relaxed occupation of the mower's leisure time. But the scythe has to be constantly resharpened, and the whetting is part of the rhythm and activity of mowing as much as the strokes cutting the grass.

The work presented is joyous. In 'L'Allegro' labour is delight. It is a vision like William Morris's haymaking in *News from Nowhere*; fulfilling, enjoyable.[33] Yet the exhausting quality of the labour is not repressed: this is not a false or purely decorative pastoral. To read of

> Mountains on whose barren breast
> The labouring clouds do often rest
>
> (73–4)

is to be reminded of the hardship of physical rural labour, of the need for rest, of the harshness of the places of rest available to the labourer. When we are shown the cottage 'hard by' the towers and battlements, the 'hard' picks up the 'barren breast' of the mountains on which the 'labouring clouds . . . rest' to remind us of the hard life of the cottager; its implications spread into the cottage life, not the castle or crenellated manor-house. And it is not easy to see how labour can be evacuated from the picture of the cottagers

---

[32] Stanley E. Fish, 'What It's Like to Read "L'Allegro" and "Il Penseroso" ', *Milton Studies*, 7 (1975), 77–99.

[33] Michael Wilding, *Political Fictions* (London, 1980), p. 59.

> Hard by, a cottage chimney smokes,
> From betwixt two aged oaks,
> Where Corydon and Thyrsis met,
> Are at their savoury dinner set
> Of herbs, and other country messes,
> Which the neat-handed Phillis dresses;
> And then in haste her bower she leaves,
> With Thestylis to bind the sheaves;
> Or if the earlier season lead
> To the tanned haycock in the mead . . .
>
> (81–90)

Brooks comments 'we do not accompany them to the haycock, nor do we feel the sun which "tans" it'.[34] But the demands of labour cannot that easily be denied. The emphatic present tense stresses the present activity of dressing the dinner and rushing off to work; the 'haste' with which Phillis leaves the bower to bind the sheaves emphatically stresses a hurried meal, hurried because of the pressing demand of labour; and the alternative 'or if the earlier season lead' similarly stresses that whatever season there is pressing work. There is always some demand.

As a result of his case, Brooks has to distort the poem further by treating unambiguous images of labour as somehow exceptions. He writes:

Nobody sweats in the world of 'L'Allegro' — except the goblin:

> *Tells how the drudging* Goblin *swet,*
> *To ern his Cream-bowle duly set,*
> *When in one night, ere glimps of morn,*
> *His shadowy Flale hath thresh'd the Corn . . .*

(Perhaps it is overingenious to suggest that in this scene — the only depiction of strenuous activity in the poem — Milton has 'cooled' it off by making the flail 'shadowy', by presenting it as part of a night scene, and by making the labourer, not a flesh-and-blood man, but a goblin. And yet the scene has been carefully patterned: it is balanced by the passage in 'Il Penseroso', where the spectator having taken refuge from the sun listens

> *While the Bee with Honied thie,*
> *. . . at her flowry work doth sing . . .*

Goblins and bees are the only creatures presented 'at work' in the two poems.)[35]

---

[34] Brooks, *The Well Wrought Urn*, p. 49.   [35] Ibid., pp. 49–50.

But rather than excepting goblins and bees, we might more profitably see them as thematic reinforcements of the image of labour. All nature labours: human male and female — ploughman and milkmaid; the labouring clouds; the insect world, the bee, type and reminder of human social labour here as in Marvell's 'The Garden'; and the supernatural world. Labour is not something separate from life, either here, or in Adam and Eve's gardening labour in Eden, or in the description of God as 'my great task-master' in Sonnet 7 (14).

The significance of Brooks's denial of the presence of labouring activity in 'L'Allegro' is brought into political focus by some comments of Raymond Williams in *The Country and the City*:

The whole result of the fall from paradise was that instead of picking easily from an all-providing nature, man had to earn his bread in the sweat of his brow; that he incurred, as a common fate, the curse of labour. What is really happening, in Jonson's and Carew's celebrations of a rural order, is an extraction of just this curse, by the power of art: a magical recreation of what can be seen as a natural bounty and then a willing charity: both serving to ratify and bless the country landowner, or, by a characteristic reification, his house. Yet this magical extraction of the curse of labour is in fact achieved by a simple extraction of the existence of the labourers. The actual men and women who rear the animals and drive them to the house and kill them and prepare them for meat; who trap the pheasants and partridges and catch the fish; who plant and manure and prune and harvest the fruit trees; these are not present; their work is all done for them by a natural order. When they do at last appear, it is merely as the 'rout of rural folke' or, more simply, as 'much poore' . . .[36]

It is this extraction of the existence of the rural labourers in the representative rural poetry of the early seventeenth century that Milton confronts and resists. Brooks attempts to subsume 'L'Allegro' to this dominant, quasi-pastoral, patrician, land-owning vision. And his attempt to do so when detected reveals the politics of Milton's vision more clearly. The labourers are present; indeed, the labourers are introduced before the landowners, gentry, and aristocrats are encountered in the poem. The labour of the rural workers is recognized, given a dignity and an aesthetic beauty in commemoration, and its hardships acknowledged. The human basis for Milton's stand against the forces of oppression — bishops,

---

[36] Raymond Williams, *The Country and the City* (1973), (St Albans, 1975), p. 45.

monarchs, all the figures of power and authority that he confronted—
lies here in a recognition and sympathy for the labouring class.

And 'labour and intent study' are the destined lot of the prophetic
poet. Inspiration works dialectically with the medium; the medium
needs to have a store of knowledge and a developed wisdom, across
which inspiration can play. Describing the first steps in his decision
to become a writer, Milton recalled in *The Reason of Church-
Government Urg'd Against Prelaty* that, encouraged by the response
his early poems had received from members of the private Academies
of Italy,

I began thus farre to assent both to them and divers of my friends here at
home, and not lesse to an inward prompting which now grew daily upon
me, that by labour and intent study (which I take to be my portion in this
life) joyn'd with the strong propensity of nature, I might perhaps leave
something so written to aftertimes, as they should not willingly let it die.[37]

Labour and intent study and inward prompting—the Protestant
drive. And prophetic millenarianism has a long tradition of radical,
revolutionary associations.[38] The surprise would be if Milton's
prophetic apocalyptic note were unpolitical. The repression of
apocalyptic commentary under Laud was from a recognition of its
revolutionary potential. In that time of brutal censorship, the political
had to be expressed covertly, in literary code. By 1645 the political
situation had changed and the code could be openly translated. From
that perspective we can rediscover the radicalism of Milton's earlier
years.

[37] *CPW* i. 810.
[38] Norman Cohn, *The Pursuit of the Millenium* (New York, 1957).

3

Comus, Camus, Commerce:
Theatre and Politics on the Border

When John Milton wrote *A Maske Presented At Ludlow Castle,*
1634: On Michaelmasse night, before the Right Honourable, Iohn
Earle of Bridgewater, Vicount Brackly, Lord Præsident of Wales,
And one of His Maiesties most honorable Privie Counsell (1637),
the political could not be a central concern of his work. Strict censorship was maintained until the Long Parliament met in November
1640 and with the abolition of the Court of the Star Chamber in
July 1641 the instrument of ecclesiastical censorship was removed.
'Before 1640 there were no printed newspapers, and publication of
home news of any sort was a legal offence. Newsletters for the rich
circulated privately at £5 *per annum*: they were suppressed in
1632.'[1] Radical ideas could only be alluded to, presented obliquely.
A strict censorship of publication and performance was enforced.

The Instructions issued in May 1633 to Bridgewater on taking up
the Lord Presidency of the 'Councell within his Maiesties dominion
and principalities of Wales, and Marches of the same' specify the
controls on free expression to be exercised, amongst the Council's
many functions:

And whereas divers Lewd and maliciouse persons have heretofore and of
Late dayes more and more devised spread abroad reported or published
many false and seditious tales newes sayeings writteings bookes letters and
libells which amongst the people have wrought and may worke great
mischieffe and inconveniences to the intent the like may bee evoided hereafter
and the inventors and settors furth thereof may bee condignly punished,
his Maiesties pleasure is that the said Lord President Vice President and
Councell as is aforesaid shall have due regarde thereof and that whensoever
any such false and sedicious tales newes sayeings Writteings bookes letters
and libells shalbee devised reported published or disperced within any the

---

[1] *The Collected Essays of Christopher Hill,* vol. i. *Writing and Revolution in*
Seventeenth Century England (Brighton, 1985), p. 39.

limits and Jurisdicions aforesaid That the Publishers and reporters thereof bee forthwith staid and all meanes vsed to attach them all from one to another vntill the first author may bee apprehended, and such offendors shalbee duely and openly punished by the said Lord President or Vice President and Councell or any three of them . . .[2]

More serious offences 'as may tend to the dainger and dishonnor of his Maiestie or the State' were to be referred to His Majesty or the Lords of his Privy Council. The Record of fines levied before the Court of the Council in the Marches between 1616 and 1637 (Harleian MS 4220) contains 'throughout' and 'more especailly towards the end . . . numerous notices of offences such as contempt, libel, the making of scandalous rhymes and so forth'.[3]

The Council was only one of many institutions, ecclesiastical and secular, empowered to control and censor thought. A concomitant of this control is that dramatic works performed by theatrical companies under royal or aristocratic patronage, and masques performed by members of the royal family and aristocracy themselves, were looked at for their political asides, their glancing allusions. Sustained allegory or sustained argument was too risky; the political could not be made explicit. But equally it could not be totally repressed, and the circumstances surrounding the patronage and production of plays and masques invited and encouraged the political speculations. The meaning of *A Maske* is that some meaning is masked, hidden — whatever other expectations of dance and formal presentation it may suggest.

Driven from the centre, the political can exist on the margins, in the aside, the oblique reference, the marginal allusion. *A Maske Presented at Ludlow Castle* invites this attention to the margins, for Ludlow Castle was the seat of the Court of the Marches, the administrative and judicial authority controlling Wales and the Marches, the border region between England and Wales.[4] It is an

[2] Caroline A. J. Skeel, 'The St. Asaph Library MS. of the Instructions to the Earl of Bridgewater, 1633', *Archaeologia Cambrensis*, 6th series, 17 (1917), 202.

[3] Caroline A. J. Skeel, 'Social and Economic Conditions in Wales and the Marches in the Early Seventeenth Century, as illustrated by Harl. MS. 4220', *Transactions of the Society of Cymmrodorion* (1916–17), 132.

[4] Though Ludlow had emerged as the administrative centre, the Court met at other towns, notably Shrewsbury. Edward Phillips, who married Milton's sister Ann, was a lawyer from Shrewsbury and leased land there, which was inherited by Milton's nephew Edward, whose education together with that of his brother John, Milton

ambiguous position and these ambiguities inevitably penetrate the
Maske. The March is the border, the mark. But though mark became
extended from the sign of the border to a sign in general, border
signs remained ambiguous, disputed. The Marches meant both a
tract of land on the border of a country, and a tract of debatable
land separating two countries. Are the children in the *Maske* lost
in the English counties on the English side of the Marches (the Court
had jurisdiction over Shropshire, Herefordshire, Worcestershire, and
Gloucestershire as well as over Wales), or in Welsh territory? Even
to ask whether such distinctions matter or are valid is to raise the
political. Ludlow is redolent of the border history, and the border
history was often the history of England. Sir John Doddridge gave
the history of the Marches in his *History of the Ancient and Moderne
Estate of the Principality of Wales* . . . (1630)

As touching the gouernment of the Marches of *Wales*, it appeareth by diuers
ancient monuments that the Conqueror after hee had conquered the English,
placed diuers of his Norman Nobility vpon the confines and borders towards
Wales, and gaue power vnto the said persons thus placed vpon those borders,
to make such conquests vpon the Welsh, as they by their strength could
accomplish, holding it a very good policy, therby not only to encourage them
to be more willing to serue him, but also to prouide for them at other mens
costs. And hereupon further ordained that the lands so conquered, should
be holden of the Crowne of England in capite, and vpon this and such like
occasions diuers of the Nobility of *England* hauing lands vpon the said
borders of Wales made roades and incursions vpon the Welsh, whereby diuers
parts of that Country neere or towards the said borders were wonne by the
sword from the Welshmen, and were planted partly with English Collonies;
and the said lands so conquered, were holden *per Baronia*, and were called
therefore Baronyes, Marchers . . .[5]

Of the establishment of the Council *c.*1473, Doddridge wrote:

And as touching the first Councell, established in the Marches of *Wales*,
it is conceived by the best and most probable opinions amongst Antiquaries,
that the same began in or about the seaventeenth yeer of king Edward the

was to undertake. The mother of Edward Phillips the lawyer came from Shrewsbury,
the father from Atcham. See Ralph E. Hone, 'New Light on the Milton-Phillips Family
Relationships', *Huntington Library Quarterly*, 22 (1958), 63–75; John C. Hobbs,
'John Milton's Shrewsbury Connections', *Transactions of the Shropshire Archaeological
Society*, 57 (1961), 26–30.

   [5] Sir John Doddridge, *The History of the Ancient and Moderne Estate of the
Principality of Wales, Dutchy of Cornewall, and Earldome of Chester* (London, 1630);
(facsimile reprint, London and New York, 1973), p. 36.

Fourth, when as Prince Edwards sonne was sent vnto the Marches of Wales, vnder the tuition of the Lord Riuers his Vncle by the Mothers side, as afore hath appeared: and at that time also *Iohn, Bishop of Worcester*, was appointed Lord President of Wales.[6]

The intention was, Hall wrote in his *Chronicles*, that by sending the Prince of Wales to Ludlow 'by the autoritee of his presence the wilde Welshemenne and eiuell disposed personnes should refrain from their accustomed murthers and outrages'.[7] But the young prince and his brother were met on the way from Ludlow to London for the former's coronation by their uncle, Richard Duke of Gloucester, who declared himself king, imprisoned the princes in the Tower of London, and had them murdered. The memory of the two princes helps establish an atmosphere of expectant menace when we encounter the two young sons of the Lord President lost on their way to Ludlow in the *Maske*.

The Council was revived by Henry VII who sent his eldest son Arthur to Ludlow, *c.*1493, and Catherine of Aragon joined him there upon their marriage. Merlin's prophecies of the return of Arthur were to be fulfilled by the Welsh-descended Tudors. But Arthur died in 1502 aged sixteen. Henry VIII sent his daughter Mary to Ludlow in 1525 but she was recalled three years later in the course of Henry's attempts to divorce Catherine of Aragon on the grounds of her previous marriage to his elder brother, Prince Arthur, which she insisted had never been consummated. This historic sexual drama of Ludlow offers a poignant background for the Lady's confrontation with Comus.

Between 1525 and 1553, when the next surviving instructions are dated, writes Penry Williams in *The Council in the Marches of Wales Under Elizabeth I*: 'the Council in the Marches changed from the household and Council of a princess, with judicial commissioners attached, into a formal institution for administering law and controlling the country'.[8] But by the time of James I, writes A. H. Dodd in *Studies in Stuart Wales*, 'the Council was in fact taking on itself

[6] Ibid., p. 39.

[7] Hall, *Chronicles* (1809), p. 347, quoted in David Lewis, 'The Court of the President and Council of Wales and the Marches from 1478 to 1575', *Y Cymmrodor*, 12 (1897), 20.

[8] Penry Williams, *The Council in the Marches of Wales Under Elizabeth I* (Cardiff, 1958), p. 27.

more and more the aspect of a mere court of law (and a pettifogging one at that), less and less that of a viceregal court'.[9]

James strongly opposed the attempts of the four English counties to be free of the Council's jurisdiction in 1608. As Caroline Skeel writes in *The Council in the Marches of Wales*:

> The interest of the case lies mainly in this, that the king's prerogative and the existence of discretionary governments were conceived to be involved. 'Discretionary governments,' it was urged on one side, 'are most dangerous, and therefore the fewer of them in any state the better.' On the other side, James laid down with emphasis the sweeping doctrine, 'All novelties are dangerous.' 'I wolde not,' he says, 'haue you medle with suche auntient Rightes of myne as I haue receaved from my predecessors, possessing them *more maiorum*.'[10]

James demanded at a meeting with the judges and Privy Council whether he had the right by his own prerogative to give power to the Lord President and Council: but

the judges refused to answer the question, even when propounded by the king. James spoke strongly of the hindrance caused to the Lord President and Council by prohibitions, and the prejudicial effect that the weakening of the Council of the Marches would have on the Council of the North, the Court of Admiralty, the Court of Requests, and the Ecclesiastical Courts. In a long and rambling speech, in which he touched on Moses and Jethro, the Emperor Constantine, the Picts and Scots, the Heptarchy, and the growth of the English law Courts, James emphatically laid down the doctrine that 'all lawe is but voluntas Regis' and 'eius est interpretare cuius est condere.' He then turned to the prince, saying, 'This conserneth you, sir, and I hope you will loose no thinge which is yours.' Coke, kneeling before the king, said that the question was one of fact, and ought to come before a jury; whereon the king 'angerly' replied that judges derived their power merely from the royal will, and that all this mischief had come about through kings not sitting in Parliament. 'Non doe oppose themselves against the Jurisdiction of the Councell in the marches but certen high-headed ffellowes calling them by a Scottish name mountinge ffellowes, in English swaggering ffellowes . . . I knowe there might be wiser Kinges and more vertuouse, and yett I knowe I am noe foole, I came not as a usurper but as a Rightfull Kinge discended out of the Loines of the Kinges of this Lande, and what prerogative to mee therin apperteigneth I will hould and mayntaine to the uttermost.'[11]

---

[9] A. H. Dodd, *Studies in Stuart Wales* (Cardiff, 1952), p. 59.

[10] Caroline A. J. Skeel, *The Council in the Marches of Wales* (London, 1904), p. 143. The 4 counties, out of 17, contributed 50% of the fines.

[11] Skeel, *Council*, pp. 144–5.

The young Prince Charles certainly followed his father's advice in regard to the Council of the Marches, which began to experience a revived importance. A. H. Dodd writes:

When the Presidency became vacant in 1631, Charles I had newly entered into the period of personal government in which he dispensed with parliament and strained every nerve to maintain the royal prerogatives it had dared to challenge. For this purpose the Councils of Wales and of the North, where he could exercise unfettered his discretionary powers, were of capital importance, and he promptly set about strengthening both. Wentworth, the chief architect of the new policy of Thorough, was given the presidency of the North even before the dissolution of parliament, and for the corresponding post at Ludlow the King chose the Earl of Bridgewater, a border lord with territorial interests extending into Wales and with nearly fifteen years' experience on the council at Ludlow and five on the Privy Council. Although far below Wentworth (as soon appeared) in weight of character, he carried bigger guns than any of his Stuart predecessors at Ludlow had done . . .

Before Bridgewater took up residence (which was not until 1633) fresh instructions had been issued which increased his Council to the unprecedented number of eighty-four, including twenty-four peers and eleven bishops, and restored to him the commission of lieutenancy in the south eastern corners of Wales which Elizabeth had alienated to the house of Raglan.[12]

The four English counties were also back under the Council's authority, together with the thirteen Welsh counties.

In the *Maske*, the attendant Spirit immediately sets the scene in terms of political control:

> Before the starry threshold of Jove's court
> My mansion is.
>
> (1–2)

His concerns may be primarily spiritual; but of all the available metaphors by which to describe the divine presence, 'court' is selected; whether monarchical or judicial, an analogy of structure is immediately created with the Court of the Marches. The attendant Spirit goes on to make explicit the areas of authority of various spiritual agencies in terms of imperial rule.

> But to my task. Neptune besides the sway
> Of every salt flood, and each ebbing stream,
> Took in by lot 'twixt high, and nether Jove,

---

[12] Dodd, *Stuart Wales*, pp. 60–1.

> Imperial rule of all the sea-girt isles
> That like to rich, and various gems inlay
> The unadorned bosom of the deep,
> Which he to grace his tributary gods
> By course commits to several government,
> And gives them leave to wear their sapphire crowns,
> And wield their little tridents, but this isle
> The greatest, and the best of all the main
> He quarters to his blue-haired deities,
> And all this tract that fronts the falling sun
> A noble peer of mickle trust, and power
> Has in his charge, with tempered awe to guide
> An old, and haughty nation proud in arms:
> Where his fair offspring nursed in princely lore,
> Are coming to attend their father's state,
> And new-entrusted sceptre, but their way
> Lies through the perplexed paths of this drear wood,
> The nodding horror of whose shady brows
> Threats the forlorn and wandering passenger.
>
>   (18–39)

'Imperial rule', 'government', 'crowns', 'princely lore', 'sceptre'; the political is intertwined immediately with the specifics of patriotism: 'this isle / The greatest, and the best'. To speak of Neptune's 'imperial rule' is to underline English imperial rule of Wales. 'All this tract that fronts the falling sun' is not simply the western region of England; it is the land of a subject people, united with England by the Acts of Union of 1536 and 1543, but clearly at a different and subordinate level of development. Masson writes of Bridgewater's position: 'Wales had been so efficiently annexed to England that the office had lost its warlike character. There were no longer fears of Welsh insurrections . . . '[13] But though organized insurrection was no longer feared, political tensions still persisted. Christopher Hill writes of 'Puritans and "the Dark Corners of the Land"':

The existence of the Council of the North and the Council in the Marches of Wales (not to mention the abortive Council of the West) shows the continuing awareness of governments that there were special problems in these areas. The frequency with which bishops were appointed to the presidency of the Council in the Marches, and the Council's attention to religious matters, suggests that the absence of religious revolt in Wales

---

[13] David Masson, *The Life of John Milton* (London, 1881), i. 608.

did not mean that there was no tension between the old and the new in the Principality.[14]

Religious, political, and military issues were intermixed:

The Civil War confirmed the worst forebodings of those who had agitated for the evangelization of the dark corners. The gentry and clergy of Wales were royalist almost to a man. Not one pamphlet sought to explain the Parliamentary standpoint in Welsh. There had been alarm about the possibility of a Spanish landing in Wales in 1587, 1597, 1598, 1599, 1603 and 1625; in 1641 a story that Welsh papists were being armed as a preliminary to a Spanish or other foreign invasion passed into English popular mythology.[15]

The journey Bridgewater's 'fair offspring' have to make 'to attend their father's state / And new-entrusted sceptre' consequently involves a journey through potentially hostile territory. How hostile remains ambiguous. The Lady fears drunken country people, 'the rudeness, and swilled insolence / Of such late wassailers' (177–8). The Elder Brother talks of 'savage fierce, bandit, or mountaineer' (425). Depending on the point of view *vis-à-vis* the ruling power structure, terms vary; what Lord Brackly, elder son of the Earl of Bridgewater, conceptualizes as a 'bandite', others might see as a freedom-fighter, a Samson attempting to deliver his people. The threats expected from drunken countryfolk, savages, bandits, and mountaineers are never presented as a threat from 'wild Welshmen' by the attendant Spirit, the Lady, the Brothers, or anyone else.[16] But the realities of the context, the actualities of Ludlow Castle's role as seat of the Council in the Marches, would make such associations inevitable. The inexpressible exists no less for being inexpressible. The threat of

[14] Christopher Hill, *Change and Continuity in Seventeenth Century England* (London, 1974), pp. 4–5.   [15] Ibid., p. 23.

[16] There is nothing in the *Maske* of that condescending and contemptuous portrayal of the Welsh such as we find in Ben Jonson's *For the Honor of Wales* (1618). However, Cedric Brown has suggested that lines 631–6 in the Bridgewater MS with 'the comparison between "this soyl" and "another Countrey" was omitted, because it could be construed as uncomplimentary to the people of the principality. There was a horrific danger of seeing "this soyl" as Wales. The same consideration applies to "dull swayn." To patronise the locals by describing their rustic dance of duck and nod was one thing, to call them stupid or slothful quite another.' 'The Shepherd, the Musician, and the Word in Milton's Masque', *JEGP* 78 (1979), 544.

> the perplexed paths of this drear wood,
> The nodding horror of whose shady brows
> Threats the forlorn and wandering passenger
>
> (37–9)

is a threat from the hostile natives—a subjugated race, a subjugated class. And though the 'drear wood' is undoubtedly associated with the Platonic mysteries of the *Maske*'s allegory of the soul's progress,[17] the local socio-political meaning is no less present for being repressed. It is there in the political context, not spelled out but on the margins.

The Lord President's role was multiple—administrative, judicial, military. 'The Council in the Marches of Wales', writes Penry Williams,

was part of the remarkable Tudor policy of creating centralized regional administrations within England. Except for a brief period during the war of 1939–45, there has been no other attempt to interpose such regional governments between the central administration and the authorities of shire and borough.[18]

During Elizabeth's reign, he writes:

The military duties of the lord president were much the same as those of any other lord-lieutenant, since he was responsible in all the shires of his commission, for the militia, which was the only source of men for home defence and foreign wars. It was his regular duty to conduct the summer musters at which the militia of every shire was assembled, inspected, and trained; and it was his frequent task to levy men for overseas service . . . the president and Council were constantly occupied with military affairs. In addition to their normal duties of supervising the musters, they had to encourage the practice of archery, to develop the breeding of horses 'for service in the wars' and to supervise the storing of each shire's equipment in a central armoury. In time of foreign wars, particularly in time of Irish rebellion, the Council had to levy men for service abroad.[19]

[17] J. B. Savage, 'Comus and Its Traditions', *English Literary Renaissance*, 5 (1975), 58–80; Sears Jayne, 'The Subject of Milton's Ludlow Mask', *PMLA* 74 (1950), 533–43; Michael Lloyd, ' "Comus" and Plutarch's Daemons', *N & Q* 205 (1960), 421–3; Philip Brockbank, 'The Measure of "Comus" ', *Essays and Studies 1968*, NS 21 (London, 1968), 46–61.   [18] Williams, *Council*, p. 3.
[19] Ibid., p. 113.

The military aspects of the Presidency were re-emphasized in Bridgewater's presidency under Charles I, as A. H. Dodd points out:

The policy of Thorough involved not only a tightening of local administration but a degree of military and naval preparedness that devoured money and man-power and re-emphasised the military character of the President's office.[20]

When Comus in his first speech declares 'let us our rites begin' (125):

> Ere the blabbing eastern scout,
> The nice Morn on th'Indian steep
> From her cabined loophole peep,
> And to the tell-tale sun descry
> Our concealed solemnity
>
> (138–42)

the imagery is inescapably military: the scout peeping through the cabined loophole. While the mention of 'th'Indian steep' brings in suggestions of American Indians or the East India Company: dark places, backward and pagan, awaiting the civilizing missions of England's imperial designs, missionaries, and trade. Sir Benjamin Rudyerd said in the House of Commons in 1628 that 'there were some places in England which were scarce in Christendom, where God was little better known than amongst the Indians'. 'Divers parts of Wales' were among such places.[21]

Cleanth Brooks and John Hardy characteristically depoliticize the passage: 'Lines 138–42 make Morning and the Sun, personified here as figures of the light of day, peepers and tattlers, irreverent goody-goodies spying upon a "solemn," religious exercise.'[22] But Milton's 'scout' insists that this is not the intrusion of village gossips, private 'peepers and tattlers'; it is a word with a specific association of military espionage and surveillance. The *Variorum Commentary on the Poems of John Milton* notes that

scout combines two meanings: 'one sent out ahead of the main force to reconnoitre' (*OED*: *sb.*[4] s), and 'One who keeps watch upon the actions of another; . . . Formerly often in opprobrious sense' (ibid. 4).[23]

---

[20] Dodd, *Stuart Wales*, pp. 63–4.
[21] Hill, *Change and Continuity*, p. 19.
[22] Brooks and Hardy, *Poems of Milton*, p. 196.
[23] A. S. P. Woodhouse and Douglas Bush, eds., *A Variorum Commentary on the Poems of John Milton*, ii 3 (New York, 1972), p. 880.

The scout can be someone operating externally against a foreign enemy, or internally as part of the system of social control. With the border setting the ambiguity is enforced. The *Variorum* remarks that 'peep' applied to the morn is 'a commonplace'.[24] But the military association brought in by 'scout' is Milton's own vision. Thomas Newton suggested that

Milton here perhaps imitated Fletcher's beginning of his fifth Act of the Faithful Shepherdess.

> See the blushing morn doth peep
> Through the window, while the sun &c.[25]

The passage may have been in Milton's mind and he may have intended that his adaptation of it should be noticed. The specific note of quasi-military surveillance is all Milton's: 'th'Indian steep' is added, and 'the window' becomes a 'cabined loophole'. J. B. Leishman[26] cited some further sources for the passage, but as with those cited by Newton, none has the military note. The idea of Ludlow Castle as a military outpost keeping watch over the surrounding area is an implication the audience could readily draw from Comus's image of dawn dramatized in just such terms; it was not an idea anyone was like to reject. 'Beyond its activities as a court,' writes Penry Williams, 'the council acted as a police organization, an administrative office, a military headquarters, and a selection board for local officials.'[27]

The note of surveillance, of informers, has a specific application to the practices of Bishop Roland Lee, 'the most celebrated of all the Marcher Council's presidents',[28] who had established a rule of terror a hundred years earlier in 1534.

Although his ultimate aim was the elimination of thieves and although his ultimate belief lay in hanging as the best deterrent, Lee realized that sometimes a judicious pardon might do more good than wholesale execution. It was more effective, he told Cromwell, to discharge a man if he could give information leading to the capture of others. By following this policy Lee

---

[24] Ibid.
[25] Thomas Newton, ed., *Paradise Regain'd. A Poem, In Four Books. To which is Added Samson Agonistes; and Poems Upon Several Occasions. The Author John Milton* (2 vols., London, 1766), ii. 102.
[26] J. B. Leishman, *Milton's Minor Poems* (London, 1969), p. 240.
[27] Williams, *Council*, p. 106.   [28] Ibid., p. 15.

built up an intelligence service which became legendary in Tudor England and was advocated for Ireland half a century later; 'yet Wales was exceeding wild until Bishop Roland's time, who, being Lord President of the Marches, maintained so many spials . . . and had so good intelligence who were the maintainers of the thieves and doing justice upon them without partiality.'[29]

Moreover, there

was the crowd of professional informers which clustered about the Council in order to gain an income from its jurisdiction. To reduce their activities the Council in 1586 limited the number of informers who were allowed to bring actions on penal statutes to two; in 1602 this number was raised to four, but in theory at least the crowd was kept down.[30]

Discussing 'The Activity of the Council in the Marches under the Early Stuarts', Penry Williams writes:

While charges for most offences were brought by private plaintiffs, almost all accusations of sexual immorality were brought by informers; in other words they were begun by men who hoped to profit financially from the outcome. Informers could obtain a legitimate profit in two ways, either by obtaining part of the fine on conviction, or by making a licensed composition out of court with the defendant before the case came to a hearing. It seems that the second way was the most usual at the Council in the Marches. There is, however, one surprising feature: in most courts, fines imposed in licensed compositions were lower than those imposed in court; the defendant, in fact, gained a reduction of his fine by pleading guilty. But at the Council in the Marches the scale of fines was the same for cases which reached the court and those which did not. Defendants must have decided to settle out of court because the expenses of conducting a defence were very high or because they were not very confident of winning. Some of the accusations thrown at the court may explain this lack of confidence. Informers were alleged to search the registers of ecclesiastical courts for offenders whom they might accuse, and to keep a flock of whores who would give evidence against their customers.[31]

As well as these informers, there is no reason to assume that the system of 'spials' established by Bishop Lee was not still in use. It was the procedure adopted against Communist guerrillas in Malaya by British Intelligence over three centuries later:

---

[29] Ibid., pp. 18–19.   [30] Ibid., p. 80.
[31] Penry Williams, 'The Activity of the Council in the Marches Under the Early Stuarts', *Welsh Historical Review*, 1 (1961), 145–6.

The Special Branch used a standard procedure for 'turning': once a target
had been identified, they set about compiling evidence of his or her complicity
in illegal activities. In due course the future agent was arrested and confronted
with the details assembled by the Branch. Little additional pressure was ever
required to achieve a successful 'turning'.[32]

In his first speech Comus declares:

> We that are of purer fire
> Imitate the starry quire,
> Who in their nightly watchful spheres,
> Lead in swift round the months and years.
> The sounds, and seas with all their finny drove
> Now to the moon in wavering morris move,
> And on the tawny sands and shelves,
> Trip the pert fairies and the dapper elves;
> By dimpled brook, and fountain-brim,
> The wood-nymphs decked with daisies trim,
> Their merry wakes and pastimes keep:
> What hath night to do with sleep?
> Night hath better sweets to prove,
> Venus now wakes, and wakens Love.
> Come let us our rites begin . . .
>
> (111–25)

The pretty picture[33] is explosive with religious and political tension.
The morris dancing and 'merry wakes' (a 'wake' was originally the
vigil or feast of a patron saint) were the focus of religious, social,
and political controversy. Denounced by Puritan clergy as pagan and
papist survivals, the traditional sports and pastimes were promoted
for political reasons by James I in his Declaration of Sports in 1618.
Charles I reasserted the Declaration in 1633, the year before the
performance of Milton's *Maske*. Christopher Hill writes in *The
Century of Revolution*:

When James justified his Declaration of Sports, his reasons were: (i) men
would associate the traditional sports with Popery, and become dissatisfied

---

[32] Jonathan Bloch and Patrick Fitzgerald, *British Intelligence and Covert Action*
(London, 1983), p. 73.

[33] Cf. A. N. Wilson, *The Life of John Milton* (Oxford, 1983), p. 51 on this
passage: 'The gaiety, and above all the supreme tastefulness of this is what lends the
verse such charm. Lovers of Milton have always regarded his Masque as his prettiest
work . . . '

with the established Church if deprived of them; (ii) 'the common and meaner sort' would become unfit for military service; (iii) they would go in disgust to ale-houses, and there indulge in 'a number of idle and discontented speeches.' The Laudian Bishop Pierce a few years later added a fourth objection: if men had no sports to occupy them on Sundays, they might meet for illegal religious discussion.[34]

Milton commented in *Of Reformation* that the Bishops

hamstrung the valour of the Subject by seeking to effeminate us all at home. Well knows every wise Nation that their Liberty consists in manly and honest labours, in sobriety and rigorous honour to the Marriage Bed, which in both Sexes should be bred up from chast hopes to loyall Enjoyments; and when the people slacken, and fall to looseness, and riot, then doe they as much as if they laid down their necks for some wily Tyrant to get up and ride. Thus learnt *Cyrus* to tame the *Lydians*, whom by Armes could not, whils they kept themselves from Luxury; with one easy Proclamation to set up *Stews*, dancing, feasting, & dicing he made them soone his slaves. I know not what drift the *Prelats* had, whose Brokers they were to prepare, and supple us for a Forreigne Invasion or Domestick oppression; but this I am sure they took the ready way to despoile us both of *manhood* and *grace* at once, and that in the shamefullest and ungodliest manner upon that day which Gods Law, and even our own reason hath consecrated, that we might have one day at least of seven set apart wherein to examin and encrease our knowledge of God, to meditate, and commune of our Faith, our Hope, our eternall City in Heaven, and to quick'n, withall, the study and exercise of Charity; at such a time that men should bee pluck't from their sobererst and saddest thoughts, and by *Bishops* the pretended *Fathers of the Church* instigated by publique Edict, and with earnest indeavour push't forward to gaming, jigging, wassailing, and mixt dancing is a horror to think. Thus did the Reprobate hireling Priest *Balaam* seeke to subdue the Israelites to Moab, if not by force, then by this divellish *Pollicy*, to draw them from the Sanctuary of God to the luxurious, and ribald feasts of *Baal-peor*.[35]

Comus's celebration of the 'wavering morris' and of 'merry wakes and pastimes' associates him with the central Stuart court policy, a policy 'flying in the face of respectable middle-class opinion, appealing to all that was unregenerate, undisciplined, and popish in men'. 'Fuller tells us that many moderate men thought the Declaration of Sports was a principal cause of the civil war.' 'Responsibility for

---

[34] Christopher Hill, *The Century of Revolution, 1603–1714* (Edinburgh, 1961), p. 85. [35] *CPW* i. 589.

the Declaration of Sports furnished one of the charges on the basis of which Laud was accused of high treason.'[36]

The dances, wakes, maypoles, and piping of popular culture were contentious issues in the confrontation of Protestant and pagan.

The controversy over Sunday sports perhaps takes on a different appearance if we think of it as a struggle between the ethos of urban civilization and the ethos of the dark corners. It was the poorer Welsh members of the Shearmen's guild in Shrewsbury who rioted in 1588 to defend a maypole which the municipal authorities had prohibited. The Welsh were often denounced for their horrible profanation of the Sabbath 'by using unlawful games even in the time of divine service, and that oftentimes in the very churchyard.' Under Elizabeth the Council in the Marches had been authorized to enforce the statutes against unlawful games.[37]

In her examination of Harleian MS 4220, ' a record of fines levied before the Court of the Council of the Marches between 1616 and 1637', Caroline Skeel notes:

Many entries refer to the keeping of unlawful and disordered alehouses and the encouragement of unlawful games . . .[38]

The Book of Fines contains entries respecting bowling on the Sabbath, singing of ribald songs in the alehouse, unlawful playing and gaming at bowls during divine service, unlawful gaming and abusing a preacher in 'Profaning of the Saboth', playing cards and unlawful games.[39]

She cites the entry:

Anthony Atwood of the p'ish of Claynes in the County of Worcester, gent, for seuerall unlawful assemblyes acting of Enterludes and Ribbauldryes upon seuerall sabboth dayes neare Church, procurement thereof, and other misdemeanours.[40]

The existence of morris dancing in Wales is confirmed *inter alia* by another entry.[41]

Richard Baxter described in his *Autobiography* the dancing and piping in Shropshire in the 1620s:

In the village where I lived the reader read the Common Prayer briefly, and the rest of the day even till dark night almost, except eating-time, was spent

---

[36] Christopher Hill, *Society and Puritanism in Pre-Revolutionary England* (London, 1969), pp. 195, 198.

[37] Hill, *Change and Continuity*, pp. 20–1.

[38] Skeel, 'Social and Economic Conditions', p. 136.   [39] Ibid., p. 137.

[40] Ibid., p. 140.   [41] Ibid., p. 141.

in dancing under a maypole and a great tree not far from my father's door, where all the town did meet together. And though one of my father's own tenants was the piper, he could not restrain him nor break the sport. So that we could not read the Scripture in our family without the great disturbance of the tabor and pipe and noise in the street. Many times my mind was inclined to be among them, and sometimes I broke loose from conscience and joined with them; and the more I did it the more I was inclined to it. But when I heard them call my father Puritan it did much cure me and alienate me from them; for I considered that my father's exercise of reading the Scripture was better than theirs, and would surely be better thought on by all men at the last; and I considered what it was for that he and others were thus derided.[42]

Comus is firmly identified with this disturbing piping. The Lady remarks at her first entrance on the sound of Comus and his crew:

> This way the noise was, if mine ear be true,
> My best guide now, methought it was the sound
> Of riot, and ill-managed merriment,
> Such as the jocund flute, or gamesome pipe
> Stirs up among the loose unlettered hinds
> When for their teeming flocks, and granges full,
> In wanton dance they praise the bounteous Pan,
> And thank the gods amiss.

> (169–76)

Hill writes in *Society and Puritanism in Pre-Revolutionary England* that

protestantism, and especially Puritanism, like Lollardy before them, went furthest in rejecting all kinds of magic and attacking those survivals of the old rituals whose existence had so long been tolerated. In this popular radical Puritanism unwittingly prepared the way for the modern scientific attitude, as well as helping to eradicate habits which unfitted men for an industrial society.

In Edward VI's reign an attempt had been made to abolish wakes, since they led to idleness, drunkenness and brawls. But Elizabeth licensed Sunday games, although more cautiously than her successors. In 1585 a clergyman who maintained in a sermon before the university of Cambridge that plays and sports were unlawful on Sundays had to account for himself before the Vice-Chancellor.

By about the time of the Armada, a puritan memorandum speaks of 'wakes, ales, greens, May games, rush-bearings, bear-baits, dove-ales, bonfires, and all such manner unlawful gaming, piping and dancing . . .

[42] *The Autobiography of Richard Baxter*, abridged by J. M. Lloyd Thomas, ed. N. H. Keeble (Everyman's Library, London, 1974), p. 6.

in all places freely exercised upon the Sabbath; by occasion whereof it cometh
to pass that the youth will not by any means be brought to attend the exercises
of catechizing in the afternoon; neither the people to be present at the evening
service.' Stubbes and a score of puritan propagandists could be quoted for
the charge that men 'could not keep their servants from lying out of their
own houses' on Sunday nights.

There were thus police arguments against permitting some of these
jollifications. In 1550 the Lord President of the Council in the Marches
instructed J.P.s to prevent assemblies or games during divine service; and
32 years later one of the four penal statutes the Council in the Marches was
allowed to execute was that aginst unlawful games—especially prevalent
in Wales.[43]

Traditional dances, merry wakes and pastimes, sports and piping
are the focus of multiple issues. Appropriated by the central Court
authority as a way of preventing the spread of subversive or radical
ideas, the games and icons also represented a popular cultural
focus of socio-political opposition. In 1642 a maypole was set up
in Ludlow as a political symbol. The phallic significance of the
maypole was noted by Hobbes as well as the Puritans.[44] Comus's
'charming rod', like the sceptre of monarchical authority, had the
same signification. When Comus says 'Venus now wakes, and
wakens Love' the reference is not merely that of classical literary
allusion, but a specific statement of the sexual licence of the wakes
and church-ales, deplored by 'Justices and judges who disliked the
brawls and bastards produced'.[45]

Comus's pagan 'rites' to Cotytto and his allusions to Venus and
Hecate are generally read as examples of a literary classicizing. The
unexamined assumption is of Milton the student of the classics,
absorbed in the literary, projecting it on to the world around him
from which he is alienated. When the Lady mentions Pan or when
Comus refers to

> My mother Circe with the Sirens three,
> Amidst the flowery-kirtled Naiades
> Culling their potent herbs, and baleful drugs
>
> (252–4)

these references are taken as placing Comus in a world purely archaic
and artificial.

---

[43] Hill, *Society and Puritanism*, pp. 182–3.   [44] Ibid., pp. 178–9.
[45] Hill, *Century of Revolution*, p. 86.

But the paganism of the classical world was not at that time thought to be confined to the classical world. There was a perceived continuity between the ancient rites and festivals and those still surviving in rural Britain. There were pagan survivals; and Roman Catholicism, having appropriated pagan festivals—Yule, Easter—maintained this continuity of the pagan impulse. Attacks on papist customs involved attacks on surviving paganism. Sir Francis Walsingham wrote to Sir Henry Sidney, Lord President, in 1580 that his laxity in acting against recusants was causing his disfavour at court:

Your lordship had neade to walk warely, for your Doings are narrowely observed, and her Majestie is apt to geve Eare to any that shall yll you. Great Howlde is taken by your Ennemyes, for Neglectyng the Executyon of this Commission[46]

In the next century Caroline Skeel notes the fine of £10 imposed by the Court of the Marches on a Denbighshire man for, *inter alia*, 'suffring his three daughters being yong girles and his maid-seruant to goe out of his house in the night tyme in superstitious manner to Wenefrides well.'[47]

As Hill reminds us in *Society and Puritanism*,

Nor should we lightly dismiss the recurrent emphasis on paganism in discussing the maypole and the traditional sports. Some of Philip Stubbes' more hysterical passages deal with this subject. Bishop Corbett wrote an 'Exhortation to Mr. John Harrison, minister of the parish of Bewdley, for battering down the vanities of the Gentiles, which are comprehended in a May-pole . . . ' The ordinance of 8 April 1644 described maypoles as 'a heathenish vanity.' . . . An understanding of this point will help us to grasp the consistency of many puritan attitudes. The traditional sports clearly were survivals of pre-Christian fertility rituals: May Day celebrations still reputedly produced their crop of bastards in seventeenth-century England. Medieval catholicism had subsumed much of the older religion, but from the fifteenth century onwards Christianity had gone over to the offensive against witches in an attempt finally to eradicate the degenerate remnants of the rival cult. The campaign against the traditional sports linked up with the campaign against witches.[48]

The pagan reference of Comus is not to be reduced to mere literary decoration, pastoral classicizing. The 'potent herbs and baleful drugs'

---

[46] Cited in Williams, *Council*, p. 267.   [47] Skeel, 'Social and Economic Conditions', p. 139.   [48] Hill, *Society and Puritanism*, p. 181.

Comus recalls his mother Circe as culling, his own 'orient liquor in a crystal glass' (65), his 'potion' (68) is part of the witches' pharmacopoeia. 'Deep skilled in all his mother's witcheries' (522) the attendant Spirit calls him. What Comus represents was a vivid contemporary issue. The repression of the pagan was part of the Christian ideology of Puritan social engineering, the attempt to impose labour discipline, the subordination of traditional nature rites to the new cash prerogatives of merchant capital and nascent industrial manufacturing, the beginnings of the control of alcohol and drugs. When the bonds with nature were cut the factory system could be imposed. Seasonal variation and celebration were subordinated to the clockwork regularity of factory production. The repression of the pagan survivals was a stage in the organized alienation of humanity from nature, and from itself. It is the attempt by the 'Presbyterian true-blue' Sir Hudibras to suppress the skimmington and bear-baiting that leads to the village riots in *Hudibras* (1662). Samuel Butler, born in Worcestershire, was steward to the Lord President of the newly revived court in Ludlow, the Earl of Carbery, in 1661. Paganism was spread through Britain; but Ludlow and the Marches bordered an especially benighted district, one of 'the dark corners of the land'.[49]

Wales and the Marches were areas notorious in the 1630s for being unenlightened by true Christianity, deprived of adequate preaching clergy, and still practising pagan customs. The attempts to evangelize these and other areas of Britain were brought to a halt by Archbishop Laud in 1633, the year before the *Maske* was performed.

Richard Baxter, born 1615, describes growing up in the country (i.e. county) of Shropshire in a village five miles from Shrewsbury.

We lived in a country that had but little preaching at all. In the village where I was born there was four readers successively in six years time, who were all my schoolmasters. In the village where my father lived there was a reader of about eighty years of age that never preached, and had two churches about twenty miles distant. His eyesight failing him, he said Common Prayer

[49] See E. P. Thompson, 'Time, Work Discipline, and Industrial Capitalism', *Past and Present*, 38 (1967), 57–97; E. S. De Beer, 'The Later Life of Samuel Butler', *RES* 4 (1928), 160; Samuel Butler, *Hudibras*, ed. John Wilders (Oxford, 1967), pp. xviii–xix. On Butler's legal associations, see Michael Wilding, 'Butler and Gray's Inn', *N & Q*, NS 18 (1971) 293–5. On paganism, see Laurence Lerner, 'Farewell, Rewards and Fairies: An Essay on *Comus*', *JEGP* 70 (1971), 617–31.

without book; but for the reading of the psalms and chapters he got a common thresher and day-labourer one year, and a tailor another year (for the clerk could not read well); and at last he had a kinsman of his own (the excellentest stage-player in all the country, and a good gamester and good fellow) that got Orders and supplied one of his places. After him another younger kinsman, that could write and read, got Orders. And at the same time another neighbour's son that had been a while at school turned minister, one who would needs go further than the rest, and ventured to preach (and after got a living in Staffordshire), and when he had been a preacher about twelve or sixteen years he was fain to give over, it being discovered that his Orders were forged by the first ingenious stage-player. After him another neighbour's son took Orders, when he had been a while an attorney's clerk, and a common drunkard, and tippled himself into so great poverty that he had no other way to live. It was feared that he and more of them came by their Orders the same way with the forementioned person. These were the schoolmasters of my youth (except two of them) who read Common Prayer on Sundays and Holy-Days, and taught school and tippled on the weekdays, and whipped the boys, when they were drunk, so that we changed them very oft. Within a few miles about us were near a dozen or more ministers that were near eighty years old apiece, and never preached; poor ignorant readers, and most of them of scandalous lives. Only three or four constant competent preachers lived near us, and those (though conformable all save one) were the common marks of the people's obloquy and reproach, and any that had but gone to hear them, when he had no preaching at home, was made the derision of the vulgar rabble under the odious name of Puritan.[50]

In an attempt to remedy the sort of situation that Baxter and many others describe, a scheme to buy up the impropriated tithes of various parishes and use the revenue to provide paid preachers was put into operation in 1625. But in 1633 the trustees of the scheme were brought to trial in the Court of Exchequer, and their funds confiscated.[51] Hill writes:

The Feoffees were inspired by John Preston, and he was acutely aware of the problems of the North and West. In a sermon preached before the House of Commons in 1625 he asked: 'Is it not a lamentable case to see how many perish for want of knowledge in Wales, in the Northern counties and in many other places besides? . . . Where doth popery abound so much as in the dark places of the kingdom?' The Feoffees' activities lasted for only eight years, and were to some extent guided by chance: by the availability of impropriations or patronage in areas known to the London merchants,

[50] *Autobiography of Baxter*, pp. 3–4.
[51] David Williams, *A History of Modern Wales* (2nd edn., London, 1977), p. 112.

lawyers and ministers who made up their number; or to their friends. In 1613 (before the formal existence of the Feoffees) Alderman Heylyn had bought an impropriation in Shropshire and used it to set up a lectureship at St. Alkmund's, Shrewsbury: two protégés of the Feoffees subsequently held this lectureship. The Feoffees were accused of spending money on lecturers in London rather than 'on those dark and far-distant corners where souls were ready to famish for lack of food of the Word;' and there is no evidence they paid special attention to Wales. Nevertheless, it is significant that of the thirty-odd ministers whom they appointed or to whom they gave augmentations, nearly half were in Wales or on its borders (six or seven in Shropshire, three in Staffordshire, one each in Pembrokeshire, Radnorshire, Worcestershire and Gloucestershire). The suppression of the Feoffees by Laud in 1633, like the execution of Penry at Whitgift's insistence forty years earlier, showed that neither government nor hierarchy would help to evangelize Wales.[52]

The activities of the Feoffees were not restricted to Wales and the Marches, though those areas were amongst their special concerns. One of the Feoffees, Rowland Heylyn, a former sheriff of London, was of Welsh descent; another was a Pembrokeshire lawyer, John White. But the simultaneous programme of publishing religious books in Welsh translation financed by Heylyn and Sir Thomas Middleton, a former Lord Mayor of London who was also of Welsh descent, showed a specific concern and 'was clearly part of a concerted policy, in which merchants took the lead'.[53]

From 1629 to 1634 there was a remarkable output from the London press, financed by Aldermen Myddleton and Heylyn, of devotional and instructive literature in simple Welsh. The central product was the *Beibl coron*, which for the first time brought the Scriptures in Welsh to the homes of those who could meet the cost and had learned to read; but with it went translations from standard religious works and short elementary manuals of faith and morals, accompanied by aids to reading in Welsh. The standards of these productions, whether moral or aesthetic, were anything but bardic standards, for the new reformers, intent on a less eclectic public than that for which the bards had written, were content with the diluted Welsh of the market place, and in morals they inculcated the middle-class virtues of sobriety and thrift, humility and self-denial, respectability and Sunday observance, in place of the aristocratic and military virtues favoured by that relic of pagan vanity and vainglory, the bardic order.[54]

[52] Hill, *Change and Continuity*, pp. 16–17.
[53] Ibid.   [54] Dodd, *Stuart Wales*, p. 62.

Laud's abolition of the Feoffees and the ending of the active programme of taking Christian and educational enlightenment into Wales is part of the context of the *Maske*. Comus represents the dangerous, threatening, pagan, papist aspects of the dark corners of the land, that will now thrive unchecked. Oliver Cromwell supposedly later referred to the common people of Wales as 'but a seduced ignorant people'. Hugh Peter found the Marches 'ripe for the Gospel' in 1646, and that same year Cradock

preached before the Commons in July:

'And what if you should spend one single thought upon poor contemptible Wales. It's little indeed and as little respected, yet time was the enemy made no small use and advantage of it . . . Is it not a sad case that in thirteen counties there should not be above thirteen conscientious ministers who in these times expressed themselves firmly and constantly faithful in the Parliament, and formerly preached profitably in the Welsh language twice every Lord's Day?'

(We note in passing Cradock's simple assumption that regular preachers would of course be constantly faithful to Parliament.) In *The Parliament explained to Wales* John Lewis complained of 'that swarm of blind superstitious ceremonies that are among us, passing under the name of old harmless customs'—worship of saints, pilgrimage to wells, superstitious veneration of chapels. It 'is still to this day undispelled, and hinders us from the primitive light of the Gospel.' The task of enlightening Wales was therefore a dual one: darkness had to be dispelled as well as truth preached.[55]

On 22 February 1650, the Act for the Propagation of the Gospel in Wales was passed 'according to the plan laid down by Hugh Peter'.[56] But in 1634 such legislation lay only in a revolutionary dream, an apocalyptic vision. In 1634 the Feoffees had been abolished, and the Book of Sports promoted. Enlightenment was being repressed, paganism licensed. Milton's comment is implicit but unavoidable: this is a climate in which Comus can flourish. The Lady may be saved but Comus escapes with his wand to roam at large, unscathed, unfettered.[57]

[55] Hill, *Change and Continuity*, pp. 28–9.
[56] Ibid., pp. 26 n. 172, 28–9, 32 n. 206.
[57] 'The palace of evil has to be escaped, and is not destroyed': John Creaser, ' "The Present Aid of this Occasion"; the setting of *Comus*', in Lindley, *The Court Masque*, p. 127.

As for Ludlow itself, the specific temptations there in the 1630s are well described by Richard Baxter, who was sent to attend the Chaplain to the Council, rather than going to university.

And though the house was great (there being four judges, the King's Attorney, the Secretary, the Clerk of the Fines, with all their servants, and all the Lord President's servants and many more), and though the town was full of temptations, through the multitude of persons (counsellors, attorneys, officers and clerks), and much given to tippling and excess, it pleased God not only to keep me from them, but also to give me one intimate companion, who was the greatest help to my seriousness in religion that ever I had before, and was a daily watchman over my Soul. We walked together, we read together, we prayed together, and when we could we lay together . . . Yet before we had been two years acquainted he fell once and a second time by the power of temptation into a degree of drunkenness, which so terrified him upon the review (especially after the second time) that he was near to despair, and went to good ministers with sad confessions. And when I had left the house and his company, he fell into it again and again so oft that at last his conscience could have no relief or ease but in changing his judgment and disowning the teachers and doctrines which had restrained him . . . And the last I heard of him was that he was grown a fuddler and railer at strict men; but whether God recovered him, or what became of him, I cannot tell.[58]

The corruptions of the Marches round Ludlow, then, involved pagan piping, a lack of preaching ministers, gambling (Baxter describes the gaming tables), and drunkenness. Comus's 'orient liquor in a crystal glass' which makes those who drink it 'roll with pleasure in a sensual sty' is not something remote, literary, fabricated, not something unconnected with the fate of Baxter's intimate companion: 'He was grown a fuddler and railer at strict men'. We recall Comus's railing:

> O foolishness of men! that lend their ears
> To those budge doctors of the Stoic fur,
> And fetch their precepts from the Cynic tub,
> Praising the lean and sallow Abstinence.

> (705–8)

The Lady's fears of encountering the 'swilled insolence / Of such late wassailers' (177–8) is realistic enough if the continual reference to unlicensed alehouses in the Council's records is taken note of. Discussing 'the activity of the Council in the Marches under the early

[58] *Autobiography of Baxter*, pp. 7–8.

Stuarts', Penry Williams remarks that 'Two offences did receive more attention in the 1630s than before. The first was the keeping of unlicensed alehouses and the negligence of the J.P.s who licensed too many. The second was the breaking of the game laws.'[59] It was a long-standing situation. Instructions sent to sheriffs and justices of the peace by the Council in 1573 declare:

Whereas the Lord President and Council are given to understand that an excessive number of alehouses exists in the counties mentioned below, many being in desert and secret places, as woods, commons, waste grounds and mountains out of any highway; and the number is still increasing by the obtaining of licences from Justices of the Peace who are far away from the affected places and ignorant of the character of the applicant or the needs of the locality. And as by this felonies are increased, thieves, murderers and women of light conversation are harboured, rogues and vagabonds maintained, whoredom, filthy and detestable life much frequented, unlawful games as Tables, Dice, Cards, Bowls, Kayles, Quoits, and such like commonly exercised, Bows and Arrows left aside to the great decay of artillery and emboldening and encouragement of the foreign army.[60]

The central sexual episode of the *Maske* had its appropriateness for a court a major part of whose business was with sexual 'offences'. Penry Williams writes

Fines on sexual offenders were relatively constant: adultery almost always cost £3. 6s. 8d.; the price of fornication was generally £2. 13s. 4d., though it sometimes fell to £1. 0s. 0d.; incest was more expensive. By Star Chamber standards these sums were moderate, even when one remembers that the fines imposed in Star Chamber were generally mitigated after the original sentence. Yet by seventeenth century standards they were heavy enough. Even 6s. 8d. could be a large sum to a poor man at a time when a labourer's daily wage might be only 6d. or 8d.; and the fines for sexual immorality would have been burdensome to all but the richest or most circumspect inhabitants of Wales and the border.[61]

Williams goes on to indicate the economic base of the concern with sexual morality:

[59] Williams, 'The Activity of the Council', p. 141.
[60] Cited in Gareth Jones, *The Gentry and the Elizabethan State* (A New History of Wales, Swansea, 1977), p. 100, modernized from Ralph Flenley, ed., *A Calendar of the Register of the Queen's Majesty's Council in the Dominion and Principality of Wales and the Marches of the same 1569–1591, from the Bodley MS No. 904* (London, 1916).
[61] Williams, 'The Activity of the Council', pp. 143–4.

Normally, such lapses were punished by the ecclesiastical courts; but the
Council in the Marches had long been empowered to fine adulterers and
fornicators . . . the number of fines for these offences was high, higher indeed
than for any other misdemeanour except non-prosecuting. As a result the
Council viewed this part of its jurisdiction with a jealous eye. When, in 1636,
the ecclesiastical courts objected that they, and not the Council, had the
sole right to the punishment of such offences, the Council defended itself
vigorously. Sir John Bridgman wrote to the Lord President that if this
jurisdiction were taken from the Council 'there will be such a decay of the
fines that they will not support the charge of the house.' Here, then, the
financial motive behind the Council's jurisdiction was especially strong.[62]

In describing the changes worked by Comus's 'orient liquor', the
attendant Spirit is quite specific:

> Soon as the potion works, their human countenance
> The express resemblance of the gods, is changed
> Into some brutish form of wolf, or bear,
> Or ounce, or tiger, hog, or bearded goat,
> All other parts remaining as they were,
> And they, so perfect is their misery,
> Not once perceive their foul disfigurement . . .
>
> (68–74)

The first mutation listed is into a wolf, as it is when the attendant
Spirit describes to the two brothers the same process resulting from
'his baneful cup'

>   whose pleasing poison
> The visage quite transforms of him that drinks,
> And the inglorious likeness of a beast
> Fixes instead, unmoulding reason's mintage
> Charactered in the face; this have I learnt
> Tending my flocks hard by i'the hilly crofts,
> That brow this bottom glade, whence night by night
> He and his monstrous rout are heard to howl
> Like stabled wolves, or tigers at their prey,
> Doing abhorred rites to Hecate
> In their obscured haunts of inmost bowers.
>
> (525–35)

Don Wolfe has remarked on the specific resonance of 'wolf' in
Milton's writings as denoting the greedy, corrupt clergy. There is no
reason to exempt the *Maske* from participating in this signification.

---

[62] Ibid., p. 144.

Applied to the greedy clergy the word *wolves* was a favourite one with Milton. In *Defensio Secunda* he writes a bitter passage on the wolves of the church 'stuffed with tithes' yet nothing can satisfy their rapacious cravings. In *The Tenure* he calls them 'ravenous wolves'. And in *Christian Doctrine*, where one always looks for Milton's most mature and considered opinions on church matters, he bluntly affirms that the exaction of tithes is the act of wolves, not of ministers.[63]

There is no problem in seeing Comus and his crew as in part representing, or composed of, corrupted clergy.[64] Comus invokes Cotytto:

> befriend
> Us thy vowed priests, till utmost end
> Of all thy dues be done, and none left out . . .
>
> (135-7)

They perform 'rites' to Cotytto (125), to Hecate (534), not to 'the Supreme Good' (216). This is interpretable both as witchcraft and as Catholicism; a perversion or parody or inversion of true religion. The *Variorum Commentary* has some difficulty in explaining the phrase 'stabled wolves'.

(1) put or sheltered in a stable: which seems possible only if we think of the 'stable' as confining rather than sheltering the wolves and of their complaining like the lions at their bonds in Virgil's description of the sounds heard from Circe's island (*Aeneid*, 7. 15–20). (2) Browne compares *Triste lupus stabulis* (Virgil, *Eclogue*, 3. 80). This Verity accepts as possibly explaining *stabl'd*, i.e., having got into the sheepfold (Lat. *stabulum*); but he also notes (3) that in *Paradise Lost* II. 752 *stabl'd* means 'made their the ⟨Sea-monsters'⟩ lair.' This meaning, [accepted by Trent], if dominant here, would make the phrase equivalent to 'wolves in their lairs' [favoured by Hughes, 1937] — not 'their haunts', as Verity infers. But *OED* recognizes no such meaning for *stable*, and strictly speaking the context in *PL* suggests no more than a shelter. The next phrase, *tigers at their prey*, supports the second meaning above. [One may not think so; the tigers are introduced by *or*, as a different kind of idea. The second meaning may seem very strained; the first, involving a recollection of Virgil, quite probable, since Milton has just been describing Circean transformations.][65]

[63] Don M. Wolfe, *Milton in the Puritan Revolution* (London, 1941), p. 109.

[64] *Variorum*, p. 955: 'a sort of priest of misrule'; Andrew Milner, *John Milton and the English Revolution* (London, 1981), p. 135: 'It is significant, too, that Milton chooses to associate the character of Comus with the notion of priesthood.'

[65] *Variorum*, pp. 921–2.

This uncertainty suggests that some other meaning might be sought. If we take 'wolves' as denoting clergy, then 'stabled' can readily be interpreted as 'established'; stabled wolves—established clergy. These are the institutionalized destroyers of Christian virtue, of the flock of innocent sheep. This reading is given confirmation when Comus rebukes the Lady after her speech on the just distribution of wealth, and is extended into the educational sphere:

> Come, no more,
> This is mere moral babble, and direct
> Against the canon laws of our foundation . . .
>
> (805–7)

The *Variorum* remarks:

Warton took this as ridicule (by Milton) of ecclesiastical establishments and the Canon Law and cited contemptuous allusions in Milton's prose of 1641–4; but, as Masson said, 'Milton had not yet figured as a church-reformer and satirist of ecclesiastical laws and law-courts.' Keightley, countering Warton, saw 'a humorous application of the language of universities and other foundations.' Todd, Verity, Wright and Hanford follow Warton; Masson follows Keightley, as Elton does with a happy phrase, Comus' 'College of Pleasure.' It seems impossible that Milton should here use such words without intending a reference to the laws of the church, as if Comus were to say: 'The rules of our foundation are as binding as the Canon Law itself.' If Comus is referring ironically to his 'foundation' as a college, then the *meer moral babble* (806) perhaps glances at the ethical instruction of other foundations (cf. 706 and n.).[66]

The roles of minister and teacher were interconnected; it was the clergyman who provided teaching in the village schools, and the university teachers were also all ordained. The two roles are inter-twined in Milton's denunciation in 'Lycidas': 'The hungry sheep look up, and are not fed' (125). He indicts 'our corrupted clergy, then in their height', as the head-note of 1645 makes clear; but he indicts, too, the educational failings of the Cambridge fellows. The 'canon laws of our foundation' allude both to a religious and to an educational institution—a papist monastery, a Laudian cathedral, or an Oxford or Cambridge college. When Comus tells the Lady

---

[66] Ibid., p. 955

> see, here be all the pleasures
> That fancy can beget on youthful thoughts,
> When the fresh blood grows lively, and returns
> Brisk as the April buds in primrose season
>
> (667–70)

the emphasis is on youthful thoughts, the spring of life. The context is of the young, exposed to temptation instead of benefiting from the moral education expected at this stage of life. The Lady Alice Egerton was fifteen. Milton had entered Cambridge at sixteen. The 'stately palace' with its 'tables spread with all dainties' resembled a college Hall readily enough. The attendant Spirit describes Comus's palace as 'the necromancer's hall' (648). There was a congruence of architecture, furnishing, and decoration in these monuments of the ruling class. Earlier the Lady referred to 'tapestry halls / And courts of princes' (323–4). The *Variorum* glosses: '*Hall* may mean either the whole mansion (*OED* 1 and 3) or one of its large public rooms (ibid. 2), which would be the part actually hung with tapestries'.[67] But the immediate specific association of 'hall' for someone who had just spent seven years at Cambridge would be of the college hall, where he dined every day. Comus's palace hall could readily evoke a college hall, something the hypothetical 'low but loyal cottage' (319) or 'lowly sheds / With smoky rafters' (322–3) could never do. The setting is the great hall at Ludlow Castle, where Richard Baxter had been sent for an education instead of to university. The Court of the Marches at Ludlow kept terms, like the University, though they were four brief ones. 'Trinity and Michaelmas terms usually lasted for about four weeks each, Lent term for two-and-a-half or three, and Hilary term for just over two.'[68] And Comus's railing

> O foolishness of men! that lend their ears
> To those budge doctors of the Stoic fur
>
> (705–6)

[67] Ibid., p. 901.

[68] Williams, 'The Activity of the Council', pp. 148–9. Comus's references to budge and stoic fur may also be taken as referring to legal robes and gowns. Cf. Ben Jonson, *For The Honor of Wales*: 'I, please your urship, is a Welshe attorney, and a preddily shcolars, a wear him his long coat line with seepskin, as you see, every days o' the week. A very sufficient litigious fellows in the terms, and a finely poets out o' the terms, he has a pring of laurel already towards his girlands.' (47–52). Ludlow is referred to in line 105. *Ben Jonson: The Complete Masques*, ed. Stephen Orgel (New Haven, 1969).

can readily be subsumed to the image of the comfortably living establishment don railing at Puritan extremist colleagues. 'Warton referred to budge, a fur (originally from the skin of lamb or goat) used to trim garments, including academic robes (*OED*: *sb.*[1]I)', the *Variorum* notes.[69] The implication of the flock of students or parishioners skinned—not even shorn—to provide the academic gown, the sheep's clothing for the wolves, has its appropriate resonances. The *Variorum* notes further of the passage, 'the whole indicating Comus' contempt for academic moralizers'.[70] The academic context is firmly established; and this does not mean that because Comus is railing at academic doctors, he is not to be seen as an academic himself. Far from it, the bitterness of his denunciation comes as readily from someone in the same business. As Chekhov shows in 'A Boring Story', criticism of fellow academics is a mark of the university life. The Trinity manuscript reading 'stoic gown', noted by Warburton, further attests the university context.[71]

We might also note that Comus's magic is not alien to the universities. Comus is another manifestation of Spenser's Archimago, the arch-magus. The power, the magic of the Magus comes from study and knowledge. In his *Witchcraft and Black Magic*, Montague Summers cites William Perkins, a fellow of Christ's College some thirty years before Milton was an undergraduate there, whose posthumous *A Discourse of the Damned Art of Witchcraft* was published in 1608:

There can, I think, be little doubt that this special course of sermons was preached or inspired in the first place by some vivid rumours of witchcraft and meddling with magic among Cambridge men, dons and undergraduates, which had come to his ears. The whole thing was kept very secret, and details have not yet been traced. That Cambridge was the headquarters of a witch society hardly admits of question. Half a century later it was discovered that the witch cult was highly developed in Cambridgeshire and the Isle of Ely, and this did not grow up in a year or two. It has persisted throughout the centuries, and in Cambridge today bands of Satanists meet for their worship of hell.[72]

With Comus representing in one of his aspects the corrupted clergy and the betrayal of education, the association with Cambridge and

---

[69] *Variorum*, p. 944.   [70] Ibid., p. 945.
[71] Newton, *Paradise Regain'd . . .* , ii. 155. Brockbank notes it is in part 'a masque about growing up', 'The Measure of "Comus" ', p. 52.
[72] Montague Summers, *Witchcraft and Black Magic* (London, 1974), p. 92.

its river spirit, 'Camus, reverend sire' as he is denoted in 'Lycidas' (103), takes on a sardonic resonance. The *Maske* has its good river-spirit, Sabrina of the River Severn; to think of the spirit of the River Cam is not to think in an alien way. Milton was not long out of Cambridge, having graduated as MA on 3 July 1632. He was now engaged in his own educational programme to remedy the inadequacies of the university. To name the arch-tempter Comus cannot but bring Camus into play. There were many other types of tempter from whom Milton could have taken a name, and avoided any accidentally pejorative allusion to his Alma Mater. When we recall that Milton was known at Cambridge as 'the Lady of Christ's', a further resonance of personal meaning emerges in the temptation of the Lady by Comus. Just as the Lady of Christ's resisted the blandishments of Camus, the Lady resists Comus. Had Milton wanted to exclude any personal implications he need not have called his tempter Comus nor his protagonist The Lady. He could have invented a name for Lady Alice Egerton's part; he could have specified her as Lady Alice, even. But Lady, *tout court*, tempted by Comus, insists on religio-educational Cambridge associations, whether at a subconscious or at an explicit, personal level; a coded rejection of Cambridge and the established church and educational structure.

The verbal play that directs us to read Camus for Comus, a sub-text revealed in the change of a letter, is there similarly in the Lady's rewriting of charity as chastity.

> O welcome pure-eyed Faith, white-handed Hope,
> Thou hovering angel girt with golden wings,
> And thou unblemished form of Chastity . . .
>
> (212–14)

The outrageous substitution of chastity for charity, the very scandalousness of the verbal play, calls out. The repressed political is drawn attention to because the repression is drawn attention to. Milton blazons the way in which a social, public, potentially political theme — charity — is replaced by the private issue of chastity. Faith, Hope, and Chastity are qualities that do not necessarily involve other people: these are victimless virtues, as it were, for the individual adept to pursue; the would-be Magus adopts chastity as a way of achieving individual power.[73] These powers may be used publicly, socially, politically later, when acquired; that possibility is not excluded. 1634 was not a good time for open political activity. The only possibilities were the private preparations for the revolution that was to come. Premature public activity would only provoke arrest, repression.

Milton's commitment to chastity may, then, have this ultimate social purpose. But generally chastity is a private virtue whereas the charity it replaces involves other people, the objects of charity. And but to conceptualize the existence of these other people is inevitably to think politically, economically.

Charity, however, was a declining social phenomenon. Christopher Hill points out how 'Milton in his Commonplace Book collected examples to show that "the most lavish alms-givers are not always truly devout"'.[74] 'George Wither included "indiscreet and fond compassion" for the poor among the passions pilloried in *Abuses Stript and Whipt*, finding men "often erring in their charity." Thomas Heywood regarded the refusal of charity to the idle as a specifically puritan attitude. Yet it was more general than that.'[75] Hill continues:

Community of goods in primitive Christianity was soon transformed into financial assistance for the less prosperous among the faithful; and as Christianity became an official religion, the Church was increasingly institutionalized. It became the recipient even more than the dispenser of alms. The process is symbolized by the degradation of the word 'charity'. It used to be the holiest of the three, holier than hope or even faith: it has become a crust of bread handed to the poor man at the gate. Adam Smith attributed the decline of clerical charity to the rise of industry, which made available commodities in exchange for agricultural products whose 'quantity exceeded greatly what the clergy could themselves consume.'[76]

And in a just society there would be no need of charity. The Lady confronts the issue in answering Comus:

> If every just man that now pines with want
> Had but a moderate and beseeming share
> Of that which lewdly-pampered Luxury
> Now heaps upon some few with vast excess,
> Nature's full blessings would be well-dispensed

[73] Cf. Francis Yates, *The Occult Philosophy in the Elizabethan Age* (London, 1983), pp. 160, 180.
[74] Hill, *Society and Puritanism*, p. 268.   [75] Ibid., p. 276.   [76] Ibid., p. 252.

In unsuperfluous even proportion,
And she no whit encumbered with her store,
And then the giver would be better thanked,
His praise due paid, for swinish gluttony
Ne'er looks to heaven amidst his gorgeous feast,
But with besotted base ingratitude
Crams, and blasphemes his feeder. Shall I go on?
Or have I said enough?

(767–79)

As William Haller points out in *The Rise of Puritanism*,

The invective of Lycidas and of the anti-prelatical tracts against the blind mouths of the church are both anticipated when the Lady says that nature's blessings are meant to be dispensed in even proportion to just men, not crammed by swinish gluttons.[77]

Mary Ann Radzinowicz similarly focuses on this passage:

The moment of most powerful intellectual energy in the work would be seen to be the moment when the mortal spokesman for all the nation rebukes the few who with 'swinish gluttony' gorge themselves and blaspheme their feeder. The Lady hates it 'when vice can bolt her arguments / And virtue has no tongue to check her pride.' (759–60) Speaking this resonant republicanism with a bravura sense of her own force ('Shall I go on? / Or have I said enough?'), the Lady prophesies the coming political age of true brotherhood and contemptuously leaves to Comus 'deer Wit and gay Rhetorick.' To her true words 'dumb things' and even the 'brute Earth' will respond in sympathy.[78]

So although 'charity' is erased from the explicit thematic concerns of the *Maske*, the very erasure draws attention to the issue. From the Lady's speech in favour of equal distribution of wealth, we realize that charity is a minor, transient, transitional virtue. If the world were ordered with political and economic justice, there would be no need of charity; it would be erased from the virtues because it would no longer be necessary; it is a purely reactive virtue, responsive to social injustice. Social justice would remove the necessity for

[77] Haller, *The Rise of Puritanism*, p. 320. And see Saad El-Gabalawy, 'Christian Communism in *Utopia*, *King Lear*, and *Comus*', *University of Toronto Quarterly*, 47 (1978), 228–38. As Lerner puts it, 'offered riches, she chooses austere socialism', 'Farewell, Rewards and Fairies', p. 622.

[78] Mary Ann Radzinowicz, *Toward Samson Agonistes: The Growth of a Poet's Mind* (Princeton, 1978), pp. 126–7. See also Norbrook, *Poetry and Politics*, pp. 257–9.

charity, allowing the substitution of chastity, a course of preparation for spiritual powers and knowledge, the true purpose of the soul's sojourn on earth. Of course, the need for charity in the context of 1634 or any other time is not minor and transient, and in such a context how can the soul be preoccupied with its own salvation alone and confine its attention to the spiritual? By indicating how charity could be dispensed with, Milton underlines how necessary it is, underlines this simply by letting the issue be raised. The social injustice and inequality is everywhere apparent and unavoidable. It is built into the very structure of the *Maske* with its range of figures from peasants (or imitated peasants) to the Lord President and his family. And though the central issue between Comus and the Lady is presented as chastity, the terms of the arguments and the dissimulations are saturated with the economic, the political, the ideological.

When Comus hears the Lady's footsteps, he takes precautions that she will not see him and his crew for what they are.

> when once her eye
> Hath met the virtue of this magic dust,
> I shall appear some harmless villager
> Whom thrift keeps up about his country gear.

(164–7)

That last line about thrift, though present in the first edition of the *Maske*, 1637, was omitted in the second edition, the text printed with the *Poems* of 1645, and is relegated to a textual note in many editions, Carey included. The line is important for the train of illusion Comus sets in motion. The magic dust allows the Lady to perceive Comus as a worthy embodiment of the puritan virtue of thrift, a hard-working, good peasant. Thrift is a basic component of Protestant ideology, and is integrally related to the critique of the clergy as devouring wolves, of magic, and of pagan festivals, that runs through the *Maske*. Jack Lindsay devotes a chapter of his *John Bunyan* to thrift:

Throughout the Protestant movements we find that the question of thrift is a root-question. From Wiclif on, the middle-class anger against the Church is based always on anger at the Church's parasitism, the maintenance of a vast unproductive organization, and the diversion of moneys into the Church's coffers . . .

Thrift was needed as part of the process of accumulation whereby industry was speeded on its course. Thrift alone would never have created industrialism. The social dynamic came from the seizure of the land by the upper classes; but the thrift of the lower middle classes was also necessary. It provided the ceaseless little petty-bourgeois centres of activity from which industrialism stemmed.

Hence the way the loose-liver, the debauchee, became the figure of evil. Recall the horror that came over Bunyan about dancing. It seems a long way from such a wildly idiosyncratic terror to an ethic of thrift based on class-needs; yet the connexion is there. William Prynne, typical Puritan moralist, clinched his condemnation of dancing with the statement: 'They that work hard all day had more need to rest than to dance all night. And yet how many there are who after a hard journey or toilsome day's work will take more pains at night in dancing than they did in labouring all the daytime.' . . . We must also remember that the games—maypoles and wakes and so on—were bound up with a general medieval viewpoint based on magic; so that the Puritans were not merely ousting innocent enjoyment, they were concerned primarily with 'idolatry', the primitive magical ideas imbedded in the revelries. Yet the revolt against magic and the ethic of thrift merge inseparably in the needs of the progressive classes. The puritan fight against junketing saints' days combined the thrift-urge with this horror of all cultural activities that had magical associations.[79]

Hill has noted that 'there was a great increase in the literature advocating thrift in the years 1600–40'.[80] It was one of the virtues inculcated by the programme of religious literature in Welsh translation published from 1629 to 1634, financed by Middleton and Heylyn.

But whatever happens to the Lady's eye, her ear remains true. She hears uproar; and she interprets the sounds she has heard as those of the traditionally drunken, rioting, sexually aroused workers, seen from her ruling-class perspective. She begins her first speech:

> This way the noise was, if mine ear be true,
> My best guide now; me thought it was the sound
> Of riot, and ill-managed merriment,
> Such as the jocund flute or gamesome pipe
> Stirs up among the loose unlettered hinds,
> When for their teeming flocks and granges full
> In wanton dance they praise the bounteous Pan,
> And thank the gods amiss. I should be loth

[79] Jack Lindsay, *John Bunyan: Maker of Myths* (London, 1937), pp. 198–9.
[80] Hill, *Society and Puritanism*, p. 127.

> To meet the rudeness and swilled insolence
> Of such late wassailers.
>
> (169–78)

The sexual threat is reinforced through the full complexity of phallic image and verbal association: ill-managed merriment, loose, teeming, wanton dance, the jocund flute and gamesome pipe, and the bounteous Pan. But the first association of the noise the Lady makes is of riot. Civil disturbance, political insurrection is given expression before the threats of sexual arousal and drunkenness. And the drunkenness with which the Lady concludes her list of complaints — riot, sex, drink — is a drunkenness that involves insubordination: 'swilled insolence'. Hers is a ruling-class perspective with all the ruling-class fear of the oppressed. And riot was a frequent enough charge in the cases before the Court of the Marches.

When Comus addresses the Lady,

> Hail, foreign wonder,
> Whom certain these rough shades did never breed
>
> (264–5)

there could not but have been a *frisson* of racial superiority running through the Ludlow Castle audience. The colonial situation of an Anglo-Saxon ruling class and a Celtic peasantry is momentarily made explicit. The Lady dismisses the praise; though significantly she does not deny or correct it:

> Nay gentle shepherd ill is lost that praise
> That is addressed to unattending ears.
>
> (270–1)

But the attending ears would read confirmation of their ruling-class English superiority.

Comus's servile, cultural-cringe attitude can be read as a mark of the defeated Welsh peasant talking to the daughter of the English regional military commander. So the Lady immediately accepts it as her due even in rejecting it, and assumes he is a local peasant, 'gentle shepherd'. Her class assumptions blind her to reality: they are Comus's magic dust, he needs no other. The mask he puts on, his act, fulfils all too readily her expectations. And recognizing the value the Lady places on Puritan virtues of thrift and hard work, Comus describes having seen her two brothers. The occasion allows him to bring in the note of exhausted labour.

> Two such I saw, what time the laboured ox
> In his loose traces from the furrow came,
> And the swinked hedger at his supper sat;
> I saw them under a green mantling vine
> That crawls along the side of yon small hill,
> Plucking ripe clusters from the tender shoots,
> Their port was more than human, as they stood;
> I took it for a faëry vision
> Of some gay creatures of the element
> That in the colours of the rainbow live
> And play i'the plighted clouds. I was awe-struck,
> And as I passed, I worshipped . . .
>
> (290–301)

Comus implies that he too has been hard at labour, like the ox and the hedger. He associates himself with the official social values of hard work; but he scrupulously avoids presenting the sons of the Lord President as working; they are posed beneath the vine, plucking ripe clusters. Aristocrats, they just pluck the produce at hand, untroubled that the fruit might be someone's hard cultivated produce. In his *Autobiography* Richard Baxter records some of his childhood sins in Shropshire 'which for the warning of others I will confess here to my shame':

2. I was much addicted to the excessive gluttonous eating of apples and pears; which I think laid the foundation of that imbecility and flatulency of my stomach which caused the bodily calamities of my life.

3. To this end, and to concur with naughty boys that gloried in evil, I have oft gone into other men's orchards and stolen their fruit, when I had enough at home.[81]

Baxter was acutely aware that these were 'other men's orchards'. But perhaps the ripe clusters devoured by the brothers were indeed the 'Berries, or such cooling fruit / As the kind hospitable Woods provide' (185–6) for which the Lady sent them. The vine of Comus's literary account suggests the grapes of some idealized classical landscape, but the word could also be applied to other climbing or

---

[81] *Autobiography of Baxter*, p. 5.

spreading plants; the Trinity manuscript had the Elder Brother say later 'here be brambles', and blackberries would have been seasonal at Michaelmas.

The Lady loves the description. 'Gentle villager / What readiest way would bring me to that place?' (303–4) She sees him as the 'gentle' villager, and everything he says fits in with her establishment vision of how such things should be: courteous, gentle shepherd, gentle, thrifty, hard-working villager, who recognizes the more-than-human qualities of the children of the ruling class.

Comus's language reveals the falsity of his claim to hard work. It is the language of artifice, of literary tradition rather than the real language of work. 'Swinked' is a literary coinage. John Carey notes 'This is the first occurrence of the word in *OED*: Milton has coined an archaistic past-participial adjective'.[82] It is derived from Spenser: 'swinck and sweat' in *The Faerie Queene*, II. vii. 8, VI. iv. 32.) But the Lady does not know the authentic language of shepherds; she takes the literary fabrication as the real thing. 'Mantling' is also a literary formation. Carey notes it as the first example in the *OED* in the sense of 'spreading and covering'; previously it had been applied only to liquids, meaning 'gathering a coating of scum' (cf. *Paradise Lost* iv. 258, v. 279, vii. 439).

The pejorative connotations are functional in Comus's negative orientation toward the brothers. But the Lady misses the clue and accepts the praise as the appropriate neologizing of literary compliment. The gross flattery of her brothers the Lady takes as proper respect. So no doubt did many of the audience. When Comus implies he has been labouring, she cannot tell that he has not. Such lower-class figures are all other: rapists, workers, the Welsh, spirits. He seems a worker to her, so she addresses him 'Nay gentle shepherd'. The negative is attached to her first social placing of him, her first utterance to him is 'Nay'. A mark of negativity that he is a nay-shepherd, not-a-shepherd, a figure of evil as it turns out to whom she must always say 'Nay'; or a mark of the Lady's class role, nay-saying, handing down prohibitions to the lower other.

Her class expectation of threat transforms into a vision of servile peasantry. What Comus manifests himself as is her projected delusion, her materialized thought-form. He offers:

[82] Carey and Fowler, *Milton*, pp. 190–1.

> I can conduct you, lady, to a low
> But loyal cottage, where you may be safe
> Till further quest.
>
> (318–20)

The 'low' hangs there; it could be taken along with loose and wanton, low life, a low trick. To a revolutionary, 'low but loyal' suggests servile dependence. But to a Lady (viz. an aristocrat) it seems like ideal truth.

> Shepherd, I take thy word,
> And trust thy honest-offered courtesy,
> Which oft is sooner found in lowly sheds
> With smoky rafters, than in tap'stry halls
> And courts of princes, where it first was named,
> And yet is most pretended . . .
>
> (321–5)

It is the Lady who politicizes the social virtue of courtesy. Charity has been erased; what else will serve to denote offering somebody a bed for the night? Comus makes the offer; the Lady glosses the offer as courtesy, and proceeds to draw a political moral. As Mary Ann Radzinowicz remarks, she is 'unmistakably associated with an ideal or republicanism, attracted to a vision of courtesy "sooner found in lowly sheds" and of the just distribution of Nature's goods to all men "In unsuperfluous even proportion." '[83]

But the Lady is deluded. This is no servile gentle shepherd but a magician with designs on her. The fact that her moralizing about courtesy being 'sooner found in lowly sheds . . . ' is a cliché is functional. The Lady's instinctive reaction to the lower orders is a class fear of riot and rape, subversion political and sexual. Now, taking Comus to be the impossible gentle villager, she comes forth with literary cliché, not valid observation. Thomas Newton notes the source

> The sentiment here is the same as in Ariosto's *Orlando Furioso*. Cant 14. St. 62. of the original, and 52 of Harrington's translation;
>
> > As courtesy oftimes in simple bow'rs
> > Is found as great as in the stately tow'rs.[84]

---

[83] Radzinowicz, *Samson Agonistes*, p. 127.
[84] Newton, *Paradise Regain'd* . . . , ii. 119.

And the Lady's etymologizing has its source as Newton likewise points out:

This is plainly taken from Spenser, *Faery Queen*, B.6 Cant. I. St. I.

> Of court, it seems, men courtesy do call
> For that it there most useth to abound;

as Mr Sympson perceiv'd with me.

Milton noticeably radicalizes these sources. Ariosto's courtesy is 'oftimes' in simple bowers as great as in stately towers; it is present in both locales, but Milton's 'oft is sooner found in lowly sheds . . . than in tap'stry halls / And courts of princes'. And Spenser's present-tense etymology — 'do call', 'most useth to abound' — is now a thing of the past for Milton — 'where it first was named' — while in the present it 'yet is most pretended'.

Arguing that Milton's *Maske* is unique in being a masque of the Country rather than the court', John Cox remarks of this passage:

> Bearing in mind the Country allegiance of Milton's *Maske*, we can better understand a number of points. Consider, for instance, the lady's initial response to Comus when she mistakes his identity . . . (321–6) We sense the dramatic irony in her misplaced trust, of course, since Comus intends to trap her in 'a stately Palace set out with all manner of deliciousness' (659 stage direction) But we also recognize the ironic appropriateness of identifying Comus with the Court, for the identification makes this scene the opposite of what it appears to be. The seeming shepherd who offers to aid an innocent in 'a wild Wood' is really the sorcerer/seducer who destroys innocence in stately palaces.[85]

But the dramatic irony serves also to discredit the Lady's fine sentiment from Ariosto. It may well be true that the Court is corrupt and courtesy not to be found there. Milton's radical republican sentiments are consistent on this point throughout his life. But the antithetical Court–Country ideology is not shown to be true here either. Comus is a fraud. The hypothesized true courtesy from a gentle shepherd is never presented. It is significantly erased. Comus is not a villager and the lowly cottage turns out to be a stately Palace and is never replaced. The absence allows us to consider what the inexpressible is. The court is corrupt, and the gentle shepherds are

---

[85] John D. Cox, 'Poetry and History in Milton's Country Masque', *ELH* 44 (1977), 627–8.

hostile, rebellious, threatening? We reconsider Comus's phrase, the 'low / But loyal cottage'. Such a thing is impossible. Since we are on the borders of an occupied, linguistically separate nation, the falsity of the tribute is even more apparent than in the merely class-hostile, English environment. And the Norman Yoke concept[86] had already mutated a class sense of exploitation into a nationalist sense of exploitation: we are invaded by foreigners, our ruling élite are illegitimate foreigners and their comprador class. It is only eight years from civil war, and the pre-existent class-war aspects of that were to be exploited by parliament and the financiers as an ideology to motivate the fighting rank and file of the army.

Comus is multi-faceted, just as the Hecate to whom the attendant Spirit says Comus performs rites is one of the facets of Artemis, goddess of the moon. One aspect of Comus is clearly associated with the Court, with monarchy. His wand and glass are a version of monarchical regalia, the orb and sceptre. After hearing the Lady sing he declares, 'I'll speak to her / And she shall be my queen' (263–4). Certainly there is an ambiguity with 'queen' in the sense of someone sexually accessible, promiscuous. But that meaning readily went along with a monarchical reference. When William Prynne had described women who acted on stage as whores in *Histriomastix* (1632) it was taken that he referred to the Queen, Henrietta Maria, who frequently performed in court masques. Convicted of treasonous libel by the Court of the Star Chamber, Prynne had both his ears cut off, was pilloried, disbarred, fined £5,000, and imprisoned for life.

The 'stately palace' to which Comus takes the Lady certainly has Court implications. Of course, palace was not restricted to a monarchical application; there were bishops' palaces, which would have its appropriateness for Comus with his crew of wolves. Ludlow Castle had been the residence of many a bishop as Lord President. But it had also been a stately palace for Prince Edward and Prince Richard, Prince Arthur, Catherine of Aragon, and Princess Mary. A Court sense is certainly present, and reaffirmed in Comus's assertion that 'Beauty is Nature's brag, and must be shown / In courts' (744–5). The Lady sees Comus as he is when the 'low / But loyal cottage' turns out to be a 'stately palace'. The social reality is

---

[86] Hill, *Puritanism and Revolution*, pp. 50–122.

now unavoidable and at last impinges. No longer does she see him
and address him as 'gentle shepherd'. He still addresses her as 'Lady'
but she replies with a peremptory, patrician 'Fool' (663) and even
stronger 'False traitor . . . was this the cottage?' (689–92) The
expectations of the low but loyal are now exploded and the social
subterfuge is confirmed as a political treachery. Comus is not a
servile, safe cottager but a palace-dwelling 'false traitor'.

The Court was certainly in Milton's consciousness as he wrote the
Maske. When the brothers hear someone call out, the elder brother
speculates, wrongly, that it is

> For certain
> Either some one like us night-foundered here,
> Or else some neighbour woodman, or at worst,
> Some roving robber calling to his fellows.
>
> (481–4)

Newton cited Warburton's note:

> The Trinity Manuscript had at first,
>   Some *curl'd man of the sword* calling &c:

which alluded to the fashion of the Court Gallants of that time: and what
follows continues the allusion,

> Had best look to his *forehead*, here be brambles.

But I suppose he thought it might give offence: and he was not yet come
to an open defiance with the court.[87]

Though the earlier version was rephrased, the presence of the 'curl'd
man of the sword' lingers on. The Elder Brother asserts of Comus:

> I'll find him out,
> And force him to restore his purchase back,
> Or drag him by the curls, to a foul death,
> Cursed as his life.
>
> (605–8)[88]

---

[87] Newton, *Paradise Regain'd . . .* , ii. 135.

[88] Andrew Milner writes: 'Comus not only sounds like a cavalier, but he also,
apparently, looks like one . . . who, in the England of the 1630s, but a cavalier,
would have "curls"?' (*Milton and the English Revolution*, p. 135). The general point
of Comus's court affiliations with his curls stands, though the term 'cavalier' was not
applied to the supporters of Charles I until 1641–2.

At the same time as being associated with the Court, Comus is also identified with bourgeois commercial interests. This was no contradiction. Isaac Rubin writes that

This transition from feudal to capitalist economy enjoyed the active promotion of the *state authorities*, whose increasing centralization ran parallel with the growing strength of merchant capital. The commercial bourgeoisie suffered greatly at the hands of the antiquated feudal regime: firstly, because the fragmentation of the country into separate feudal estates made commercial relations between them difficult (aggressions from the lords and their knights, the levying of duties, and the like) and secondly, because the right of access to the individual towns was refused to traders from other cities. To smash through the privileges of the estate holders and towns, a strong crown was essential. But the bourgeoisie also needed a powerful state to protect its international trade, to conquer colonies, and to fight for hegemony over the world market. And so the youthful bourgeoisie came out as a partisan of the strong royal houses in the latter's struggle against the feudal lords. The transition from the closed-off town and regional economy to a truly national one demanded the transformation of the weak feudal monarchy into a centralized state which could rely on its own bureaucracy, army, and navy. Thus the age of *merchant capital* was also the age of *absolute monarchy*.[89]

Comus reduces everything to cash terms. Beauty and morality are degraded to commodities, to cash, and the language of capitalism is the language in which he presents them. The attempted seduction of the Lady is phrased in these utterly bourgeois terms:

> Why should you be so cruel to yourself,
> And to those dainty limbs which Nature lent
> For gentle usage, and soft delicacy?
> But you invert the covenants of her trust,
> And harshly deal like an ill borrower
> With that which you received on other terms,
> Scorning the unexempt condition
> By which all mortal frailty must subsist,
> Refreshment after toil, ease after pain . . .
>
> (678–86)

The money-lender's son expressed here the way cash values had penetrated and degraded everything. The sexual implications of 'dainty limbs . . . for gentle usage' mutate into an image of borrowed money which must be put to work to generate the interest payments

---

[89] Isaac Rubin, *A History of Economic Thought* (London, 1979), p. 25.

that must be returned. Nature 'lent' the limbs, and that to the bourgeois is a financial arrangement, a loan with terms spelled out in 'the covenants of her trust'. The Lady is an 'ill borrower' because she will not use what she has borrowed to generate more cash and repay the interest on the loan. Sexual usage becomes usury.

> Beauty is Nature's coin, must not be hoarded,
> But must be current, and the good thereof
> Consists in mutual and partaken bliss,
> Unsavoury in the enjoyment of itself.

> (738–41)

The New Testament parable of the talents was taken as the ideology of capitalism. Put your capital to work for you to generate more cash. Simply to hoard money is not to participate in the necessary circulation of money; hoarded coin will not appreciate. It must be put to use. Dudley North wrote in *Discourses Upon Trade* (1691):

No Man is richer for having his Estate all in Money, Plate, &c. lying by him, but on the contrary, he is for that reason the poorer. That man is richest, whose Estate is in a growing condition, either in Land at Farm, Money at Interest, or Goods in Trade: If any man, out of an humour, should turn all his Estate into Money, and keep it dead, he would soon be sensible of Poverty growing upon him.[90]

Usury was a live, contentious issue. The Middletons,

though an old enough Denbighshire family, did not easily live down the taunt that their new dignity as lords of Chirckland (conferred in face of opposition from conservative-minded neighbours) had been bought with the profits of 'usury'.[91]

Thomas Culpeper's *Tract Against Usury* was published in 1621. Usury had not become naturalized as normal social practice; for us, in a world where credit-card interest-rates are 18–25 per cent per annum contentions about the morality of usury seem remote. Rubin writes:

the medieval laws forbidding the exaction of interest payments were repealed in England by Henry VIII in 1545. Interest could now be charged on loans, although it could not exceed 10% per annum. At the beginning of the

----

[90] Ibid., p. 60.   [91] Dodd, *Stuart Wales*, p. 113.

seventeenth century the legal ceiling was lowered to 8%, and to 6% in 1652. Especially persistent in their pressure for further reduction in the rate of interest were the landed aristocracy, whose prodigal living and constant borrowings dropped them straight into the usurer's clutches.[92]

'This unhallowd air' the Lady refers to (756) is in its one aspect the unhallowed air of usury, the money-lenders in the temple. Comus's arguments would have had a particularly immediate social relevance in 1634, and the landed aristocracy of the Bridgewaters and their guests would more readily have seen the usurious evil of Comus than twentieth-century literary critics. The fact that lines 678–86 were omitted from the Bridgewater manuscript of the *Maske* might suggest a certain sensitivity to the issue rather than a deletion on the grounds of sexual modesty. Milton noted in his commonplace book:

Dante says that usury is a sin against nature and against art: against nature because it makes money beget money, which is an unnatural begetting; against art because it does not work &c. See cant: 11. inferno and Daniell: in that place. / of the popes cruell usurers or merchands call'd: Caursini see Speed. p 352
    Whether it should be allowed, Rivet discusses at length. praelection. in decalog. p. 276. and he supports the affirmative.[93]

'Ease and leasure was given thee for thy retired thoughts out of the sweat of other men', he wrote in 1641.[94] He was aware of the economic realities. That Milton did not enter the church because of its corruptions is often enough remarked; he also chose not to enter his father's profession of scrivener, lawyer, and money-lender, unlike his younger brother Christopher, who withdrew from Cambridge at the same time as John and entered the Inner Temple as a law student in September 1632.[95]

In discussing shepherds in seventeenth-century English literature, we readily read them metaphorically: spiritual pastors, clergy, teachers, poets. The material referent is generally unexamined. Yet sheep were the basis of the primary capitalist accumulation of wealth. The English cloth industry had taken first place from the Flemish industry by the beginning of the seventeenth century. Cloth was England's major export commodity. When the attendant Spirit asks

[92] Rubin, *Economic Thought*, p. 61. [93] *CPW* i. 418–19.
[94] *The Reason of Church-Government*, *CPW* i. 804.
[95] William Riley Parker, *Milton*, (2 vols., Oxford, 1968), i. 119; ii. 781.

the Elder Brother the whereabouts of the Lady, the economic
importance of the woollen industry and sheep rearing is attested:

> I came not here on such a trivial toy
> As a strayed ewe, or to pursue the stealth
> Of pilfering wolf, not all the fleecy wealth
> That doth enrich these downs, is worth a thought
> To this my errand, and the care it brought.
>
> (501–5)

There are some things more important than making money from
sheep, declares the attendant Spirit, habited like a Shepherd, played
by the musician Henry Lawes. But this proto-Augustan periphrasis,
'Not all the fleecy wealth / That doth enrich these downs', stresses
in its repetition—wealth, enrich—the cash-value of sheep-farming.
The basis of Welsh agricultural income was from cattle sales, as
A. H. Dodd writes:

Next in importance to the sales of cattle came those of butter and woollens
. . . woollen cloth woven and spun by unorganised peasants of the north
in the upland districts of Merioneth, Montgomery and Denbigh went
overland to Shrewsbury to be sold by the municipal Drapers' Company
. . . an old and powerful corporation who could base their claim to the sole
right of selling Welsh cloth on an Elizabethan charter; and in their numerous
efforts during the first two Stuart reigns to stop the London merchants from
buying cloth in Wales itself, and so saving the middleman's profit, they
generally had the sympathy of the crown . . . and the monopoly lingered
on till the middle of the next century. It enabled Welsh cloth even in the
seventeenth century to reach a market extending over most of Western
Europe and as far as Archangel and the Guinea coasts; but the profits stuck
with the Shrewsbury middlemen and the London exporters, and did little
to enrich the Welsh countryside.[96]

Litigation involving different aspects of the cloth trade often came
before the Court of the Marches.

When Comus refers to Nature having

> set to work millions of spinning worms,
> That in their green shops weave the smooth-haired silk
> To deck her sons
>
> (714–16)

[96] Dodd, *Stuart Wales*, pp. 24–5.

he is at the same time expressing the situation of the poor cloth-workers, the weavers, the first wave of the exploited proletariat of Britain's industrialization. He picks up the image again at the end of his speech when he says that beauty 'must be shown in courts':

> It is for homely features to keep home,
> They had their name thence; coarse complexions
> And cheeks of sorry grain will serve to ply
> The sampler, and to tease the housewife's wool.
> What need a vermeil-tinctured lip for that
> Love-darting eyes, or tresses like the morn?
>
> (747–54)

The class assumptions are clear: aristocratic ladies are beautiful and should be on display, not working; the production of clothes, functional and beautiful, is to be left to worms, to the lower orders, housewives, with homely features and coarse complexions. Both factory-workshops and cottage industry are encompassed. Rubin writes:

In the seventeenth century many English mercantilists found themselves in complete agreement with the land-owners in advocating high corn prices as a means of compelling the workers to toil. They even advanced the paradoxical claim that *dear corn makes labour cheap*, and vice versa, since dear corn would cause the worker to apply himself with greater exertion.

According to Petty, writing in the second half of the seventeenth century: 'It is observed by Clothiers, and others who employ great numbers of poor people, that when Corn is extremely plentiful, the labour of the poor is proportionably dear: And scarce to be had at all (so licentious are they who labour only to eat, or rather to drink.)'[97]

The *Variorum* notes that the 'green shops' of Comus's speech are 'the mulberry trees, their workshops' (Verity).[98] But this anthropo-morphizing of silkworms tells us more about the way mankind is treated as worms, than the way silkworms are like mankind. It is a vision of mass exploitation; while the explanation of the silk production—'all to please, and sate the curious taste' (713)—evokes the unnecessariness of this sort of commodity production. This is activity of capitalist wealth-production, not the useful labour of man's subsistence and survival but useless toil.

---

[97] Rubin, *Economic Thought*, pp. 39–40.   [98] *Variorum*, p. 945.

Dr Leavis, notoriously hostile to Milton's verse, waxed lyrical about the worms:

> Its comparative sensuous richness, which is pervasive, lends itself fairly readily to analysis at various points; for instance:
>
>> And set to work millions of spinning Worms,
>> That in their green shops weave the smooth-hair'd silk . . .
>
> The Shakespearean life of this is to be explained largely by the swift diversity of associations that are run together. The impression of the swarming worms is telescoped with that of the ordered industry of the workshop, and a further vividness results from the contrasting 'green', with its suggestion of leafy tranquility. 'Smooth-hair'd' plays off against the energy of the verse the tactual luxury of stroking human hair or the living coat of an animal. The texture of actual sounds, the run of vowels and consonants, with the variety of action and effort, rich in subtle analogical suggestion, demanded in pronouncing them, plays an essential part, though this is not to be analysed in abstraction from the meaning. The total effect is as if words as words withdrew themselves from the focus of our attention and we were directly aware of a tissue of feelings and perceptions.[99]

Leavis responded positively to this vision of organized wealth-production, naturalized by organic metaphors, the workers reduced to compliant worms: ordered industry. 'It shows, in fact, the momentary predominance in Milton of Shakespeare'[100] he writes. Shakespeare the corn and malt speculator, we recall.[101] The cloth industry, wrote Rubin,

> had started to flourish in the towns of Italy and Flanders (and later on, in England) even by the end of the middle ages. Even then the master weaver could no longer depend on the immediate consumption of the local market for sales, and so he sold his cloth to middlemen, who transported large consignments to areas where demand existed. The *buyer up* now occupied an intermediary position between the consumer and producer, gradually asserting his domination over the latter. At first he purchased individual batches of commodities from the craftsman as the occasion arose; later he bought up everything the craftsman produced. With the passage of time he began to provide the raw materials at his own expense (e.g. thread or wool), farming them out to individual craftsmen (spinners, weavers, etc.) who were then paid a remuneration for their labour. From this moment the *independent craftsman* was turned into a *dependent handicraft worker*, and the *merchant* into a *buyer up-putter out*. In this way the merchant capitalist, moving from

---

[99] F. R. Leavis, *Revaluation* (London, 1936), pp. 48–9.   [100] Ibid., p. 48.
[101] S. Schoenbaum, *William Shakespeare: A Documentary Life* (Oxford, 1975), pp. 178–9.

the sphere of trade, worked his way into the production process, organized it and gained control over the labour of large numbers of handicraft workers working in their own homes.[102]

This is the economic reality of 'the ordered industry of the workshop . . . "green" with its suggestion of leafy tranquillity'.

As English and Flemish cloth manufacturers increased their demand for wool, so prices shot up and sheep breeding became a more profitable undertaking than cultivating the soil. 'Sheep swallow down the very men themselves,' said Thomas More at the beginning of the sixteenth century. Another of his contemporaries wrote: 'Gentlemen do not consider it a crime to drive poor people off their property. On the contrary, they insist that the land belongs to them and throw the poor out from their shelter, like curs. In England at the moment thousands of people, previously decent householders, now go begging, staggering from door to door.'[103]

The increase in sheep-farming led to an increase in dispossessed peasants. The Council in the Marches heard enclosure cases in Elizabeth's reign; the Instructions to Sir Henry Sidney in 1574 specify:

Furthermore the said Lord President or Vice-President and Council shall, from time to time, make due and diligent inquisition, who hath taken and inclosed any commons or decayed tillage, or habitations for husbandry, against the form of the laws and statutes. And leaving all respect and affections apart, they shall take such order for the redress of the enormities used in the same, as the people be not oppressed for lack of habitation, but that they may live after their sortes and qualities.[104]

By the seventeenth century, however, writes Penry Williams:

the Marcher court was no longer authorized to hear cases of illegal enclosure; and when such cases did come up, the Council was usually occupied in punishing the men who destroyed, rather than those who erected, enclosures.[105]

And, as A. H. Dodd notes, 'riots provoked by the enclosure of common (especially in North Wales) were frequent subjects of complaint in the Star Chamber or the Council at Ludlow'.[106]

As well as cloth-production, Comus celebrates that other basic of capitalist wealth-accumulation, mining: he moves on from

---

[102] Rubin, *Economic Thought*, p. 24.   [103] Ibid., p. 23.
[104] Skeel, *Council*, p. 93.   [105] Williams, 'The Activity of the Council', p. 141.
[106] Dodd, *Stuart Wales*, p. 18. Norbrook, *Poetry and Politics*, notes 'extensive agrarian disturbances in south-west England in protest against illegal enclosures' in the 1620s–30s (p. 257).

Nature's 'full and unwithdrawing hand' shown in setting the silkworms to work,

> and that no corner might
> Be vacant of her plenty, in her own loins
> She hutched the all-worshipped ore, and precious gems
> To store her children with.
>
> (716–19)

'All-worshipped' comes readily enough from Comus, worshipper of evil; to a Christian 'all-worshipped' can properly be applied only to the divine. Comus's application of the phrase testifies to his corruption and to the corrupting quality of a preoccupation with 'ore', gold ('or'), in particular of the precious metals. The imagery of sexual procreation in the production of precious stones allows the establishment of a negative orientation to the exploitation of these mineral resources. The sense of incestuous sexual interference in mining is brought out strongly in *Paradise Lost* when the fallen angels are led by Mammon to dig for gold:

> by him first
> Men also, and by his suggestion taught,
> Ransacked the centre, and with impious hands
> Rifled the bowels of their mother earth
> For treasures better hid. Soon had his crew
> Opened into the hill a spacious wound
> And digged out ribs of gold.
>
> (i. 684–90)

The Elder Brother's earlier reference to 'goblin, or swart faëry of the mine' (435), and the attendant Spirit's opening speech with its mention of 'the sea-girt isles / That like to rich, and various gems inlay / The unadorned bosom of the deep' (21–3) establish a continuity of image. From Elizabethan times there was active operation of silver, lead, and coal mines and iron works in Wales. 'The right to search for copper and precious metals in Wales and other places was granted to Daniel Hochstetter, a German, who together with English associated, formed in 1568 the Society of Mines Royal', writes David Williams.[107] In 1617 Sir Hugh Middleton

---

[107] Williams, *History of Modern Wales*, p. 92.

began to extract silver from the lead mines of Cardiganshire. A. H. Dodd writes that Middleton

took a lease from the Mines Royal Company, extended his activities as far as south Caernarvonshire, and made fabulous profits, which he used (with no great advantage to himself) to improve London's water supply in preference to sinking further capital in his native soil.[108]

Caroline Skeel notes in *The Council of the Marches* that

In 1623 the king ordered the Master and Officers of the Mint that all bullion sent up from the lately discovered mines of Wales should be coined weekly into pieces bearing the arms of the prince, to distinguish them from the others. The Lord President and Council with others, were authorised to apprehend all persons found encroaching on the mines of Sir Hugh Middleton, in Cardiganshire, from which he had been able to extract silver and lead to the employment of many poor and the general benefit of the kingdom.[109]

The two primary forms of bourgeois wealth-production in seventeenth-century Britain, sheep and mines, have a firmly established place in the language and imagery of Milton's *Maske*. Comus mutates not only into Camus but also into Commerce.

The Court of the Marches had its traditions of mask and ceremony. Princess Mary's court had its Lord of Misrule. When the court met at Shrewsbury in 1581 there was a pageant with recited verses and schoolboys as water-nymphs among the Severn reeds. 'At the Christmas court in 1596 . . . Pembroke gave a feast at which the guests, an "honourable and gentlemanlie companie", impersonated King Arthur's knights.' The creation of Charles as Prince of Wales at Whitehall in 1616 was marked at Ludlow by ceremonies involving a sermon, music, and Latin and English verses.[110] As D. Lleufer Thomas noted, a number of Presidents 'notably Bishop Smith, Sir Henry Sidney and Lord Carbery, associated with their office a generous patronage of literature, and they aimed at making Ludlow, so far as possible, a congenial meeting place for learned men from the universities'.[111] And the Court had its distinguished literary associations. Sir Henry Sidney was Lord President from 1560 to 1586, and though much of that time he was absent as Lord Deputy

---

[108] Dodd, *Stuart Wales*, p. 26.   [109] Skeel, *Council*, pp. 146–7.
[110] Ibid., pp. 52, 207; Dodd, *Stuart Wales*, p. 52; Skeel, *Council*, pp. 188–9.
[111] D. Lleufer Thomas, 'Further Notes on the Court of the Marches', *Y Cymmrodor*, 13 (1900), 109–10.

in Ireland, his children Philip, the poet, and Mary 'the Subject of
all Verse' grew up at Ludlow. Philip was educated at Shrewsbury
grammar school, twenty miles away, together with Fulke Greville,
and it was Sir Henry's influence that created a footing at the court
for Greville, from which he came 'to monopolize the administrative
offices in the Council of the Marches. They proved the major source
of his public income for the rest of his life.'[112] Sidney was succeeded
as Lord President by Henry Herbert, second Earl of Pembroke, who
married Mary Sidney as his third wife. Pembroke had a theatrical
company, and his personal representative in the Marches was
Arthur Massinger, father of the playright. It was to Pembroke's two
sons, 'the Most Noble and Incomparable Pair of Brethren, William
and Philip Herbert', that the first folio of Shakespeare's plays was
dedicated in 1623. The dedication still stood in the second folio that
carried Milton's 'On Shakespeare'. Pembroke was succeeded as Lord
President in 1602 by Ben Jonson's friend, Lord Zouch.

The Shakespearian nature of the language of Comus has often
enough been remarked.

Milton seems in this poem to have imitated Shakespeare's manner more than
in any other of his works; and it was very natural for a young author
preparing a piece for the stage to propose to himself for a pattern the most
celebrated master of English dramatic poetry. (*Thyer.*)

Milton has here more professedly imitated the manner of Shakespeare in
his faery scenes than in any other of his works: and his poem is much the
better for it, not only for the beauty, variety and novelty of his images, but
for a brighter vein of poetry, and an ease and delicacy of expression very
superior to his natural manner. (*Warburton.*)[113]

But what was the meaning of Shakespearian in 1634? The Shakespearian
achievement had been fetishized in the expensive, assertively splendid
folios, the aesthetic appropriated by the establishment. The mode
is theatrical and out of date. The Shakespearian is used by Milton

---

[112] Ronald A. Rebholz, *The Life of Fulke Greville* (Oxford, 1971), p. 23.
[113] Newton, *Paradise Regain'd* . . . , ii. 89. On Milton and Shakespeare see
Alwin Thaler, *Shakespeare's Silences* (Cambridge, Mass., 1929), pp. 139–208, and
'Shakespeare and Milton Once More', *SAMLA Studies in Milton* (Miami, 1953),
80–99; George Coffin Taylor, 'Shakespeare and Milton Again', *Studies in Philology*,
23 (1926), 189–99; Ethel Seaton, 'Comus and Shakespeare', *Essays and Studies by
Members of the English Association*, 31 (1945), 68–80; John M. Major, '*Comus*
and *The Tempest*', *Shakespeare Quarterly*, 10 (1959), 177–83.

for the position to be rejected. Similarly with *Paradise Lost*, the easily accessible, self-consciously rhetorical mode of Satan is a manner that proclaims itself to be poetic, heroic epic. And just as the positive values emerge from the contrast with that style in the comparative simplicities of Adam and Eve and in the last two books of the epic,[114] so Comus's overblown manner is opposed at the *Maske*'s and by the simple, translucent clarities of Sabrina's songs. Comus's language is not quite a pastiche of the theatrical high style; but it is a high style that embodies its own undermining criticism, its overripeness demonstrates its decadence. The metaphoric richness, the heaping of image on image is a verbal indulgence. The writer sees it as temptation, self-regarding, narcissistic writing, too much writing. It is so obviously style, and style with a lot of possessions, material referents, overstuffed.

> The earth cumbered, and the winged air darked with plumes,
> The herds would over-multitude their lords,
> The sea o'erfraught would swell, and the unsought diamonds
> Would so emblaze the forehead of the deep,
> And so bestud with stars, that they below
> Would grow inured to light, and come at last
> To gaze upon the sun with shameless brows.
>
> (729–35)

Milton's attitude to the theatre is at least ambivalent. 'On Shakespeare' expresses his admiration, his attraction to the great writer. But when Eve has eaten the apple in *Paradise Lost* she is described in theatrical terms:

> in her face excuse
> Came prologue, and apology to prompt,
> Which with bland words at will she thus addressed.
>
> (ix. 853–5)

In his own 'dramatic poem' *Samson Agonistes*, Samson is described as pulling down a theatre on top of himself and the audience; 'The building was a spacious theatre' (1605). The ultimate in anti-theatre, in self-destroying art, though 'this work never was intended' for 'the stage'. (45–6)

---

[114] Cf. Louis L. Martz, *The Paradise Within* (New Haven, 1964), pp. 117–19.

This ambiguity is structural in the *Maske*. It has been remarked
time and again that conventional radical puritan opinion was
generally hostile to the theatre — Prynne's *Histriomastix* (1632), for
example, and the closing of the theatres by the Long Parliament.
Milton's writing in this contentious form has been explained
variously: adding a new moral seriousness to the masque, writing
a Puritan masque in confrontation to the court masques of Charles
I.[115] He groups the court masques with other sorts of loveless
sexuality in *Paradise Lost*. Love is to be found

> not in the bought smile
> Of harlots, loveless, joyless, unendeared,
> Casual fruition, nor in court amours
> Mixed dance, or wanton mask, or midnight ball,
> Or serenade, which the starved lover sings
> To his proud fair, best quitted with disdain.
>
> (iv. 765–70)

The ambiguity of the situation was unavoidable. Milton confronts it:

> Beauty is Nature's brag, and must be shown
> In courts, at feasts, and high solemnities
> Where most may wonder at the workmanship.
>
> (744–6)

The words are Comus's, as the Lady sits on display in his 'stately
Palace'. But the setting is the stately Ludlow Castle, where the Lady
sits on display, her beauty constantly and insistently remarked, in
a masque performed at the official vice-regal residence of the Lord
President of the Court of the Marches. Ludlow has been a royal court
and a judicial court. Comus's 'courts' exploits this ambiguity.

The attendant Spirit tells the Lady upon her rescue:

> And not many furlongs thence
> Is your father's residence,
> Where this night are met in state
> Many a friend to gratulate
> His wish'd presence.
>
> (945–9)

---

[115] David Norbrook, 'The Reformation of the Masque', in Lindley, *The Court
Masque*, pp. 94–110.

So what Comus asserts to be the proper place of beauty is what indeed eventuates. The Lady and her brothers are presented to the Earl of Bridgewater and his wife:

> Noble Lord, and Lady bright,
> I have brought ye new delight;
> Here behold so goodly grown
> Three fair branches of your own.
>
> (965–8)

And whatever moral instruction may be imparted by the *Maske*, the Lady is none the less on display, her beauty shown at the court, the feast, the high solemnity on Michaelmas night.[116]

The ambiguities, the internal contradictions, are an important part of the *Maske*. In them we see the tensions of Milton's radical politics and literary aspirations.[117] There is no reason to believe that Milton had any respect for the Court of the Marches—abolished along with other prerogative courts like the Star Chamber in 1641—or for the Bridgewaters. The Earl declared for the king at the outbreak of civil war. And the Elder Brother noted in a copy of Milton's *Defense of the English People* (1651) 'Liber igni, Auctor furca, dignissimi'. 'This book is most worthy of the fire, its author of the gallows.'[118] A writer's attitude to his patron must always have been at the least as ambiguous as it is to his twentieth-century publisher, editor, or film-producer.

But the ambiguity was also functional. Shakespeare was certainly in Milton's consciousness when he wrote the *Maske* but it was Spenser he was later to acknowledge to Dryden as his model, the sage and serious Spenser, who is the positive force. And the immediate structural feature of the *Faerie Queene* is its ambiguity. Fidessa and Duessa, the Bower of the Bliss and the Garden of Adonis. The issue in the *Faerie Queene* is of discriminating the true from

---

[116] On the significance of Michaelmas night, see James G. Taafe, 'Michaelmas, the "Lawless Hour," and the Occasion of Milton's Comus', *ELN* 6 (1969), 257–62; William B. Hunter, Jr., 'The Liturgical Context of *Comus*', *ELN* 10 (1972), 11–15; M. S. Berkowitz, 'An Earl's Michaelmas in Wales', *Milton Quarterly*, 13 (1979), 122–5. Taafe cites customs at Kidderminster in Worcestershire.

[117] Cf. Thomas N. Corns, 'Milton's Quest for Respectability', *Modern Language Review*, 77 (1982), 769–79, and 'Ideology in the Poemata (1645)', *Milton Studies*, 19 (1984), 195–203.   [118] Parker, *Milton*, ii. 975.

the false, the real from the imitation, the face from the mask. So the potential parallel of Comus's stately palace with Ludlow Castle can be explained as a Spenserian structure: the false court and the true court. That the indictment of the false court leaks into the portrayal of the true court is yet a further ambiguity of the structural use of ambiguity. The indictment is there for those who want to recognize it; and it can always be explained as the moral of the story: take care Ludlow doesn't end up like Comus's palace. From Baxter's evidence we might speculate that it already had. And the Castlehaven scandal of 1631 with the execution of the Earl of Castlehaven and two of his servants for their sexual activities with his wife and daughter, the Lady Alice Egerton's aunt and cousin, made the ambiguities even murkier.[119]

The issue of discriminating the true from the false runs throughout the *Maske*. The Attendant Spirit presents himself as a shepherd to the brothers, and Comus is seen as a shepherd by the Lady. There are good shepherds and bad shepherds, good priests and bad priests, good academics and bad academics, but it is not easy to tell which are which. Comus's crew dance 'The Measure', which is a corrupt, orgiastic dance, possibly with Court associations in its denotation as measure; but not all dancing is presented as bad. The Attendant Spirit takes the freed Lady and her brothers to the Michaelmas night celebrations at Ludlow.

> All the swains that there abide,
> With jigs, and rural dance resort,
> We shall catch them at their sport.
>
> (951–2)

It is an acceptable version of the 'wanton dance' (175) feared by the Lady when she heard 'the sound of riot and ill managed merriment' (170–1):

> When for their teeming flocks, and granges full
> In wanton dance they praise the bounteous Pan,
> And thank the gods amiss.
>
> (174–6)

---

[119] Barbara Breasted, 'Comus and the Castlehaven Scandal', *Milton Studies*, 3 (1971), 201–24; Dean A. Reilein, 'Milton's Comus and Sabrina's Compliment', *Milton Quarterly*, 5 (1971), 42–43; John Creaser, 'Milton's *Comus*: The Irrelevance of the Castlehaven Scandal', *N & Q*, NS 31 (1984), 307–17.

And so 'The scene changes, presenting Ludlow Town and the President's Castle; then come in Country Dancers . . . '. It is the first recorded use of the term 'country dancers'.[120]

But just as the riotous 'wanton dance' is replaced by the controlled 'jigs and rural dance', so these country dancers are replaced by

> Other trippings to be trod
> Of lighter toes, and such court guise
> As Mercury did first devise
> With the mincing Dryades . . .
>
> (960–3)

And this class triumph, the repression of the common people — 'Back, shepherds, back, enough your play' (957) — is mutated yet again into an asserted and implicitly analogous moral triumph. The Lady and her brothers have come

> through hard assays
> With a crown of deathless praise,
> To triumph in victorious dance
> O'er sensual folly, and intemperance.
>
> (971–4)

And just as Comus's magic fettered the Lady, Sabrina's magic freed her. We are told of Sabrina that 'the Shepherds at their festivals / Carol her goodness loud in rustic lays . . . ' (847–8). These are good festivals with carols, to be discriminated from the bad festivals and rites of Comus.

But there are, naturally, two sorts of ambiguity. There is the ambiguity of stasis, or irony, the debased New Critical model of seeing two sides of an issue and avoiding commitment to either. But there is also that politically strategic ambiguity, in which something said can always be cancelled by the careful, ambiguous signification. What might be read as a criticism of the Bridgewaters having their daughter on public display on stage, like Queen Henrietta Maria, can instantly be retracted by saying that the display at Ludlow is the celebration of true, divine beauty, allegorically presented, of course, compared with the materialist corruptions of Comus's palace.

[120] Jane Garry and Fred R. Shapiro, 'Earlier Uses of Terms Relating to English Folk-Dance', *N & Q*, NS 31 (1984), 304.

Those who would try to minimize Milton's radicalism return again and again to his alleged love of hierarchy. At first sight the *Maske* might seem to support such a case. The Attendant Spirit tells us in the opening lines:

> Before the starry threshold of Jove's court
> My mansion is, where those immortal shapes
> Of bright aërial spirits live ensphered
> In regions mild of calm and serene air,
> Above the smoke and stir of this dim spot,
> Which men call earth . . .
>
> (1-6)

The Spirit 'descends or enters' from this high realm and tells us how

> some there be that by due steps aspire
> To lay their just hands on that golden key
> That opes the palace of eternity.
>
> (13-15)

The pattern of ascent to better things is established. This is followed by the establishment of a chain of command. Neptune controls the sea and 'the sea-girt isles' (21):

> Which he to grace his tributary gods
> By course commits to several government,
> And gives them leave to wear their sapphire crowns,
> And wield their little tridents . . .
>
> (24-7)

It is hardly a celebration of the might of the tributary gods. The stress is on their concessional power, permitted by Neptune, who 'gives them leave'. And the leave they are given to 'wield their little tridents' in no way ennobles them. Even if 'little tridents' is not reductive, it is certainly not glorifying their power. The stress is on the virtuous power of the highest: Jove, Neptune. The account is absolutely concomitant with Milton's vision in the early revolutionary period that governmental power, the tenure of kings and magistrates, is a concessional power, a job to be done, not an absolute right. The presentation of the tributary gods here suggests analogies with monarchy and the fancy-dress aspects of monarchy: 'gives them leave to wear their sapphire crowns, / And wield their little tridents'. The delegation of power by Neptune to the tributary gods sets the model for Charles I's delegation to Bridgewater:

> And all this tract that fronts the falling sun
> A noble peer of mickle trust, and power
> Has in his charge . . .

$$(30-2)^{121}$$

Significantly Milton does not stress the vice-regal nature of the appointment. Nowhere does he say that the noble Peer receives his power from, to quote the St Asaph Cathedral library manuscript of Instructions, 'our moste gratious Soveraigne Lord Charles by the grace of God Kinge of England, Scotland, ffraunce and Ireland defendor of the ffaith, etc.'[122] Neptune and his tributary gods provide analogies for the chain of command, but Charles is excluded. If anything, it is implied that the 'noble Peer' gets his authority directly from Neptune's 'blue-haired deities' (29). This may not be rampant republicanism, but it is certainly scrupulously not endorsive of royalism, monarchy, absolute power.

Re-examining the implicit hierarchy, we might ask who are they 'that by due steps aspire'. The assumed context of the fixed hierarchy, the great chain of being, dissolves: what we have is a series of steps upwards. There is not a rigid, reified, immovable hierarchy; but a process, a movement. Not a ladder, but the movement of ascent. The concept is made clearer in the Elder Brother's 'divine philosophy' (475):

> So dear to heaven is saintly chastity,
> That when a soul is found sincerely so,
> A thousand liveried angels lackey her,
> Driving far off each thing of sin and guilt.
> And in clear dream, and solemn vision
> Tell her of things that no gross ear can hear,
> Till oft converse with heavenly habitants
> Begin to cast a beam on the outward shape,
> The unpolluted temple of the mind,
> And turns it by degrees to the soul's essence,
> Till all be made immortal . . .

$$(452-62)$$

Warburton remarked: 'This is agreeable to the system of the materialists, of which Milton was one', and Thyer noted:

---

[121] Cf. Creaser in Lindley, *Court Masque*, p. 129.
[122] Skeel, 'Social and Economic Conditions', p. 193.

The same notion *of body's working up to spirit* Milton afterwards introduc'd
into his Paradise Lost, V. 469 &c. which is there, I think, liable to some
objection, as he was entirely at liberty to have chosen a more rational system,
and as it is also put into the mouth of an Arch-Angel.[123]

This is Milton's 'fundamental idea' as B. A. Wright puts it, 'that body
and spirit are not different kinds but only different degrees in the
scale of existence'.[124]

> To whom the winged hierarch replied.
> O Adam, one almighty is, from whom
> All things proceed, and up to him return,
> If not depraved from good, created all
> Such to perfection, one first matter all,
> Indued with various forms, various degrees
> Of substance, and in things that live, of life;
> But more refined, more spiritous, and pure,
> As nearer to him placed or nearer tending,
> Each in their several active spheres assigned,
> Till body up to spirit work, in bounds
> Proportioned to each kind. So from the root
> Springs lighter the green stalk, from thence the leaves
> More airy, last the bright consummate flower
> Spirits odorous breathes . . .
>
>   (v. 468–82)

This idea is basic to Milton's thinking. Having cited Wright the
Variorum quite unaccountably asserts of the passage in the *Maske*:
'But it is unlikely that his thought had as yet taken this direction'.[125]
But there is no reason not to recognize a continuity of thought here.
That reference to the body as 'the unpolluted temple of the mind'
contains implicitly a radical puritan rejection of material temples,
churches, and cathedrals; the body is the only true temple, the rest
is material corruption.

The hierarchical scheme of the universe in Milton's account is a
moral hierarchy, the good ascends to the divine, the bad sinks down.
There is not a fixed hierarchy but a process of ascent or descent.
And the process is not one of climbing an external ladder to the

---

[123] Newton, *Paradise Regain'd* . . . , ii. 32.

[124] B. A. Wright, *Milton's Paradise Lost* (London, 1962), cited in *Variorum*,
p. 915.

[125] *Variorum*, p. 915. Carey and Fowler, *Milton*, however, cross-reference
A Maske, 458–62 and *Paradise Lost*, V. 497–500.

higher good, but of every created thing being transmuted within itself to a purer essence, or sinking to a more depraved state. The hierarchy is within the individual; the process of moral development is the movement up and down the hierarchy. This is the divine model which provides no justification for the imitation earthly or Satanic hierarchies, where monarchical and class distinctions are reified into a fixed social order. The divine order is not fixed but in continual refining motion. Raphael's assertion that

> time may come when men
> With angels may participate, and find
> No inconvenient diet, nor too light fare:
> And from these corporal nutriments perhaps
> Your bodies may at last turn all to spirit,
> Improved by tract of time, and winged ascend
> Ethereal, as we, or may at choice
> Here or in heavenly paradises dwell
>
> (v. 493–500)

is an assertion that denies any claimed divine justification for social rank, earthly hierarchy. We are all composed of the same substance; angels are not something remote, separate. There is a continuity of creation; the body, the material, is simply unrefined spirit. In its full implications the belief is utterly revolutionary in earthly terms. It subverts the legitimacy of every earthly hierarchical system.

And the *Maske* ends with a final comment on hierarchy:

> Mortals that would follow me,
> Love Virtue, she alone is free,
> She can teach ye how to climb
> Higher than the sphery chime;
> Or if Virtue feeble were,
> Heaven itself would stoop to her.
>
> (1017–22)

Again the stress is on a flexible hierarchy, not an unbending one. Milton wrote 'bow' for 'stoop' originally, which suggests the analogy with earthly hierarchical rituals more explicitly. The theological meanings of the passage have been well worked over, but in the context of the Court of the Marches there are immediate social implications. Heaven will stoop to help the feeble but virtuous; the suggestion that Bridgewater should administer his judicial and governmental role with the same flexibility, concern, and generosity is unmistakable. 'Height with a certain grace doth bend', Andrew Marvell wrote in 'Upon Appleton House'. Divine grace, social concern.

'Jove's court' of the *Maske*'s opening line is seen able to stoop to help the beleaguered virtuous in the closing line. As above, so below, is Milton's implication, adjuration even. The *Maske* has come full circle. The descent of the Attendant Spirit to help the Lady has been the enactment of Heaven's stooping.

4

Religio Medici
in the English Revolution

I

Not only radicals wrote in a coded, careful, cautious way. Sir Thomas Browne, generally deemed to offer an escape from the political strife of his age, emerges upon analysis, as so many supposedly apolitical figures so often do emerge, as deeply, committedly, and indeed polemically, conservative. Commentator after commentator has accepted Browne's statement 'To the Reader', which prefaces the authorized edition of *Religio Medici* (1643), that the work was written 'about seven yeares past' and thus has read it as a product of the 1630s, as a late metaphysical meditation.[1] Yet in this very stress on times past—and he repeats his assertion, 'it was set downe many yeares past'—Browne is emphasizing times present, the time of publication, the time of his readers. In stressing how things may have changed, how 'there might be many things therein plausible unto my passed apprehension, which are not agreeable unto my present selfe', he is inviting a comparison between times past and times present, and any such comparison in 1643 inevitably invoked the circumstances of revolution and civil war.

There is no doubt about the 1640s context: the preface, as C. A. Patrides has pointed out, 'supplies both the immediate context and the degree of personal involvement':[2] 'the name of his Majesty defamed, the honour of Parliament depraved, the writings of both depravedly, anticipatively, counterfeitly imprinted'. And Browne's complaint about the 'tyranny' of the press is the expression of a definite, partisan position in the political conflict. It followed Charles I's proclamation at the beginning of the revolutionary period, in February 1639: 'For whereas the Print is the King's in all Kingdoms, these

---

[1] C. A. Patrides, ed., *Sir Thomas Browne: The Major Works* (Harmondsworth, 1977), p. 59. All quotations from Browne are from this edition. [2] Ibid., p. 24.

seditious Men have taken upon them to print what they please, though we forbid it'.[3] A supporter of the King and of Archbishop William Laud might lament the 'tyranny' of the press, but the press, together with the pulpit and the petition, was one of the Puritans' main weapons of propaganda. For the Puritans, separatists, and radicals, the 'tyranny' had been the censorship and licensing of the press by Charles and Laud.

In 1637, by decree of Star Chamber, the number of authorised printers in London was reduced to twenty, and savage corporal penalties were denounced against illegal printing. All foreign books imported were to be vetted by the Bishops before they were put on the market. John Lilburne, later the Leveller leader, was flogged through the streets of London for breaking this regulation. No book was to be reprinted, even if previously licensed, without a new licence. Laud was alleged to have refused licences to print Luther's *Table Talk*, Foxe's *Book of Martyrs*, Bishop Jewell's *Works*, and Bishop Bayley's *Practice of Piety*. The Geneva Bible, with its anti-authoritarian marginal notes, had to be smuggled from Holland.[4]

The breakdown in censorship after 1640 was a liberation: 'Nothing gave more resounding emphasis to the overthrow of Laud's power in the state than the collapse of his power over the press'.[5]

Browne appropriated the outraged note of 'tyranny' for new purposes. Under the guise of complaint, he took the opportunity to reissue 'a full and intended copy of that Peece, which was most imperfectly and surreptitiously published before'. The unauthorized edition had appeared in December 1642, a year from which George Thomason collected some 2,134 publications, 'the highest total in any year up to the Restoration', Perez Zagorin remarks, 'a fact that sufficiently demonstrates the accelerated preoccupation with political-ecclesiastical issues in the first stages of the revolution's progress'.[6]

To situate *Religio Medici* in the context of the pamphlet war at the time of its publication, rather than in the mid-1630s when it was hypothetically composed, is to realize its ideological significance, and

[3] William Haller, *Liberty and Reformation in the Puritan Revolution* (New York, 1955), p. 9.

[4] Christopher Hill, *The Century of Revolution, 1603–1714*, pp. 98–9. For a fuller discussion of the topic see 'Censorship and English Literature' in id., *The Collected Essays of Christopher Hill*, (Brighton, 1985), i. 32–71.

[5] Haller, *Liberty and Reformation*, p. 33.

[6] Perez Zagorin, *The Court and the Country: The Beginning of the English Revolution* (New York, 1970), p. 204.

to see Browne's participation in the socio-political debate of the English Revolution. The changes between the 1642 and 1643 editions provide ready access to politically sensitive passages. As Simon Wilkin pointed out, 'In all the manuscript copies are to be found, without exception, those passages of the surreptitious edition which have been omitted in that of 1643, but not one of the numerous additions nor of the most important alterations it contains'.[7]

Jean-Jacques Denonain calculated that Browne made more than 650 changes from the 1642 to the 1643 edition.[8] Some of the changes involved a word or phrase, some involved additional passages, and four entire new sections (8, 28, 43, 56) were added in Part 1. The first of the four added sections occurs early: 'That Heresies should arise we have the prophecy of Christ, but that old ones should be abolished wee hold no prediction'. Browne is not concerned with the nature of particular heresies, but with their multiplication:

even in Doctrines hereticall there will be super-heresies, and Arians not onely divided from their Church, but also among themselves: for heads that are disposed unto Schisme and complexionally propense to innovation, are naturally indisposed for a community, nor will ever be confined unto the order or œconomy of one body; and therefore when they separate from others they knit but loosely among themselves; nor contented with a generall breach or dichotomie with their church, do subdivide and mince themselves almost into Atomes.

(68–69)

'Innovation' was the contemporary term for revolution ('revolution' retained the sense of returning to the same point), and 'separate' alludes to the separatists, those who wished to separate from the Church of England rather than work for Puritan reforms within the Church. The language has its political specificities. Historians are agreed that the proliferation of sects did not occur until the impeachment of Laud on 18 December 1640. 'Until 1641 separatism was numerically insignificant and without much influence upon religious life', Zagorin wrote, but, as Brian Manning stated, 'during 1641 the

---

[7] *The Works of Sir Thomas Browne*, ed. Simon Wilkin (London, 1846), ii, pp. vi–vii.

[8] *Religio Medici*, ed. Jean-Jacques Denonain (Cambridge, 1953), p. xxvii.

separatists increased dramatically in numbers and influence'.[9] Both cite a report from Thomas Knyvett, dated 17 January 1641, on Browne's home town: 'Conventicles every night in Norwich, as publicly known as the sermons in the daytime, and they say much more frequented'. Browne's correction of the 1642 text here is not the restoration of a passage that had been 'by transcription successively corrupted untill it arrived in a most depraved copy at the presse' ('To the Reader'), but a new observation written for the 1643 edition.

Both the sentiments and the imagery of atoms are similar to Bishop Hall's *An Humble Remonstrance* of January 1641:

But stay; Where are we, or what is this we speak of, or to whom? Whiles I mention the Church of *England*, as thinking it your honour, and my own, to be the professed sons of such a Mother, I am now taught a new Divinity, and bidden to ask, Which Church we mean? My simplicity never thought of any more Churches of *England* but one; Now this very dayes — wiser discovery tells us of more; There is a Prelaticall Church (they say) for one; and, which is the other? Surely it is so young, that as yet, it hath no name; except we shall call it indefinitely, as the Jews were wont to style the creature they could not abide to mention, That other thing; And what thing shal that be, think we? Let it be called, if you please, the Church Antiprelaticall; but leave *England* out of the style; Let it take a larger denomination, and extend to our friends at *Amsterdam*, and elsewhere, and not be confined to our *England*: Withall, let them be put in mind, that they must yet think of another subdivision of this division; some there are (they know) which can be content to admit of and orderly surbordination of severall Parishes to Presbyteries, & those again to Synods; others are all for a Parochiall absoluteness, and independence; Yea, and of these, there will be a division, in *semper divisibilia*; till they come to very Atomes: for to which of those scores of separated Congregations, knowne to be within and about these walls will they be joyned? and how long without a further scissure? . . .

Why will ye be so uncharitable, as by these frivolous and causeless divisions, to rend the seamlesse coat of Christ? Is it a Title, or a Retinue, or a Ceremony, a garment, or a colour, or an Organ-pipe, that can make us a different Church, whiles we preach and professe the same saving Truth . . . [10]

Joseph Hall was one of the twelve bishops the Commons impeached and sent to the Tower on 30 December 1641, after they had tried

[9] Zagorin, *The Court and the Country*, p. 232, and Brian Manning, *The English People and the English Revolution*, (Harmondsworth, 1978), p. 51.

[10] Joseph Hall, *An Humble Remonstrance To The High Court of Parliament By A dutifull Sonne of the Church* (facsimile reprint, Amsterdam, 1970), pp. 39–41.

to reverse the vote of 28 December that it was still 'a free parliament', by complaining (correctly enough) that 'they have been at several times, violently menaced, affronted, and assaulted, by multitudes of people, in their coming to perform their service in that honourable House; and lately chased away, and put in danger of their lives'.[11] Hall's participation in the political manœuvre to reverse the 'free parliament' vote and so invalidate its decisions indicates the ideological significance of his hostility to the separatist sects and to the politics of mass action — a crowd of more than ten thousand was estimated to have prevented all but one or two bishops from taking their seats in the Lords on December 28. After his release from the Tower on 5 May 1642 Hall took up the bishopric of Norwich, where he became acquainted with Browne. 'My honord friend' Browne called him in *Repertorium*.[12] Browne's hostility to the sects and the multitude can be read in the same ideological context. The destructiveness of sectarian schism is Browne's theme in this added section, as it is in another entirely new section (56) added in 1643, which concludes:

'Tis true we all hold there is a number of Elect and many to be saved, yet take our opinions together, and from the confusion thereof there will be no such things as salvation, nor shall any one be saved; for first the Church of *Rome* condemneth us, wee likewise them, the Sub-reformists and Sectaries sentence the Doctrine of our Church as damnable, the Atomist, or Familist reprobates all these, and all these them againe. Thus whilst the mercies of God doth promise us heaven, our conceits and opinions exclude us from that place. There must be therefore more than one Saint *Peter*, particular Churches and Sects usurpe the gates of heaven, and turne the key against each other, and thus we goe to heaven against each others wills, conceits and opinions, and with as much uncharity as ignorance, doe erre I feare in points, not onely of our owne, but one anothers salvation. (130)

Wilkin quotes *Gurney's Observations*: 'The spirit of charity which pervades this section is truly characteristick of its author'.[13] But the whole passage is characteristic of Browne's university-educated, élitist contempt for the 'ignorance' of the clashing sects, for the 'vulgarity of those judgements' stressed in the opening line of the section, for the social implications of the theological belief of the

---

[11] Manning, *The English People*, pp. 100–1.
[12] F. L. Huntley, *Sir Thomas Browne* (Ann Arbor, 1962), p. 177.
[13] Wilkin, *The Works of Sir Thomas Browne*, ii. 82.

radical sects. As Christopher Hill remarks, 'in the early 1640s attitudes towards the lower-class heresy of Familism were almost the test of radicalism'.[14] For the theological positions had their political implications:

The Family of Love and the Grindletonians had taught that prelapsarian perfection could be attained in this life. But before the 1640s such doctrines had been kept underground. Now nothing could be suppressed. Plebeian materialist scepticism and anticlericalism could express themselves freely, and fused with theological antinomianism. The result was a rejection of clerical control of religious and moral life.[15]

Joan Bennett, who at the opening of her *Sir Thomas Browne* declares 'there is nothing in his published writings to remind us of the Civil War',[16] none the less recognizes that this 'new section, explicitly attacking mutual exclusiveness and sectarian arrogance, was probably prompted by the increased animosities of the Civil War'; she stresses, however, that

this does not represent any change of mind since the composition of the work in 1635: the section formerly following upon 55 (now sect. 57) opens in the same sense: 'I believe many are saved who to man seeme reprobated, and many reprobated, who, in the opinion and sentence of man, stand elected'.[17]

Browne's distaste for the sects is characteristic of the whole of *Religio Medici*. It is there from the beginning, appearing as early as Section 6 of Part I:

I could never divide my selfe from any man upon the difference of an opinion, or be angry with his judgement for not agreeing with mee in that, from which perhaps within a few dayes I should dissent my selfe: I have no Genius to disputes in Religion. (65)

The addition in 1643 of 'love to' and 'I hope . . . not' (italicized in the following quotation) are additions of emphasis that underline the message of happy conformity to the established church:

[14] Christopher Hill, *The World Turned Upside Down* (Harmondsworth, 1975), pp. 35–6.   [15] Ibid., p. 166.
[16] Joan Bennett, *Sir Thomas Browne* (Cambridge, 1962), p. 1.
[17] Ibid., p. 94.

In Philosophy where truth seems double-faced, there is no man more paradoxicall than my self; but in Divinity I *love to* keepe the road, and though not in an implicite, yet an humble faith, follow the great wheele of the Church, by which I move, not reserving any proper poles or motion from the epicycle of my own brains; by this meanes I leave no gap for Heresies, Schismes, or Errors, of which at present, *I hope* I shall *not* injure Truth, to say, I have no taint or tincture. (66)

The pacific note has often been remarked upon. But in the context of the book's publication, it is a tendentious peacefulness. The implication is that all would be well if heretics and schismatics and dissenters would stop being troublesome and disturbing the peace. Browne's peaceableness is the peaceableness of the conservative who is satisfied with the arrangement of society — an arrangement suiting his own class. All *other* opinions that disturb this peace are heretical, schismatic, dissident. And it is the peaceability of the élitist who argues that disputes in religion are not for everyone, not for the ignorant, not for those with 'inconsiderate zeale':

Every man is not a proper Champion for Truth, nor fit to take up the Gantlet in the cause of Veritie: Many from the ignorance of these Maximes, and an inconsiderate zeale unto Truth, have too rashly charged the troopes of error, and remaine as Trophees unto the enemies of Truth: A man may be in as just possession of Truth as of a City, and yet bee forced to surrender; 'tis therefore farre better to enjoy her with peace, than to hazzard her on a battell. (65–6)

The rejection of conflict employs the imagery of conflict; such imagery is rare in *Religio Medici*; Cecile Sloane has collected only a dozen such examples: 'in literary practice, Browne's distaste for active conflict is reflected in his use of imagery. Within *Religio Medici*, either aggression is presented pejoratively or the value of non-aggression affirmed'.[18] J. S. Morrill has shown that Norfolk was one of the counties that attempted a conservative neutralist stance when war broke out in 1642.[19] And, as Lawrence Stone stresses, 'There can be no doubt that the great majority of the propertied classes viewed the war with horror and apprehension'.[20]

[18] Cecile A. Sloane, 'Imagery of Conflict in *Religio Medici*,' *ELN* 8, (1971), 260–2.
[19] J. S. Morrill, *The Revolt of the Provinces: Conservatives and Radicals in the English Civil War 1630–1650* (London, 1976), pp. 38, 95–7, 165–6.
[20] Lawrence Stone, *The Causes of the English Revolution 1529–1640* (London, 1972), p. 141.

Browne singles out certain aspects of sectarian beliefs for specific rejection. Of the 'Heresies, Schisms, or Errors' that he is preserved from by following 'the great wheele of the Church',

I must confesse my greener studies have been polluted with two or three, not any begotten in the latter Centuries, but old and obsolete, such as could never have been revived, but by such extravagant and irregular heads as mine. (66)

Following on from this, he opens Section 7 thus: 'Now the first of mine was that of the Arabians, that the soules of men perished with their bodies, but should yet bee raised againe at the last day' (p. 67). But this was no 'obsolete', obscure or purely foreign heresy.

Norman T. Burns, discussing Richard Overton in *Christian Mortalism from Tyndale to Milton*, writes 'Although *Man's Mortalitie* made a great stir among the Presbyterians when it appeared in late 1643 or early 1644, its doctrine was by then commonplace enough among many sectaries'.[21] Discussing Milton's mortalism, Christopher Hill notes how 'in the forties mortalism appeared above the surface. By 1644 it was alarming the House of Commons' and 'in 1648 two Royalist newspapers declared that the mortalist heresy had been partly responsible for the revolutionary nature of the Civil War'. Not only was mortalism current, it was specifically associated with the emerging radical Protestants: 'nomenclature varies, but the radical tendency of the heresy, whose best-known spokesman was a Leveller leader, is clear'.[22]

Similarly, Browne's anti-millenarianism and scepticism about Antichrist indicate his consistent opposition to the world-view of the radical sects, whose millenarian beliefs inexorably sought a political expression. Browne's scepticism about the possibility of millenarian prediction is associated with his sad amazement at the propensity of Christianity to produce sects:

And herein I must accuse those of my own Religion; for there is not any of such a fugitive faith, such an unstable belief, as a Christian; none that do so oft transforme themselves, not unto severall shapes of Christianity and of the same Species, but unto more unnaturall and contrary formes,

[21] Norman T. Burns, *Christian Mortalism from Tyndale to Milton* (Cambridge, Mass., 1972), p. 45.
[22] Christopher Hill, *Milton and the English Revolution* (London, 1977), pp. 318, 321, 319. The Leveller Overton wrote *Man's Mortalitie*.

of Jew and Mohametan, that from the name of Saviour can condescend to the bare terme of Prophet; and from an old beliefe that he is come, fall to a new expectation of his comming: It is the promise of Christ to make us all one flock; but how and when this union shall be, is as obscure to me as the last day. (93)

He returns to the theme later, stressing the impossibility of predicting the end of the world:

Now to determine the day and yeare of this inevitable time, is not onely convincible and statute madnesse, but also manifest impiety; How shall we interpret *Elias* 6000 yeares . . . ?

. . . it hath not onely mocked the predictions of sundry Astrologers in ages past, but the prophecies of many melancholy heads in these present, who neither understanding reasonably things past or present, pretend a knowledge of things to come, heads ordained onely to manifest the incredible effects of melancholy, and to fulfill old prophecies, rather than be the authors of new. 'In those dayes there shall come warres and rumours of warres', to me seemes no prophesie, but a constant truth, in all times verified since it was pronounced: There shall bee signes in the Moone and Starres, how comes he then like a theefe in the night, when he gives an item of his comming? That common signe drawne from the revelation of Antichrist is as obscure as any; in our common compute he hath beene come these many yeares, but for my owne part to speake freely, I am halfe of opinion that Antichrist is the Philosophers stone in Divinity, for the discovery and invention whereof, though there be prescribed rules, and probable inductions, yet hath hardly any man attained the perfect discovery thereof. That generall opinion that the world growes neere its end, hath possessed all ages past as neerely as ours. (118–19)

The assurance of the 1642 text that 'no man' had 'attained the perfect discovery' of Antichrist was typically softened in 1643 to 'hardly any man'. As W. A. Greenhill remarked of the alterations, Browne 'took the opportunity of modifying various positive and strongly worded propositions by the substitution of less dogmatic expressions'.[23] But Browne's overall scepticism about the Antichrist remained unchanged from 1642 to 1643. He never calls the Pope Antichrist, he assures us, and he declares that 'that opinion, that Antichrist should be borne of the Tribe of *Dan* by conjunction with the Devill, is ridiculous, and a conceit fitter for a Rabbin than a Christian' (65, 98). This scepticism is not without its political implications. Hill points out

---

[23] *Religio Medici: A Facsimile of the First Edition*, ed. W. A. Greenhill (London, 1883), p. xxvi.

that 'after Laud's rise to dominance the English church no longer proclaimed the Pope to be the Antichrist'.[24] Publication of studies of Daniel and Revelation was prevented. The traditional Protestant identification of the Pope with Antichrist was opposed by Laud and, Hill records, 'it was not until December 1640 that London citizens could subscribe to the Root and Branch Petition complaining of prelates and others who "plead and maintain that the Pope is not Antichrist". Next month a clergyman was denounced to Parliament for declaring positively that the Pope was not Antichrist.'[25] The Root and Branch Petition also 'proposed the abolition of bishops as "members of the Beast"' and 'in May 1641 a libel was set up at the entrance to Parliament, denouncing bishops as limbs of Antichrist'.[26] The image of Antichrist was a highly political image.

Antichrist stood for bad, papal, repressive institutions: exactly which institutions was anybody's choice. This vagueness had security advantages. In the England of 1530–1640 critics of the hierarchy were in fact attacking the monarchy and the legally established government, as their enemies did not fail to point out. 'The Beast' was a much less specific enemy than 'the system of church government approved by Queen Elizabeth'.[27]

Browne not only rejects the Protestant identification of Pope and Antichrist, he is sceptical of all attempts at identification. A useful nationalistic propaganda image for Queen Elizabeth's regime, a focusing of hate on to the foreign papal enemy, Antichrist by the 1640s was out of control: 'the peculiar political circumstances of the early forties, when Parliament needed to win popular support, led to an increasing stress on Antichrist's impending downfall, giving Messianic overtones to what had previously not necessarily been a revolutionary idea'.[28] The separatists had their own definition of Antichrist: 'they thought the whole Church of England so permeated with the relics of Antichrist that it was impossible for the children of God to remain in communion with it';[29] and after 1641 the sectaries were preaching in the open and spreading in influence. The emergence of Antichrist, identified with the great Beast of Revelation, indicated the world was in its last days. The destruction of Antichrist would mark the beginning of Christ's thousand-year rule. 'The

[24] Christopher Hill, *Antichrist in the Seventeenth Century* (London, 1971), p. 37.
[25] Ibid., p. 39.   [26] Ibid., p. 73.   [27] Ibid., pp. 44–5.
[28] Ibid., p. 78.   [29] Ibid., p. 52.

time-tables of Napier, Brightman, Mede, Archer put the rule of Christ on earth in the near future. This gave a utopian perspective for political action.'[30] The correct identification of Antichrist developed a political urgency. 'Johann Hilten, a fifteenth-century prophet popular among protestants, had predicted the end of the world for 1651. John Swan in 1635 noted that some gave 1657 for the date, though he was not himself convinced.'[31]

Religio Medici appeared amidst a flood of millenarian speculations. 'Thy Kingdome is now at hand, and thou standing at the dore', Milton wrote in 1641 of Christ's Second Coming, attacking Bishop Hall in *Animadversions Upon the Remonstrants Defence, Against Smectymnuus*.[32] The same year saw the publication of *A Revelation of Mr. Brightman's Revelation . . . ,* and *Brightman's Reign of Christ upon Earth*, among others, and these were followed in 1642 by a summary of Johann Alsted's work, *The World's Proceeding Woes*, by Francis Potter's *An Interpretation of the Number 666*, and by Joseph Mede's *The Apostasy of the Latter Times*.[33] 1643 saw the publication of Alsted's *The Beloved City, Or, The Saints Reign on Earth A Thousand Years* and Mede's *Key of the Revelation* in English translation.[34] Grotius was told that eighty such treatises had appeared in England by 1649.[35] This was the context in which Browne derided computations of the end of the world as decisively as he did the identifications of Antichrist.

Browne's three references to Antichrist are in both the 1642 and the 1643 texts. And he deals with millenarian predictions in Section 43, added in 1643:

the whole world, whose solid and well composed substance must not expect the duration and period of its constitution, when all things are compleated in it, its age is accomplished, and the last and generall fever may as naturally destroy it before six thousand, as me before forty. (114)

Denying the possibility of the computation in i. 46, in this new section he accepts '*Elias* 6000 yeares' as 6,000 years. But this seeming contradiction is the expression of Browne's conservative consistency. *Religio Medici* now both tells us that the millennium cannot be predicted, but at the same time tells us it is due after 6,000 years—that

[30] Ibid., p. 163.   [31] Ibid., p. 111.   [32] *CPW* i. 707.
[33] Hill, *Antichrist*, p. 26.   [34] Ibid., pp. 28–9.
[35] Christopher Hill, *Puritanism and Revolution* (London, 1958), p. 325.

is, *c.* AD 2,000, given the accepted date of Creation as 4004 BC. The political activism of his millenarian contemporaries is thus challenged. The end of the world cannot be computed and anyway it has been computed for years ahead, so predictions of 1653 or 1656 or 1666 are absurd. Browne's anti-millenarianism can hence be seen in its socio-political context: a conservative dismissal of that millenarianism developing into a radical activism among the sects. He even has a disparaging aside on the book of Revelation: 'Saint *Johns* description by Emeralds, Chrysolites, and pretious stones, is too weake to expresse the materiall Heaven we behold' (122). In the preceding sentence St Paul by contrast had been given a positive categorization, 'that elegant Apostle'.

II

Part II of *Religio Medici* deals with 'that other Vertue of Charity', and its first section develops into a denunciation of the 'multitude'. This hostility to mass action, directly following the rejection of the beliefs of the radical sects, establishes Browne's firm, anti-populist stance:

If there be any among those common objects of hatred I doe contemne and laugh at, it is that great enemy of reason, vertue and religion, the multitude, that numerous piece of monstrosity, which taken asunder seeme men, and the reasonable creatures of God; but confused together, make but one great beast, & a monstrosity more prodigious than Hydra; it is no breach of Charity to call these fooles, it is the stile all holy Writers have afforded them, set downe by *Solomon* in canonicall Scripture, and a point of our faith to beleeve so. (134)

Browne's condemnation certainly had a long tradition behind it. C. A. Patrides, discussing 'the beast with many heads', cites examples ranging through such writers as Barnaby Rich, Shakespeare, Lancelot Andrewes, Arthur Warwick, and Pierre Charron.[36] But, in the context of *Religio Medici*'s publication, Browne's condemnation attained a new pertinence. J. S. Morrill says of 1640–1, 'It is unclear whether rioting and violence were more extensive than hitherto, but most gentlemen certainly *believed* that they were. Disruption, often

[36] ' "The Beast with Many Heads": Renaissance Views on the Multitude', *Shakespeare Quarterly*, 16 (1965), 241–6.

with an overt class bias, was certainly widespread.'[37] Discussing 'the many-headed monster', Christopher Hill remarks that Browne was 'thoroughly orthodox in thinking it was "no breach of charity" to call the multitude fools'; but, Hill stresses, 'this contemptuous attitude thinly concealed the fears of the propertied class'.[38]

Brian Manning's study *The English People and the English Revolution* has documented the increasing involvement of the multitude in direct action from the huge crowds that in November 1640 welcomed the release by the Long Parliament of Prynne, Burton, and Bastwick; 'the first instance of popular intervention in the affairs of the Long Parliament' described by Clarendon as 'an insurrection (for it was no better) and frenzy of the people . . . '.[39] Fifteen thousand people signed the petition for the abolition of episcopacy 'root and branch' in November 1640 and it was delivered to the House of Commons by some one thousand two hundred to one thousand five hundred citizens.[40] Though the delivery was made without tumult or disorder, Lord Digby complained 'I am confident, there is no man of judgement, that will think it fit for a parliament, under a monarchy, to give countenance to irregular, and tumultuous assemblies of people', and he urged the house 'not to be led on by passion to popular and vulgar errors . . . '[41] But the mass action escalated. Laud was mobbed on the way to the Tower on 1 March 1641. Some 20,000–30,000 signatures were attached to a petition demanding justice against the Earl of Strafford and it was brought to London on 21 April 1641 'by a great multitude' of 10,000 people. A crowd estimated at between 5,000 and 15,000 assembled at Westminster on 3 May 1641 demanding Strafford's execution, and Charles 'who purposed to be at the House that morning . . . by reason of the tumult did not come'.[42] The pressure of mass action led the Lords to condemn Strafford, and Charles to agree to his execution, which took place on 12 May 1641 amid widespread rejoicing and 'breaking the windows of those persons, who would not solemnize this festival with a bonfire'.[43]

[37] Morrill, *The Revolt of the Provinces*, p. 34.
[38] Christopher Hill, *Change and Continuity in Seventeenth-Century England* (London, 1974), pp. 186, 189.   [39] Manning, *The English People*, p. 15.
[40] Ibid., pp. 16–17.   [41] Ibid., p. 18.   [42] Ibid., p. 24.
[43] Ibid., p. 31.

Popular protest continued throughout 1641, the multitude threatening to kill the Spanish ambassador and burn down his house, and later attacking the houses of the French and Portuguese ambassadors. The Queen Mother asked for a guard against the multitude and in August she followed the Commons' advice and left England. In November there was a succession of demonstrations at Westminster, with citizens armed with swords and staves calling 'Down with the Bishops—Down with Antichrist'.[44] On 9 December Charles ordered the London JPs and sheriffs to stop the 'many riots and unlawful assemblies . . . daily made at the City of Westminster and within the City of London'.[45] The closing days of December 1641 were marked by sustained demonstrations and riots at Westminster, provoked by Lunsford's appointment to control the Tower. 'Many hundreds of apprentices and others came down to the parliament, with swords and staves and other weapons';[46] 'ten thousand prentices were betwixt York House and Charing Cross with halberds, staves and some swords'.[47] On 28 December the crowd prevented the bishops from taking their seats in the Lords and some moved on to attack Westminster Abbey, and on 29 December parliament was again surrounded by an armed crowd calling out 'No Bishops! No Popish Lords!' as the members arrived.[48] The three days of rioting had died down when Charles on 3 January 1642 charged Lord Mandeville and the five members of the Commons with treason: one of the charges against them was having 'actually raised and countenanced tumults against the king and parliament' using 'a multitude of Brownists, Anabaptists, and other sectaries about London'.[49] The result was massive direct action and a general strike of shopkeepers. When Charles dined with the Sheriff of London, the house 'was beset, and the streets leading unto it thronged with people, thousands of them flocking from all parts of the city' and afterwards Charles's coach was followed and mobbed and the Lord Mayor 'plucked off his horse, and some of the aldermen' returning from escorting the king.[50] On 10 January Charles fled from London.

The pattern of mass demonstration and marching on Parliament with petitions continued through 1642. Nor was the activity confined to London. Norfolk fishermen cast down salt-marsh enclosures, and

[44] Ibid., p. 66.   [45] Ibid., p. 78.   [46] Ibid., p. 91.   [47] Ibid., p. 92.
[48] Ibid., p. 97.   [49] Ibid., pp. 105–6.   [50] Ibid., p. 111.

rioting against Royalists and papist property-owners occurred on a large scale in Essex and Suffolk. The houses of the Countess of Rivers at St Osyth in Essex and at Long Melford in Suffolk, of Sir Francis Mannock at Stoke-by-Nayland in Suffolk, and of Sir John Lucas near Colchester were attacked and sacked.[51]

It was in this climate of direct action by the multitude that *Religio Medici*, with its attacks on the multitude, appeared. Hill points out that 'Charles I in his Declaration of 23 October 1642 played on social anxieties by speaking of "endeavours . . . to raise an implacable malice and hatred between the gentry and commonalty of the kingdom . . . insomuch as the highways and villages have not been safe for gentlemen to pass through without violence or affront" '.[52] One of Browne's resonant additions to the 1643 edition that might seem to be simply the philosophic play of metaphysical wit takes on a more specific paranoia in this context:

'Tis not onely the mischiefe of diseases, and the villanie of poysons that make an end of us, we vainly accuse the fury of Gunnes, and the new inventions of death; 'tis in the power of every hand to destroy us, and wee are beholding unto every one wee meete hee doth not kill us. (115)

The passage had a particular relevance for a society divided by class hostilities and, after Charles raised his standard in August 1642, embroiled in civil war.

Browne's contempt for the multitude is one part of his thought that commentators have seen in some political context. Dunn, having earlier claimed that Browne 'completely ignores the political situation',[53] none the less sees a political significance here.

In other words the spectacle of English democracy in the making had turned Browne, as it had many of his generation, into something of a Stoic. He has retired from the tumult. He despises the whole tone of the society that was disintegrating the old social order, with its shifting standards of life, its fortune hunters, its political adventurers, and on the other hand its rising tide of raw plebeians with their uncouth religious and insolent political ambitions.[54]

[51] Ibid., pp. 141, 182, 189–95, 205–6.
[52] Hill, *Change and Continuity*, p. 196.
[53] William P. Dunn, *Sir Thomas Browne* (Minneapolis, 1950), p. 14.
[54] Ibid., p. 74.

Edward Dowden and Joan Bennett both argue that in detecting 'a rabble even amongst the Gentry' (134) Browne showed that his antipathy for the multitude was 'not a class-feeling'; the multitude was not 'any particular class of men'.[55] Contemporary accounts of the crowds that assembled on 3 May 1641 at Westminster demanding the execution of Strafford were agreed that the crowds comprised 'for the most part men of good fashion'; 'many of them captains of the City and men of eminent rank'; 'many thousand of the most substantial of the citizens'; 'citizens of very good account, some worth £30,000, some £40,000'. The following day 'the well-to-do demonstrators . . . sent their servants'; this 'rabble amongst the Gentry' remained involved.[56]

Browne's inclusion of 'gentry' in the rabble, then, rather than demonstrating his lack of class feeling, can be seen as expressing a specific socio-political position, a reaction against the multitude that parliamentarians were suspected of manipulating. And though Browne includes gentry in his rabble, it is quite clear that his distaste and contempt for the multitude is a distaste for the style of the plebeians, the mechanics, the 'ignorant': 'a sort of Plebeian heads, . . . men in the same Levell with Mechanickes' (134). He cannot assert the wisdom of God without sneering at the ignorance of the 'vulgar', the crowd: 'The advantage I have of the vulgar, with the content and happinesse I conceive therein, is an ample recompence for all my endeavours, in what part of knowledge soever' (74). In 1643 he added to this passage a further ten lines on God's wisdom, 'his most beauteous attribute'. He also toned down his élitism in that famous assertion of the value of intellectual inquiry, a passage arguing for the religious value of scientific investigation while at the same time condemning yet again the vulgar, the rude, the rustic:

The wisedome of God receives small honour from those vulgar heads, that rudely stare about and with a grosse rusticity admire his workes; those highly magnifie him whose judicious enquiry into his acts, and deliberate research into his creatures, returne the duty of a devout and learned admiration. (75)

In 1642 'small honour' had been 'no honour', and 'those highly magnifie him' had been 'those onely magnifie him'. The contempt

[55] Edward Dowden, *Puritan and Anglican* (London, 1900), p. 53; Bennett, *Sir Thomas Browne*, p. 99.   [56] Manning, *The English People*, p. 25.

for the unlettered remains in the 1643 version, but its finality, its intransigence, is slightly modified. It was always there with Browne, and we can find it again in *Pseudodoxia Epidemica*.

The literary tradition gave the weight of traditional authority to class prejudice and allowed contemporary events to be alluded to without any dangerous specificity, avoiding reprisal under the cover of generality. But just because there was a literary tradition we should not forget that opposite opinions were also expressed — and increasingly so at this time. In 1641, interpreting Revelation 19: 6, *A Glimpse of Sion's Glory* proclaimed that

The voice, of Jesus Christ reigning in his Church, comes first from the multitude, the common people. The voice is heard from them first, before it is heard from any others. God uses the common people and the multitude to proclaim that the Lord God Omnipotent reigneth. As when Christ came at first the poor received the Gospel — not many wise, not many noble, not many rich, but the poor — so in the reformation of religion, after Antichrist began to be discovered, it was the common people that first came to look after Christ . . .

You that are of the meaner rank, common people, be not discouraged; for God intends to make use of the common people in the great work of proclaiming the kingdom of his Son.[57]

And in April 1642 Milton in his final contribution to the debate on episcopacy between Bishop Hall and Smectymnuus, *An Apology against a Pamphlet Called a Modest Confutation of the Animadversion of the Remonstrant against Smectymnuus*, part of the controversy provoked by Hall's *Humble Remonstrance* 'commended parliament for its considerate reception . . . of the petitions even of its humblest citizens'.[58]

Insomuch that the meanest artizans and labourers, at other times also women, and often the younger sort of servants assembling with their complaints, and that sometimes in a lesse humble guise then for petitioners, have gone with confidence, that neither their meannesse would be rejected, nor their simplicity contemn'd, nor their urgency distasted either by the dignity, wisdome, or moderation of that supreme Senate; nor did they depart unsatisfi'd. And indeed, if we consider the generall concourse of suppliants, the free and ready admittance, the willing and speedy redresse in what is possible, it will not seeme much otherwise, then as if some divine commission

---

[57] Stuart Prall, ed., *The Puritan Revolution: A Documentary History* (New York, 1968), p. 87. [58] Haller, *Liberty and Reformation*, p. 25.

from heav'n were descended to take into hearing and commiseration the
long remedilesse afflictions of this kingdom . . . [59]

The acceptance of the 'meanest' is a mark of 'divine commission'.
How unlike Browne's 'charity'.

In *The Causes of the English Revolution*, Lawrence Stone notes
that 'the last peasant revolt serious enough to send the gentry fleeing
from their homes in terror had been in 1549, when risings had taken
place all over southern England. Brutal repression quickly snuffed
out the fires of rebellion in all but the one county of Norfolk, but
memories of this alarming experience died hard . . . ' [60] Though
Stone writes that 'by 1640 . . . memories had grown dim' he goes
on to note how

On the very eve of the outbreak of open war, Simonds D'Ewes vainly warned
his fellow members of Parliament: 'We know not what advantage the meaner
sort also may take to divide the spoils of the rich and noble among them.'
The looting of the houses of some Catholic noblemen in East Anglia by
undisciplined mobs seemed evidence that D'Ewes' prophecy was coming true.
It has even been argued that the Parliamentary Ordinance for the raising
of troops—in practice against the King—was accepted by the Suffolk gentry
as guarantee of the maintenance of internal order.[61]

That the poor, the propertyless, the 'meanest artizans and labourers'
might take it into their own hands to acquire what was denied them
was the great fear of the propertied. Stone cites Sir John Oglander's
comments on 1642:

I believe such times were never before seen in England, when the gentry
were made slaves to the commonalty and in their power, not only to abuse
but plunder any gentleman . . .

O the tyrannical misery that the gentlemen of England did endure from July
1642 till April 1643, and how much longer the Lord knoweth! They could
call nothing their own and lived in slavery and submission to the unruly
base multitude. O tempora, o mores . . . [62]

This fear of the multitude lies beneath Browne's contempt for the
multitude. The social vision he asserts is one that requires the meaner
sort to be firmly in their 'place'.

---

[59] *CPW* iii. 339–40.   [60] Stone, *Causes*, p. 76.   [61] Ibid., p. 77.

Statists that labour to contrive a Common-wealth without poverty, take away the object of charity, not understanding only the Common-wealth of a Christian, but forgetting the prophecy of Christ (159)

A note in Wilkin's MS 'W' annotates the passage with 'The poore ye shall have always with you'—'an unlikely adaptation of Luke 6: 20', as Patrides remarks. Luke 6: 20, 21, if that indeed be the prophecy intended, declared 'Blessed be ye poor: for yours is the kingdom of God. Blessed are ye that hunger now: for ye shall be filled.'

Browne's rejection of the millenarian interpretations of his time is part of his rejection of any idea of the poor establishing God's kingdom on earth. 'The poor existed as objects of the charity of the rich, Browne and many others tell us: but this charity must be reasonable, socially responsible. The assumption, sharply contrasting with early protestant hopes, is that poverty will continue.'[63] The poor exist to be the object of charity for the rich; they are part of the social hierarchy. Browne wrote:

Let us speake like Politicians, there is a Nobility without Heraldry, a naturall dignity, whereby one man is ranked with another, another Filed before him, according to the quality of his desert, and preheminence of his good parts. (134)

Browne presents this social hierarchy as part of the natural order of things, 'for there is in this Universe a Staire, or manifest Scale of creatures, rising not disorderly, or in confusion, but with a comely method and proportion' (101). These may well be 'time-honoured commonplaces', as Patrides remarks (26–7), but Browne reasserts them with a credo that suggests their contemporary urgency: 'I beleeve there shall never be an Anarchy in Heaven, but as there are Hierarchies amongst the Angels, so shall there be degrees of priority amongst the Saints' (131). It is 'the corruption of these times' that has disturbed the orderly hierarchy of the 'first and primitive Common-wealths', but the hierarchical principle

is yet in the integrity and Cradle of well-ordered politics, till corruption getteth ground, ruder desires labouring after that which wiser considerations

[62] Lawrence Stone, *Social Change and Revolution in England 1540–1640* (London, 1965), p. 126.
[63] Christopher Hill, *Society and Puritanism in Pre-Revolutionary England* (London, 1969), p. 281.

contemn, every one having a liberty to amasse & heape up riches, and they a license or faculty to doe or purchase anything. (134–5)

The 1643 preface opened with a reflection on the 'times wherein I have lived to behold . . . the name of his Majesty defamed, the honour of Parliament depraved'. The context was spelled out by which the reader could interpret 'the corruption of these times' in Section 1 of Part II as referring to the events of the 1640s.

With this reading of *Religio Medici*'s hostility to the radical sects and to the multitude, it is worth reconsidering Browne's much-proclaimed toleration. W. K. Jordan claims that 'the noble latitudinarianism and moderation which were being raised as the reply to bigotry are everywhere manifest in Browne's writing'.[64] But Browne's toleration of Roman Catholics is but part of his intolerance for the sectarians and his contempt for the multitude. It is all of a piece with his acceptance of Laudian ceremony and of the hierarchical, authoritarian, social meanings of that policy.

In the forms of worship, stress was laid on the revival of hieratic ritual and visual ornament, in ways which had not been seen for over sixty years. Communion tables were put back in the east end of churches, and protected by altar rails; the erection of organs and stained-glass windows was encouraged; the clergy were ordered to use the surplice and the laity to kneel at the altar rails to receive the sacrament.[65]

Browne proclaims his ceremonialism and explains the social uses of it:

I am, I confesse, naturally inclined to that, which misguided zeale termes superstition . . . at my devotion I love to use the civility of my knee, my hat, and hand, with all those outward and sensible motions, which may expresse, or promote my invisible devotion. I should violate my owne arme rather then a Church, nor willingly deface the memory of Saint or Martyr. At the sight of a Crosse or Crucifix I can dispence with my hat, but scarce with the thought or memory of my Saviour; I cannot laugh at but rather pity the fruitless journeys of Pilgrims, or contemne the miserable condition of Friers; for though misplaced in circumstance, there is something in it of devotion: I could never heare the *Ave Marie* Bell without an elevation . . . There are questionlesse both in Greek, Roman, and African Churches, solemnities, and ceremonies, whereof the wiser zeales doe make a Christian use, and stand condemned by us; not as evill in themselves, but as allurements and baits of superstitions to those vulgar heads that looke asquint on the face

     [64] W. K. Jordan, *The Development of Religious Toleration in England* (Cambridge, Mass., 1936), ii. 447.   [65] Stone, *Causes*, p. 119.

of truth, and those unstable judgements that cannot consist in the narrow point and centre of vertue without a reele or stagger to the circumference. (63–4)

Ceremonials, then, are baits for the ignorant vulgar. But the ignorant vulgar were less attracted to the images of social control than was Browne. Hill remarks on 'the popular iconoclasm which broke out whenever opportunity offered: in the late 1630s and 40s altar rails were pulled down, altars desecrated, statues on tombs destroyed, ecclesiastical documents burnt, pigs and horses baptized'.[66] The 1642 text contained a much more specific reference to this icono-clasm with its vocabulary of explicitly physical violence and its specific reference to the so breakable 'church window', which in 1643 became simply 'church': 'I should cutt off my arm, rather than violate a Church window, then deface or demolish the memory of a Saint or Martyr'. The 1643 text allows the possibility of physical violence within its more abstract expression, but its language is not as unavoidably physical as the 1642 'cut off' and 'demolish'.

It may be that Browne wanted to avoid validating iconoclasm by giving expression to it; or it may be that by removing the specific terminology, he is allowing the reader to believe that he is speaking merely metaphorically, not referring to specific incidents. On 22 February 1641 'the Cathedral Blades of Norwich' rushed to the defence of the cathedral, believing 'the Apprentices . . . would have pulled down their Organs'.[67] Norwich Cathedral was in fact ransacked three years later, its windows broken, monuments torn up, and icons smashed. The Puritan feeling was there, and Browne may have cautiously preferred not to antagonize it; he did not remove the passage altogether, but simply made its unavoidable physicality ambiguously metaphorical. But the changes did not alter the basic standpoint, the reverence for the church building. It is in pointed contrast to the radical sectarian view we find in George Fox's revelation of 1646: 'it was opened in me, "That God, who made the world, did not dwell in temples made with hands" ';[68] or in *Paradise Lost* where the 'upright heart and pure' is asserted as preferred before all temples (i. 18). 'His people were his temple, and he dwelt in them', as Fox put it.

---

[66] Hill, *The World Turned Upside Down*, p. 29.
[67] Huntley, *Sir Thomas Browne*, p. 27.
[68] George Fox, *Journal* (Leeds, 1836), i. 89.

Browne's comments on church music have to be seen in this politically charged context. Indeed Browne's tone becomes combative against those who 'disclaime against all Church musicke' (149). 'All' had been 'our' in 1642, and the number of other detailed changes in this passage suggest the political sensitivity of the topic. For it was highly sensitive. 'Choral singing and the playing of organs in church were the work of Antichrist, introduced by the Pope in the significant year 666', according to Henry Burton in a sermon preached before the House of Commons and published in 1641 as *Englands Bondage and Hope of Deliverance* and to William Thomas in a speech to Parliament in June 1641.[69] Against this radical puritan position Browne asserts that

Whatsoever is harmonically composed, delights in harmony; which makes me much distrust the symmetry of those heads which declaime against all Church musicke. For my selfe, not only from my obedience but my particular genius, I doe imbrace it. (149)

'From my obedience' replaces 'for my Catholike obedience' of 1642, lest 'Catholike' should be interpreted as papist, and the implication of Laudian enforcement followed grudgingly which might be deduced from 'I am obliged to maintaine it' in 1642 is replaced by 'I doe imbrace it'. It is one of the rare occasions that Browne's emendations make the 1643 text more challenging, more combative; and the reference a couple of lines further on to 'my Maker' in 1642 is changed to 'the first Composer', asserting the divinity of church music. Browne may be echoing Hermes Trismegistus here. Libellus XVIII of the *Corpus Hermeticum* speaks of 'God, who is by nature a musician, and not only works harmony in the universe at large, but also transmits to individuals the rhythm of his own music'.[70] If Browne is alluding to the Hermetica here, it is an allusion with political resonance. The writer of Libellus XVIII declares:

The aim of my endeavour is the glory of kings; and it is the trophies which our kings have won that make me eager to speak. Onward then! for so God wills; and the melody that the musician makes will sound the sweeter by reason of the greatness of his theme.[71]

[69] Hill, *Antichrist*, p. 75.
[70] *Hermetica*, ed. Walter Scott (Cambridge, 1924), i. 275-7.
[71] Ibid., i. 279.

Not only is Browne inclined toward tolerance of ceremonial and various Roman Catholic practices such as 'the prayer for the dead; whereunto I was inclined from some charitable inducements' (67–8); compare 1642: 'enclined by an excess of charity'. Negatively, the Puritan stress upon preaching finds no echo in his work. Preaching was central to Puritanism. Hill opens his chapter on 'The Preaching of the Word' in *Society and Puritanism in Pre-Revolutionary England*, with 'Preaching is necessary to salvation, said Hus in 1412'.[72] Hus is mentioned by Browne in a passage of studied ambiguity that, whatever its positive meaning, negatively removes Hus from any sure eminence of authority.

Now as all that die in warre are not termed Souldiers, so neither can I properly terme all those that suffer in matters of Religion Martyrs. The Councell of *Constance* condemns *John Husse* for an Heretick, the Stories of his owne party stile him a Martyr; He must needs offend the Divinity of both, that sayes hee was neither the one nor the other: There are many (questionlesse) canonized on earth, that shall never be Saints in Heaven . . . (94)

Neither Protestant martyrs nor preaching find endorsement in *Religio Medici*. When preaching is mentioned, it is negatively:

those usuall Satyrs, and invectives of the Pulpit may perchance produce a good effect on the vulgar, whose cares are opener to Rhetorick then Logick, yet doe they in no wise confirme the faith of wiser beleevers, who know that a good cause needs not to be patron'd by a passion, but can sustaine it selfe upon a temperate dispute. (65)

Preaching for Browne is identified with 'those popular scurrilities and opprobrious scoffes of the Bishop of *Rome*, whom as a temporall Prince, we owe the duty of good language' (65). The radical implications of encouraging disrespect for authority disturb him; implicitly he endorses the bishops' opposition to preaching. In September 1641 the Commons passed a motion, made by Cromwell, voting 'general permission to the people of any parish to "set up a Lecture" and maintain a preacher at their own charge "to preach every Lords Day, where there is no Preaching; and to preach One week Day in every Week, where there is no weekly Lecture"'.[73] But preaching is no part of the *Religio Medici*; it is a significant absence. While the

---

[72] Hill, *Society and Puritanism*, p. 31.
[73] Haller, *Liberty and Reformation*, pp. 24–5, 360.

toleration for Roman Catholicism in a context of widespread fears of popish plots, documented by Manning,[74] similarly forms part of a hostility to radical, sectarian Puritanism. As Ruth Wallerstein wrote, Browne's 'view of the Apostolic succession, his attitude toward Roman Catholicism, his whole tone, mark him as a Laudian Anglican, very susceptible to the traditions and instrumentalities of devotion'.[75]

To place the components of Browne's 'toleration' against the grievances expressed in the 'Root and Branch' petition presented to Parliament on 11 December 1640 is to see his conservative, oppositional stance. The signatories complained, among other things, of:

7. . . . the want of preaching ministers in very many places both of England and Wales . . .

9. The hindering of godly books to be printed . . . the restraint of reprinting books formerly licensed, without relicensing.

11. The growth of Popery . . .

13. the prelates here in England, by themselves of their disciples, plead and maintain that the Pope is not Antichrist, and that the Church of Rome is a true Church . . .

14. The great conformity and likeness both continued and increased of our church to the Church of Rome, in vestures, postures, ceremonies, and administrations . . .

15. The standing up at *Gloria Patri* and at the reading of the Gospel, praying towards the East, the bowing at the name of Jesus, the bowing to the altar towards the East, cross in baptism, the kneeling at the Communion.[76]

III

This reading is a preliminary attempt to situate *Religio Medici* in the context of the English Revolution, in the context in which it was published and first read. Browne's claim, which he perhaps too emphatically repeats, that the work was composed many years before publication in 1642, may be true; it may be that the work was begun many years earlier and progressively added to. Certainly the work was added to between the 'unauthorized' editions of 1642 and the authorized edition of 1643, with passages that relate to contemporary social upheavals; and contemporary readers could not have read

---

[74] Manning, *The English People*, pp. 33 f.

[75] Ruth Wallerstein, *Studies in Seventeenth-Century Poetic* (Madison, 1950), p. 245.   [76] Prall, *The Puritan Revolution*, pp. 98–9.

references to 'the present antipathies between the two extreames' (64) without thinking of the antipathies between Charles I and Parliament. *Religio Medici* is not a work that puts forward an explicit or positive political position; but negatively, in its rejection of sectarianism, mass action, millenarianism, the multitude, and any manifestations of plebeian Puritan activism, it is possible to locate the work in a cautious, conservative, law-and-order context. Under the guise of religious apology and intellectual speculation, through 'wit', a political picture is presented. The attacks on the sects and the multitude are the iconography, the shared language, of the emerging conservative party of law and order that provided the basis of the Royalist movement,[77] but that was careful enough not to be too explicitly assertive. Who knew what forces might eventually dominate? I am not arguing that this is the only or the total meaning of *Religio Medici*; it is in part a covert meaning, but it is not an esoteric one. I have drawn my historical evidence from the standard historians of the period—Haller, Hill, Manning, Morrill, Stone, Zagorin— for Browne embodies a recognized, mainstream political response to the documented political circumstances and events of his time. In part, no doubt, this is why *Religio Medici*, apart from the eight extant manuscript copies—none in Browne's hand—went through five editions between 1642 and 1645 and, after an interval of eleven years, another three editions between 1656 and 1659.[78] But this is in no way to deny or reduce its spiritual meanings, though it may indicate some of the material, political uses to which spiritual insights can be attached.

[77] Stone, *Causes*, p. 141.
[78] *Religio Medici*, ed. Denonain, pp. ix–xxi, and Geoffrey Keynes, *A Bibliography of Sir Thomas Browne, Kt, M.D.* (Cambridge, 1924), pp. 9–14.

5

Marvell's 'An Horatian Ode upon Cromwell's Return from Ireland', The Levellers, and the Junta

No less than *Religio Medici*, Andrew Marvell's 'An Horatian Ode upon Cromwell's Return from Ireland' has become a privileged text of the apolitical, the art that allegedly transcends the mere political or historical. Yet to look at the poem's own history is to realize how problematical a work it is.

The circumstances of its composition are unknown and it is likewise unknown whether Cromwell ever saw it. In the course of its first publication in Andrew Marvell's posthumous *Miscellaneous Poems* (1681), the sheets containing it were removed from the volume and survive in only two known copies. In July or August 1681 the printer of the book, Robert Boulter, was arrested, having allegedly said that 'he knew those engines at work that would very soon depose the King, and that he did not question to see the monarchy reduced into a commonwealth and very speedily'.[1] We may assume that 'An Horatian Ode', 'The First Anniversary of the Government under O.C.', and 'A Poem upon the Death of O.C.' were removed from *Miscellaneous Poems* because of their pro-Cromwellian qualities. The 'Horatian Ode' did not appear in print until Thompson's edition of Marvell in 1776. One of the earliest known comments on it, William Hazlitt's in *Lectures on The English Comic Writers* (1818–19) stresses, however, not the ostensible subject of its title, but its tribute to King Charles:

There is a poem of Marvel's on the death of King Charles I which I have not seen, but which I have heard praised by one whose praise is never high

---

[1] *The Poems and Letters of Andrew Marvell*, ed. H. M. Margoliouth, revised by Pierre Legouis with Elsie Duncan-Jones (Oxford, 1971), p. 214. All quotations from Marvell's poems from this edition.

but of the highest things, for the beauty and pathos, as well as generous frankness of the sentiments, coming, as they did, from a determined and incorruptible political foe.[2]

The poem on Cromwell's return from Ireland becomes transformed into a poem on the death of King Charles. Although Hazlitt had not seen the poem, his critical reversal prefigures the note for later readings of the poem. The tribute to Charles encouraged a belief that Marvell was a Royalist at this point in his career. And so Muriel Bradbrook and M. G. Lloyd Thomas wrote: 'the poem may well represent the steps of reasoning by which the friend of Lovelace threw in his lot with the Roundheads: it is only after this date that we hear of Marvell as being definitely on their side'.[3] And J. M. Newton offered the ultimate Royalist interpretation: 'Is the action being urged on the forward youth an almost suicidally desperate one, like joining other young Royalist hot-heads in an attempt to catch and assassinate Cromwell in London . . . ?[4]

It might be stressed at this point that at no date do we ever hear of Marvell's being a Royalist; this is purely critical conjecture to explain the 'tribute' to Charles, the poem on Tom May's death (in which the hostility to May could be the result of internecine struggles within the Cromwellian camp), the poem to Lovelace (which regrets the passing of the times of peace but makes no political comment), and the poem to Villiers (not included in the *Miscellaneous Poems* and ascribed to Marvell on slender evidence).[5]

---

[2] *The Complete Works of William Hazlitt*, ed. P. P. Howe (London, 1931), v. vi. 54. Charles Lamb is usually assumed to be the person who praised the ode. On Marvell's critical reputation, see Elizabeth Story Donno, ed., *Andrew Marvell: The Critical Heritage* (London, 1978), John Carey, ed., *Andrew Marvell* (Harmondsworth, 1969) and Michael Wilding, ed., *Marvell: Modern Judgements* (London, 1969).

[3] M. C. Bradbrook and M. G. Lloyd Thomas, *Andrew Marvell* (Cambridge, 1940), p. 73.

[4] J. M. Newton, 'What do we know about Andrew Marvell?', *Cambridge Quarterly*, 6 (1973), 129.

[5] Nicholas Guild, 'The Context of Marvell's Early "Royalist" Poems', *Studies in English Literature*, 20 (1980), 136: 'how much do these early poems indicate about Marvell's political opinions prior to the "Horatian Ode"? And the answer seems to be, not much. They do suggest that he had contact with royalist circles, but the poems themselves are not inconsistent with the assumption that he himself favoured Parliament.' On 'Tom May's Death' see E. E. Duncan-Jones, 'A Great Master of Words: Some Aspects of Marvell's Poems of Praise and Blame', *PBA* 61 (1975), 17–21.

In Cleanth Brooks's account of the poem in 1946, the argument moved from hypothetical history to an examination of 'the ambiguity of the compliments' paid to Cromwell.

The ambiguity reveals itself as early as the second word of the poem. It is the 'forward' youth whose attention the speaker directs to the example of Cromwell. 'Forward' may mean no more than 'high-spirited', 'ardent', 'properly ambitious'; but the *New English Dictionary* sanctions the possibility that there lurks in the word the sense of 'presumptuous', 'pushing' . . .

The speaker, one observes, does not identify Cromwell himself as the 'forward youth', or say directly that Cromwell's career has been motivated by striving for fame. But the implications of the first two stanzas do carry over to him. There is, for example, the important word 'so' to relate Cromwell to these stanzas:

> So restless *Cromwel* could not cease . . .

And 'restless' is as ambiguous in its meaning as 'forward' and in its darker connotations even more damning . . . And this thirst for glory, merely hinted at here by negatives, is developed further in the ninth stanza:

> Could by industrious valour climbe
> To ruine the great Work of Time

'Climb' certainly connotes a kind of aggressiveness.[6]

The direction of Brooks's analysis is not, however, to argue for Marvell the crypto-Royalist, but for Marvell the proto-New Critic: aware of complexity, subtlety, ambiguity, irony, and avoiding a final commitment.

In short, the more closely we look at the 'Ode', the more clearly apparent it becomes that the speaker has chosen to emphasize Cromwell's virtues as a man, and likewise those of Charles as a man. The poem does not debate which of the two was right, for the issue is not even in question.[7]

The ultimate drift is to depoliticize Marvell's poem.

It is a poem essentially dramatic in its presentation, which means that it is diagnostic rather than remedial, and eventuates, not in a course of action, but in contemplation. Perhaps the best way therefore in which to approach it is to conceive of it as, say, one conceives of a Shakespearean tragedy.[8]

---

[6] Cleanth Brooks, 'Literary Criticism', *English Institute Essays 1946* (New York, 1947), p. 137.   [7] Ibid., p. 142.
[8] Ibid., p. 151.

Brooks's reading has been immensely influential. Douglas Bush's reply, questioning the stress on the 'pejorative choice among "ambiguous" possibilities'[9] in the vocabulary of the compliments paid Cromwell, none the less offers an overall reading of the poem much the same as Brooks's:

The poem is not a conventional eulogy but a subtle portrait of its subject, warts and all. At a time when Cromwell aroused violently conflicting passions among Englishmen (as indeed he has ever since), Marvell was able to contemplate both him and King Charles with a mixture of warm admiration and cool, analytical detachment.[10]

'Now with this statement I am in complete agreement', responded Brooks.[11] What is assumed in all these critical readings, is the basic polarization between Charles and Cromwell. And the stress on Marvell's ambiguity served to create the impression that there are two possible political stances (for Charles or for Cromwell) which Marvell was able to balance. A. Alvarez wrote:

The main element in Marvell's poetry is its balance, its pervading sense of intelligent proportion. He is, I think, the foremost poet of judgment in the English language, and 'An Horatian Ode' is his foremost poem. By *judgment* I mean quality which presents, balances and evaluates a whole situation, seeing all the implications and never attempting to simplify them . . .

It is this impression of the mind detachedly at play over a number of possible choices that earns Marvell the title of poet of judgment. Another way of putting it would be to call him a political poet. Certainly, 'An Horatian Ode' is one of the two finest political poems in the language; the other is *Coriolanus*.[12]

Ambiguity, balance, detachment, judgement: these are the qualities that the 'Horatian Ode' has been seen to possess. And this is not a false reading of the poem; this is the reading that the poem is designed to elicit. It is a reading that has proved so appealing, that has taken so tenacious a hold, because this is the reading the poem's rhetoric sought. The poem gives the impression of dispassionately considering all the political possibilities; but its full political nature

---

[9] Douglas Bush, 'Marvell's Horatian Ode', *Sewanee Review*, 60 (1952), 336.
[10] Ibid.
[11] Cleanth Brooks, 'A Note on the Limits of "History" and the Limits of "Criticism"', *Sewanee Review*, 61 (1953), 129.
[12] A. Alvarez, *The School of Donne* (London, 1961), pp. 105–7.

lies not in its created 'impression of the mind detachedly at play over a number of possible choices', but in its skilful exclusion of certain possibilities and manipulation of others.

Cromwell's victories in Ireland were not just routine military activities. To re-establish the historical context of Marvell's poem is to see something of its political resonance.

In November 1641 a rebellion took place in Ireland, at last liberated from Strafford's iron hand. Many hundreds, probably many thousands, of Englishmen were killed. The opposition group in Parliament refused to trust a royal nominee with command of an army to conquer Ireland. So the question of ultimate power in the state was raised. In the panic caused by news of the Irish rebellion the Grand Remonstrance was adopted, a comprehensive indictment of royal policy. It passed the Commons by only eleven votes. For by now parties had formed. Charles replied by bringing a body of armed men to the House in an attempt to arrest Pym, Hampden, and three other leaders of the opposition group. They took refuge in the City and resolutions in their support poured in from all over the country. Charles quitted London, of which he had lost control; the Five Members returned in triumph.[13]

The Irish rebellion was a crucial event in escalating the confrontations that led to the outbreak of Civil War in 1642. But the war itself meant that no army was raised to put down the Irish uprising: Ireland remained a potential staging-post for invasion of England until Cromwell's successful campaign. So Marvell's celebration of the victorious return from Ireland is also a celebration not only of the battles and sieges and massacres there, but of the bringing to an end of a whole phase of recent history: of suppressing the rebellion that had triggered off the revolution within England. Lucy Hutchinson's recollections of the rising indicate the strength of Puritan feeling.

While the king was in Scotland, that cursed rebellion in Ireland broke out wherein above 200,000 were massacred in two months' space, being surprised, and many of them most inhumanly butchered and tormented; and besides the slain, abundance of poor families stripped and sent naked away out of all their possessions.[14]

[13] Christopher Hill, *The Century of Revolution 1603–1714* (Edinburgh, 1961), pp. 111–12.

[14] Lucy Hutchinson, *Memoirs of the Life of Colonel Hutchinson*, ed. C. H. Firth (London, 1906) p. 76. Richard Baxter also claimed 200,000 were murdered, *The Autobiography of Richard Baxter*, abridged by J. M. Lloyd Thomas, ed. N. H. Keeble (London, 1974), p. 32.

Like many other Puritans, she believed that the king

obstructed all its [parliament's] proceedings for the effectual relief of Ireland. Long was he before he could be drawn to proclaim these murderers rebels, and when he did, by special command, there were but forty proclamations printed, and care was taken that they should not be much dispersed; which courses afflicted all the good protestants in England, and confirmed that the rebellion in Ireland received countenance from the king and queen of England.[15]

But the Irish campaign was to become a contentious issue. Attempts to raise an army to send to Ireland in 1647 and 1649 both resulted in army mutinies. H. N. Brailsford writes of 1647:

For a variety of reasons the men were not keen to enlist for Ireland. Some of them had served for nearly five years and were eager to get back to their homes and their trades. Others were willing to serve in England as long as might be necessary to assure its liberties, but they were not yet what Cromwell's veterans afterwards became, professional soldiers who would go anywhere and fight for anything at the word of command . . . In the end, after the case for and against enlistment for Ireland had been hotly debated by all ranks through several weeks, it turned out that only 167 officers out of the 2,320 in the New Model—a trifle over seven per cent— would volunteer . . . Though five of them were colonels in command of regiments, they failed to induce more than a negligible number of soldiers to follow them.[16]

The renewal of civil war within England postponed the attempt to raise an army for Ireland in 1648. When attempts were made again, organized political resistance came from a radical group working both within and outside the army, named by its opponents as Levellers. William Walwyn, one of the leaders, was alleged to have said:

That the sending over Forces to Ireland is for nothing else but to make way by the blood of the Army to enlarge their territories of power and Tyranny, that it is an unlawful War, a cruel and bloody work to go to destroy the Irish Natives for their Consciences . . . and to drive them from their proper natural and native Rights . . .[17]

---

[15] Hutchinson, *Memoirs*, pp. 76–7.
[16] H. N. Brailsford, *The Levellers and the English Revolution* (1961), (Nottingham, 1976), pp. 169–70.
[17] *Walwin's Wiles* (1649) in William Haller and Godfrey Davies, *The Leveller Tracts 1647–1653* (New York, 1944), pp. 288–9.

And it was reported of Walwyn that it was

> his constant endeavour to hinder the relief of Ireland, by exhibiting arguments
> and reasons in justification of that bloody rebellion, and in puzzling the
> judgements and Consciences of those that otherways would promote that
> happy work, arguing that the cause of the Irish Natives in seeking their
> just freedoms, immunities, and liberties, was the very same with our
> cause here, in endeavouring our own rescue and freedom from the power
> of oppressors . . .[18]

The Leveller pamphlet, *The English Soldiers Standard* (1649), asked:

> For consider, as things now stand, to what end you should hazard your
> lives against the Irish: have you not been fighting these seven years in England
> for Rights and Liberties, that you are yet deluded of? and that too, when
> as none can hinder you of them but your own Officers, under whom you
> have fought? and will you go on stil to kil, slay and murther men, to make
> them as absolute Lords and Masters over Ireland as you have made them
> over England? or is it your ambition to reduce the Irish to the happiness
> of tythes upon trebble damages, to Excise, Customs and Monopolies in
> Trades? or to fill their prisons with poor disabled prisoners, to fill their land
> with swarms of beggers; to enrich their Parliament-men, and impoverish
> their people; to take down Monarchical Tyranny, and set up an Aristocratical
> Tyranny; or to over-spread that Nation as this yet is, with such Wasps and
> Hornets as our Lawyers and their Confederates?[19]

Situating that memorable description of Charles's execution at the
central point of the 'Horatian Ode' serves to support the impression
of a simple, binary opposition between Charles and Cromwell. The
full political context is thus reduced to a set of alternatives; and
since Charles is now dead, the alternatives collapse into the single
possibility of Cromwell. This, without doubt, is the intended effect;
giving prominence to an already dead opponent serves to deflect
attention from the living ones. The radical voices opposed to the
Irish campaign are given no part in the ode. This may have success-
fully suppressed them for later literary critics, but a contemporary
audience (assuming that there was an audience for the poem) could

---

[18] *Walwin's Wiles*, Haller and Davies, p. 310.

[19] A. L. Morton, ed., *Freedom in Arms: a Selection of Leveller Writings* (London,
1975), pp. 238–9. The radicals who opposed the Irish campaign were in a minority;
'many of the most radical supporters of parliament applauded the conquest'.
Christopher Hill, 'Seventeenth-century English radicals and Ireland', in *Radicals, Rebels
and Establishments*, ed. Patrick J. Cornish (Belfast, 1985), p. 40.

not but have been aware of the controversiality of the campaign, of the vocal opposition, of the ensuing mutinies and their swift suppression. Their absence from the ode is a significant absence. But though their voices, their beliefs, are excluded, their destruction by Cromwell is memorialized.

> And, like the three-fork'd Lightning, first
> Breaking the Clouds where it was nurst,
>   Did thorough his own Side
>   His fiery way divide.
> For 'tis all one to Courage high
> The Emulous or Enemy;
>   And with such to inclose
>   Is more then to oppose.
>
> (13–20)[20]

The Oxford edition of Marvell's poems glosses this: 'Cromwell's emergence from among the other Parliamentary leaders became marked at and after Marston Moor (1644) . . . To shut in and cramp a man of high courage is worse (less tolerable for him) than to oppose him. That is why Cromwell burst through his own party.'[21]

It may be that Cromwell's struggle against the Parliamentary generals Essex and Manchester is referred to in these lines. Manchester held back from prosecuting the war to a decisive end. 'If we beat the King ninety nine times, yet he is King still; but if the King beat us once, we shall all be hanged,' Manchester said, to which Cromwell replied, 'My Lord, if this be so, why did we take up arms at first?' And Cromwell complained to the House of Commons that Manchester's lack of decisive success 'was neither through accidents (which could not be helped) nor through his improvidence only, but through backwardness to all action', and he accused Manchester of 'some principle of unwillingness in his Lordship to have this war prosecuted unto full victory'. As soon as Cromwell finished, a proposal was made to exclude a member of either House of Parliament from military command—removing from control those who held their military position by reason only of rank, not of ability, and allowing the formation of what became known as the New Model Army. Fairfax,

[20] Christopher Ricks suggests that the self-reflexive image here relates to the tensions of civil war; 'Its Own Resemblance' in C. A. Patrides, ed., *Approaches to Marvell: The York Centenary Lectures* (London, 1978), pp. 129–30.
[21] *Poems and Letters of Andrew Marvell*, i. 298.

with a major engagement against the Royalist army imminent, petitioned Parliament to allow Cromwell to be given military command and be exempted from the ordinance; and Cromwell remained exempted.[22]

But though the divisiveness within the Parliamentary army may be referred to here by Marvell, it is hard to see that 'emulous' can easily be applied to the dilatory generals. But 'emulous' might readily be applied to the army radicals in the rank and file, the mutinous lower orders. The destructive violence of lightning applies less well to Cromwell's parliamentary strategies than to his savage suppression of Leveller mutiny.

At the first of the three army rendezvous promised after the Putney debates, in November 1647,

two regiments specifically not invited to the rendezvous had turned up, including that of Lilburne's elder brother Robert, men notorious for their disaffection. Many of the soldiers actually arrived with copies of the *Agreement* and the pertinent motto: 'England's freedom! Soldier's right!' stuck into their hats. It was hardly the sort of situation which any General who believed in discipline was likely to tolerate; Cromwell reacted in a fury not only to the audacious headgear but also to the straightforward disobedience of the unbidden regiments in making an appearance in the first place. When the men refused to remove their favours, he drew his sword on them with zest. The four ringleaders were seized, and after casting lots, one was shot as an example to the rest.[23]

Cromwell and Fairfax acted with equal swiftness in the suppression of radical and Leveller-based mutinies in the next wave of unrest in 1649.

When the decision had been taken to send an army to Ireland, the occasion was seized to weed out the Leveller influenced regiments. There was a mutiny in London, and Robert Lockyer, who had fought all through the civil war, was shot as ringleader. Despite this, in May there were mutinies in four more regiments, which turned into a full-scale Leveller revolt. Parliament declared mutiny in the Army to be treason. The revolt was suppressed after a lightning night attack by Cromwell on the rebels at Burford, not without suggestions of treachery on his part. Three leaders were shot after the

[22] Christopher Hill, *God's Englishman: Oliver Cromwell and the English Revolution* (Harmondsworth, 1972), pp. 69–70.
[23] Antonia Fraser, *Cromwell* (New York, 1973), p. 224.

surrender, and a fourth, William Thompson, was caught and shot three days later.[24]

The swiftness of the attack on the Levellers at Burford — a fifty-mile march in one day followed by a surprise attack in the middle of the night — and the fact that the suppression of the Levellers was a removal of opposition to the Irish campaign, suggest that Cromwell's breaking through his own side like lightning is most appropriately applied to this defeat of the radical opposition within the army. After the suppression,

> The relief felt by the rich supporters of the Grandees, whether Presbyterian or Independent, was immense. Oxford gave Fairfax and Cromwell honorary degrees and a banquet. The City another banquet and rich gifts of plate. Not even the victory at Naseby had been greeted with such unmixed enthusiasm — for them, after all, Levellers were far more dangerous enemies than Royalists.[25]

The Levellers' own account of the suppression of the Burford mutiny, *The Levellers (Falsely so called) Vindicated*, declared:

> for the Sword convinceth not, it doth but enforce; it begetteth no love, but fomenteth and engendreth hatred and revenge; for bloud thirsteth after bloud, and vengeance rageth for vengeance, and this devoureth and destroyeth all where it cometh.[26]

In absolute opposition is Marvell's celebration of the sword:

---

[24] Hill, *God's Englishman*, p. 105.

[25] Morton, *Freedom in Arms*, p. 68.

[26] Ibid., p. 315. Is there an allusion to the Leveller opposition to the enclosure of traditional common land in 'And with such to inclose / Is more then to oppose'? Richard Overton wrote '*Concerning Commons inclosed*. That all grounds which anciently lay in Common for the poore, and are now impropriate, inclosed, and fenced in, may forthwith (in whose hands soever they are) be cast out, and laid open againe to the free and common use and benefit of the poore': 'Certaine Articles for the good of the Common wealth, presented to the consideration of his Excellencie, Sir Thomas Fairfax, and to the Officers and Souldiers under his Command', appended to Overton's *An Appeale from the degenerate Representative Body . . . to . . . The free People . . . of England (1647)*, in Don M. Wolfe, ed., *Leveller Manifestoes of the Puritan Revolution* (New York, 1944), p. 194. And in the account of the falcon later, is the Levellers' insignia of the sea-green ribbon alluded to? The immediate suggestion of peaceable nature in the 'green bough', associating the falcon with positive growth rather than destruction, is no doubt the dominant meaning; John S. Coolidge interprets it as representing 'civilized peace' in 'Marvell and Horace', *Modern Philology*, 63 (1965), 111–20.

And for the last effect
Still keep thy Sword erect.
(115–16)

To introduce the Levellers and the opposition to the Irish campaign is to qualify the impression of Marvell's 'seeing all the implications and never attempting to simplify them'.[27] Whether or not the army radicals are referred to in 'the emulous' and in Cromwell's driving 'thorough his own side', they are part of the context of the poem's subject; the objection to the Irish campaign is something consciously excluded from the poem. Certain political implications are significantly absent from the poem. These political exclusions are a characteristic of the 'Horatian Ode'.

Commentators[28] have pointed out how Cromwell is described as a natural force: as lightning, as a falcon. This makes a profound contrast with the portrayal of Charles as 'Royal Actor': natural as against artificial. The elegant, dignified, tragic, theatrical impression, sustained in 'tragic scaffold', the clapping as at a performance, the 'memorable Scene', serve to identify Charles with the leisured arts of the past. The theatres had been closed by parliamentary order since 1642. Now he has played his last part before the Banqueting House in which he had participated in so many court masques.

---

[27] Alvarez, *The School of Donne*, p. 106.

[28] Among the critical readings drawn on are Ruth Wallerstein, *Studies in Seventeenth-Century Poetic* (Madison, 1950); L. D. Lerner, 'An Horatian Ode' in *Interpretations*, ed. John Wain (London, 1955); A. J. N. Wilson, 'Andrew Marvell: "An Horatian Ode upon Cromwell's Return from Ireland": the thread of the poem and its use of classical allusion', *Critical Quarterly*, 11 (1969), 325–41; C. K. Stead, 'The Actor and the Man of Action—Marvell's Horatian Ode', *Critical Survey*, 3 (1967), 145–50; Robin Grove, 'Marvell', *Melbourne Critical Review*, 6 (1963), 31–43; Raman Selden, 'Historical Thought and Marvell's Horatian Ode', *Durham University Journal*, 34 (1972–3), 41–3; J. E. Siemon, 'Art and Argument in Marvell's "Horatian Ode upon Cromwell's Return from Ireland"', *Neuphilologische Mitteilungen*, 73 (1972), 823–35; Warren L. Chernaik, *The Poet's Time: Politics and Religion in the Work of Andrew Marvell* (Cambridge, 1982); Dennis Davison, *The Poetry of Andrew Marvell* (London, 1964); Christopher Hill, 'Society and Andrew Marvell' in *Puritanism and Revolution* (London, 1958); Judith Richards, 'Literary Criticism and the Historian: Towards Reconstructing Marvell's Meaning in "An Horatian Ode"', *Literature and History*, 7 (1981), 25–47; Robert Wilcher, *Andrew Marvell* (Cambridge, 1985), pp. 113–24.

The contrast also helps enforce those impressions of dissimulation, of acting a part, of the untrustworthiness and dishonesty of which many in Parliament and the army accused Charles. Cromwell, however, is shown as someone without pretence, as an instrument of God, 'angry Heavens flame'. Whereas Charles keeps the front of the stage till the last possible moment, Cromwell is presented as impersonal, as not pursuing any cult of the individual but as agent of the historical process, an elemental force. Charles's unbending monarchical pride is present as much as any tragic dignity in '*He* nothing common did or mean'; he is impassably distant from anything common, mean, vulgar; whereas Cromwell is in respectful relationship to them:

> He to the Commons Feet* presents
> A Kingdome, for His first years rents:
> And, what he may, forbears
> His Fame to make it theirs.
>
> (85–8)

* Common Feet *1681 Folio*

Cromwell renounces personal fame, and transfers it to the common feet, to the people, to the House of Commons.

The formalist critics, seeing the work as of purely poetic concern, miss much of the impact here. The discriminations between Charles and Cromwell, and the subtleties of implication, have been firmly established in the various critical readings. But the images raise— though they are designed to obscure—the question, Is this true? They present an impression of Cromwell as a natural phenomenon; a natural phenomenon, moreover, that is an instrument of God. The lightning is glossed as the 'force of Angry heavens flame'; the falcon was known, among other associations, as Jove's servant. Auceps declares in *The Compleat Angler* (1653) of falcons:

in the Air my troops of Hawks soar up on high, and when they are lost in the sight of men, then they attend upon and converse with the gods; therefore I think my *Eagle* is so justly styled *Joves servant in ordinary*: and that very Falcon, that I am now going to see deserves no meaner a title, for she usually in her flight endangers her self, (like the son of Daedalus) . . .[29]

---

[29] Izaak Walton and Charles Cotton, *The Compleat Angler*, ed. John Buxton (World's Classics, Oxford, 1982), pp. 24–5.

Controlled first by God, Cromwell is now the instrument of Parliament, the Commons, the public:

> And has his Sword and Spoyls ungirt
> To lay them at the *Publick's* skirt.
>
> (89–90)

Cleanth Brooks accurately expresses what the imagery is doing:

The thunderbolt simile, of the first part of the poem, gives way here to the falcon simile in this second part of the poem. The latter figure revises and qualifies the former: it repeats the suggestion of ruthless energy and power, but Cromwell falls from the sky now, not as the thunderbolt, but as the hunting hawk. The trained falcon is not a wanton destroyer, nor an irresponsible one. It knows its master: it is perfectly disciplined.[30]

Yet the army of Cromwell and Fairfax was certainly not in the hand of Parliament; if anything, the reverse was rapidly becoming the case. The images of control that the falcon is designed to enforce need to be put in the context of events leading up to the Irish campaign.

When Parliament began to plan the Irish campaign in 1647, it was decided to disband the New Model Army and raise a new force. But the army refused to disband until arrears of pay had been met, and while assembled with a view to disbandment, presented a petition for past arrears and for indemnity for actions committed during the war. Cromwell assured the Commons in March 1647 'In the presence of Almighty God, before whom he stood, that he knew that the Army would disband and lay down their Arms at their door, whensoever they should command them'.[31] But the army refused to disband; and as arguments about back-pay and about the command of the Irish campaign continued, the army became increasingly threatening. In June 1647 Cornet Joyce captured Charles I from Parliamentary custody where he had been since the Scots sold him to Parliament.

At this point Cromwell fled from the Commons to avoid arrest by the Presbyterian faction, and took shelter with the army. The army resolved not to disband or divide until their grievances had been redressed, and began to advance on London. A letter, sent to the Lord Mayor of London from St Albans, was

---

[30] Brooks, 'Literary Criticism', pp. 144–5. See also Michael McKeon, 'Pastoralism, Puritanism, Imperialism, Scientism: Andrew Marvell and the Problem of Mediation', *Yearbook of English Studies*, 13 (1983), p. 53.   [31] Fraser, *Cromwell*, p. 188.

signed by Cromwell and Hammond and eight colonels. In this letter Cromwell openly claimed for the army an equal right with Parliament to settle the government of the country. He says, 'We have as much right to demand a happy settlement as we have to our money'; and adds that, to attain its desires, the army is approaching near the City, and that if the citizens take up arms in hindrance of the just undertakings of the army they must take the consequences.[32]

As the army advanced on London in July 1647, the eleven Presbyterian members most hostile to the army withdrew from the House of Commons. But the Presbyterians organized a London mob of disbanded soldiers, apprentices, and others which demanded the restoration of Charles and invaded Parliament; and nine peers and fifty-seven members fled to shelter with the army. The army proceeded to occupy London on 6 August, the eleven Presbyterians withdrew again from Parliament, and the nine peers and fifty-seven members returned. The image of Cromwell as falcon responsive to the control of Parliament has to be read in the context of these events. They were events, moreover, which were triggered by the attempts to organize an army to send to Ireland. It may be that the image of the controlled falcon is designed to allay suspicions about army power, and to reassure that Cromwell's army is now responsive to control by Parliament; to expunge those anxieties of 1647. But whether or not Marvell believed things were different in 1650, the impression of the controllable falcon is there to counter the memory of the army resisting Parliament's orders to disband, and ultimately marching on London and occupying it.

But even more significant than the events of 1647 were those of 1648 which culminated in the episode known as Pride's Purge. David Underdown in his study of that episode[33] records that from early in November 1648 there had been troop movements threatening an imminent march on London. The Army's *Remonstrance* pronounced Charles 'guilty of all the bloodshed in these intestine wars' and the army radicals were determined to see him brought to justice. The march began at the end of November. On 6 December a thousand troops were stationed around Parliament. On the stairs leading to

[32] Clements R. Markham, *A Life of the Great Lord Fairfax* (London, 1870), p. 287.
[33] David Underdown, *Pride's Purge: Politics in the Puritan Revolution* (Oxford, 1971).

the House Colonel Pride stood with a list of members to be excluded
or secured. 'Altogether, something approaching one hundred members
were either arrested or secluded in the first two days of the Purge.'
'Many more than 100 effectively removed themselves without waiting
for the Army.' At least nine more members were excluded on the
12th. Underdown estimates that 45 members were imprisoned and
186 secluded but not imprisoned at Westminster.[34] As Blair Worden
puts it,

Pride's Purge deprived the House of Commons of well over half its membership. Although only about 110 M.P.s seem to have been forcibly prevented
by the army from entering the house, these were a minority of the members
whose active participation came to an end in December 1648 . . . Of the
470 or so M.P.s qualified to sit at the beginning of December 1648, the
purge permanently removed about 270. Temporarily it removed nearly 100
more, who stayed away from parliament in the weeks between the purge
and the king's execution . . .[35]

Cromwell declared 'that he had not been acquainted with the
design; yet since it was done he was glad of it'.[36] Fairfax recalled
later in his *Short Memorials*:

To prepare a way to this Work, this Agitating Council did first intend to
remove all out of the Parliament who were like to oppose them, and carried
it on with such Secrecy, as I had not the least Intimation of it till it was
done, as some of the Members of the House can witness, with whom I was
at that very time upon special Business, when that Attempt was made
by Colonel *Pride* upon the Parliament, which I protest I never had any
knowledge of till it was done. The Reason why it was so secretly carried,
that I should have no notice of it, was, because I always prevented those
Designes when I knew them.[37]

'This Work' that Fairfax refers to was the trial of the king. The
execution of Charles is a centre-piece of the 'Horatian Ode'; Pride's
Purge of a month earlier is certainly not outside the poem's range
of reference, even if the events of 1647 might seem some time back.
As Fairfax records, the military purging of Parliament was a direct
preparation for the trial and execution of King Charles.

[34] Ibid., pp. 152, 159, 212.
[35] Blair Worden, *The Rump Parliament 1678–1653* (London, 1974), p. 23.
[36] Hill, *God's Englishman*, p. 96.
[37] *Short Memorials of Thomas Lord Fairfax written by Himself* (London, 1699),
p. 121.

To see how the recent history of the army marching on and purging Parliament is transmuted into an image of Cromwell as falcon responsive to the instructions of Parliament the falconer is to see the political manipulations behind the poetical images. And this is not something that should cause any surprise, when Cromwell's political manipulativeness is so explicitly admired in the poem.

> And *Hampton* shows what part
> He had of wiser Art.
> Where, twining subtile fears with hope,
> He wove a Net of such a scope,
> That *Charles* himself might chase
> To *Caresbrooks* narrow case.
> That thence the *Royal Actor* born
> The *Tragick Scaffold* might adorn.
>
> (47–54)

That twentieth-century historians are uncertain as to whether Cromwell masterminded Charles's disastrous escape from Hampton Court is unimportant; the point is that Marvell, along with many contemporaries, believed that Cromwell had planned the episode and admires him for doing so.[38]

Charles was imprisoned at Hampton Court, a trump card for the army. None the less it was the army radicals who had kidnapped him, and it was their position which was strengthened by holding him. It certainly suited Cromwell that Charles should escape to Carisbrooke Castle on the Isle of Wight, commanded by a cousin of Cromwell's, Robert Hammond. Before the escape, Cromwell had

[38] John Buchan, *Oliver Cromwell* (London, 1934), p. 259: 'The view that Oliver deliberately frightened him (Charles) into escape to further his own ambition was widely held at this time, and has been given currency by Andrew Marvell, who was more puritan than royalist . . . It is a view for which there is no atom of proof.' Hill, *God's Englishman*, p. 92: 'The whole episode played so completely into Cromwell's hands that many believed that he contrived the King's escape. This cannot be proved: but there is evidence, apart from its convenience for Oliver, that makes one wonder.' Joseph Anthony Mazzeo, in 'Cromwell as Machiavellian Prince in Marvell's "An Horatian Ode" ', *Journal of the History of Ideas*, 21 (1960), 1–17, cites Flecknoe, Carrington, and Henry Fletcher as seeing with Marvell 'an example of the highest skill in statecraft' (p. 11 n. 12) in Cromwell's luring Charles to Carisbrooke. 'It is part of Cromwell's cunning,' writes John Carey ('Reversals Transposed', in Patrides, *Approaches to Marvell* (London, 1978), p. 144). Milton, in *A Second Defence of the English People* (1654), repudiated the charge that Cromwell persuaded the King to flee: *CPW* iv/1. 663.

written to another cousin, Edward Whalley, who was in charge of the King's guards at Hampton Court: 'Dear Cos Whalley, There are rumours abroad of some intended attempt on his Majesty's person . . . ' Whalley immediately showed the letter to Charles, and Charles made his escape that night. Aided by Ashburnham and Berkeley, who had earlier been involved with Cromwell in various negotiations, he headed for Carisbrooke Castle. But Hammond, instead of providing a boat to take Charles to France, accepted him as a prisoner.[39]

The timing of the escape helped Cromwell and the army grandees against the radicals. With the escape of Charles and the ignorance of the rank and file of the army as to his whereabouts, the dominant issue at the army rendezvous in November 1647 was that Charles might have summoned his supporters and joined the Scots to begin a new war. The army consequently accepted demands for unity against the common Royalist foe, and the radical initiatives were lost. But not only did Charles's escape remove him from the radicals and make him the grandees' bargaining instrument, it also — and this is Marvell's stress — served as a way of giving Charles enough rope to hang himself, by demonstrating his untrustworthiness in escaping, and in attempting yet again to rally supporters and renew war. At Carisbrooke Charles signed a secret agreement with the Scots, according to which they undertook to send an army to his aid, he to call the Cavaliers to arms once more. The secret agreement soon leaked out, and the growing sense that Charles could not be trusted not to try to revive military hostilities led to his being brought to trial and condemned to death. The escape from Hampton Court was the beginning of the inevitable path to execution:

> That *Charles* himself might chase
> To *Caresbrooks* narrow case.
> That thence the *Royal Actor* born
> The *Tragick Scaffold* might adorn.
>
> (51–4)

The simple causal connectives, 'That . . . That', laconically summarize the history. The political manipulativeness of Cromwell's that could plan such an inexorable chain of cause and effect is his 'wiser Art'. It

---

[39] Fraser, *Cromwell*, pp. 221–3; Hill, *God's Englishman*, pp. 92–3.

is superior to Charles's masquing art. These are the new politico-military arts that have now superseded the old aesthetic arts.

> So restless *Cromwel* could not cease
> In the inglorious Arts of Peace,
> But through adventrous War
> Urged his active Star.
>
> (9–12)

The Ode opens with a forsaking of the contemplative art of poetry, the Muses dear, and concludes with a reassertion of the new, active, practical politico-military arts.

> The same *Arts* that did *gain*
> A *Pow'r* must it *maintain.*
>
> (119–20)

But while recognizing the poetic art with which Marvell plays on his theme of the transmutation of aesthetic arts into the new arts of the military junta, rejecting as 'inglorious' the 'Arts of Peace', we might also remember that there were others who used the word 'arts' with less admiration. So Lilburne could refer to politicians as the 'Arts-men and Craftsmen of the world',[40] and the Leveller *Manifestation* (1649) declared:

All our Desires, Petitions and Papers . . . (are) not moulded nor contrived by the subtill or politick Principles of the World, but plainly produced and nakedly sent, without any insinuating arts.[41]

The terms of Marvell's vocabulary in the Ode, 'moulded . . . subtil . . . arts', are here explicitly rejected.

It is not my argument that Marvell should have included Leveller attitudes in his poem. But by establishing this contemporary context of radical, Leveller activity, we can see more clearly what Marvell's position is. By retrieving what is excluded, we can situate this political poem in its politics.

The prominence given to Charles here is important. To pay tribute to Charles's dignity at his execution is not to be crypto-Royalist. There were many amongst the army and the supporters of Parliament

---

[40] *The Just Defence of John Lilburn* (1653) in Morton, *Freedom in Arms*, p. 324.
[41] Wolfe, *Leveller Manifestoes*, p. 392.

who were unhappy about the execution. The commander in chief
of the Parliamentary army, Fairfax, Marvell's later employer, wrote:

> On the Fatal day
> Jan: 30 1648
>
> Oh lett that day from time be blotted quite
> And lett beleefe of 't in next Age be waved
> In deepest silence th'Act Concealed might
> Soe that the King-doms Credit might be saued
> But if the Power devine permitted this
> His will's the law & ours must acquiesce
>
> Curae loquuntur leves
> Ingentes stupent[42]

And he recalled in *Short Memorials*:

This way being made by the Sword, the *Trial of the King* was easier for
them to accomplish.

My afflicted and troubled Mind for it, and my earnest Endeavours to
prevent it, will, I hope, sufficiently testify my dislike and abhorrence of
the Fact: And what will they not do to the Shrubs, having cut down the
Cedar?[43]

Marvell's account of the execution stresses Charles's tragic dignity,
the royal actor playing out the role he was born to; it is an individual
performance—there is no suggestion of its extension to the 'shrubs';
fears of a spread of judicial executions, of a purge, are excluded.
And there is nothing of the radicals' vision of Charles here, the
'Man of Blood'. There is nothing stressing that validification of the
execution that we find, for instance in Milton's *Tenure of Kings and
Magistrates*.

But this I dare owne as part of my faith, that if such a one there be, by
whose Commission, whole massachers have been committed on his faithfull
Subjects, his Provinces offered to pawn or alienation, as the hire of those
whom he had sollicited to come in and destroy whole Citties and Countries;
be he King, or Tyrant, or Emperour, the Sword of Justice is above him;
in whose hand soever is found sufficient power to avenge the effusion, and
so great a deluge of innocent blood.[44]

---

[42] MS Fairfax 40, fos. 600–601, Bodleian Library. Transcript of the poems in
Transactions of the Connecticut Academy of Arts and Sciences, 14 (1909), 237–90.
[43] Fairfax, *Short Memorials*, p. 121.   [44] *CPW*, iii. 197.

And though Cromwell's 'wiser Art' is presented as responsible for the King's fate, his hands are left clean; it is the lower orders, the rank and file soldiers amongst whom the radical element flourished, who are given the taint of blood.

> While round the armed Bands
> Did clap their bloody hands.
>
> (55–6)

The critics concerned with patterns of imagery will point out the extension of the theatrical image here, the applause at a performance. Brooks notes 'The generally received account is that the soldiers clapped their hands so as to make it impossible for Charles's speech to be heard'.[45] But the couplet is also part of the manipulative strategy with which Cromwell is presented; any taint of blood-guilt is skilfully displaced in the poem from Cromwell to the 'armed Bands', they are the ones with 'bloody hands', the rank and file soldiers, the lower orders.[46]

To allow a sympathetic portrayal of Charles at his execution in a poem commemorating Cromwell's return from Ireland was a bold and daring strategy. In uniting the unexpected extremes it shows a fine flowering of applied metaphysical wit. It ensured that the poem would find some favour with pragmatic Royalists as well as with committed supporters of Cromwell. Only the radical element could find little pleasurable in it; the celebration of the loss of the Irish people's liberties, the sympathetic portrayal of the 'Man of Blood' with no indication of his crimes, and the elevation of another single power-figure ready to take his place.

> Nature that hateth emptiness
> Allows of penetration less.
>
> (41–2)

Implicitly, Cromwell is there to step into the gap created by the removal of Charles. The very downplaying of any cult of the individual in Cromwell, the naturalizing of him as a physical phenomenon like lightning, as a natural creature like a falcon, is

[45] Brooks, 'Literary Criticism', p. 143.

[46] Rosalie Colie remarks how 'curiously neutralized the scene is, and how it does not seem to reflect on Cromwell': 'My Echoing Song': Andrew Marvell's Poetry of Criticism (Princeton, 1970), p. 65.

skilful propaganda for the emergent powerful individual. The falcon image has always seemed problematical. How can so inescapably a traditional, ruling-élite image be applied to the new revolutionary leader? 'Fair Princesse of the spacious Air', Lovelace addresses the falcon.[47] But it is just Cromwell's suitability as a continuer of a traditional ruling-élite role that is being stressed. Revolutionary elements, the radical wing, the Levellers, the Diggers, are excluded from the Ode. The falcon emphatically reasserts traditional monarchical and aristocratic associations, the sport of the ruling élite, even when it purports to be stressing Cromwell's controllability, his being an impersonal instrument of power. As John Wallace writes:

clearly the movement which was to culminate in the Protectorship and the offer of the crown had begun.
     In the light of the opposition to him, Marvell's account of Cromwell's humility should read not only as part of the proof that a man rules well who least seeks to govern but also as a refutation of the attack on his alleged ambition . . .[48]

By presenting Charles as the prime (but dead) opponent to Cromwell, attention is diverted from any other possibilities. By focusing on individuals, Parliament is displaced into the murky background; any democratic, radical, communistic, or egalitarian possibilities are altogether excluded. And just as the political opposition to the Irish campaign is excluded from the poem, so is any recognition of the opposition to the campaign against the Scots. Fairfax had resigned command of the Commonwealth's forces because, he said,

I think it doubtful whether we have a just cause to make an invasion upon Scotland. We are joined with the Scots in the National League and Covenant, and for us, contrary thereunto, and without sufficient cause given us by them, to enter their country and make war upon them, is that which I cannot see the justice of.[49]

But Fairfax's scruples about invading the territory of an ally are displaced by an assertion of the duplicity of the Scots: 'party-colour'd Mind' invokes the crossed pattern of the plaid, implying contradictory, unreliable commitments; not straight and loyal.

---

[47] *The Poems of Richard Lovelace*, ed. C. H. Wilkinson (Oxford, 1953).
[48] John M. Wallace, *Destiny His Choice: The Loyalism of Andrew Marvell* (Cambridge, 1968), p. 92.   [49] Markham, *Life of Fairfax*, p. 360.

> The *Pict* no shelter now shall find
> Within his party-colour'd Mind;
>   But from this Valour sad
>   Shrink underneath the Plad.

(105–8)

T. S. Eliot picked out this passage and lines 29–36 for praise as examples of Marvell's wit:

There is here an equipoise, a balance and proportion of tones, which, while it cannot raise Marvell to the level of Dryden or Milton, extorts an approval which these poets do not receive from us, and bestows a pleasure at least different in kind from any they can often give. It is what makes Marvell a classic: or classic in a sense in which Gray and Collins are not; for the latter, with all their accredited purity, are comparatively poor in shades of feeling to contrast and unite.[50]

The wit, the equipoise, balance, proportion, the complexity of contrasted and united shades and feeling are here without doubt. But they are here functionally, politically; they are part of the manipulative art, for they serve to distract attention from the contentiousness of the Scots campaign, and the divisiveness of the issue that Fairfax's resignation highlighted. The wit is to the fore, the tendentious political case of attacking an ally displaced.

The stress on the 'sword' takes on a clearer significance when the political context of the poem is restored. Those who read the ode as containing implied criticism of Cromwell make much of the following lines:

> And for the last effect
> Still keep thy Sword erect.
> Besides the force it has to fright
> The Spirits of the shady Night,
>   The Same *Arts* that did *gain*
>   A *Pow'r* must it *maintain*.

(115–20)

Brooks argued that they contain the implication that 'those who take up the sword shall perish by the sword'.[51] It is unlikely that such a note would be used to conclude a poem commemorating military

---

[50] T. S. Eliot, 'Andrew Marvell' (1921), *Selected Essays* (London, 1961), p. 302.
[51] Brooks, 'Literary Criticism', p. 150.

victory. Rather the lines conclude the Ode on a resonant assertion of militarism.

This takes on especial force in the context of the Leveller's equally forceful insistence on peace. 'Blessed are the Peace-makers for they shall be called the Children of God' is the epigraph from Matthew 5: 9 on the title-page of the third *Agreement of the Free People of England. Tendered as a Peace-Offering to this distressed Nation* (1649).[52] Its opening declaration begins: 'After the long and tedious prosecution of a most unnatural cruell, homebred war, occasioned by divisions and distempers amongst our selves . . .'[53] and it ends with the hope to 'produce the lasting Peace and Prosperity of this Commonwealth'.[54] The first *Agreement* (1647) had similarly stressed 'that there may be no grounds for future quarrels, or contentions to occasion warre and bloud-shed' and looked forward to a time when 'those occasions of endlesse strifes, and bloudy warres, shall be perfectly removed':

Now because we are earnestly desirous of the peace and good of all our Country-men, even of those that have opposed us, and would to our utmost possibility provide for perfect peace and freedom . . .[55]

And the *Manifestation* (1649) declares: 'Peace and Freedom is our Designe; by War we were never gainers, nor never wish to be.'[56]

But Marvell's victory ode allows no place for peace. It opens with a call to arms, celebrates one military campaign, looks forward to another, and concludes with an assertion of the sword. The appeal at the poem's opening to

> oyl th'unused Armours rust
> Removing from the Wall
> The Corslet of the Hall
> (6–8)

can now be seen in a specific context. As an appeal to take up arms for the Parliamentary army, it is obviously somewhat belated, since fighting had begun some eight years earlier and was now for the

---

[52] Wolfe, *Leveller Manifestoes*, p. 400.   [53] Ibid., p. 402.
[54] Ibid., p. 410.   [55] Ibid., pp. 229–30.   [56] Ibid., p. 396.

moment concluded within England. It might be read as a recruiting call for the Scots campaign, but it makes better sense read as a wider appeal to support the military junta: as an appeal to the poet-intellectuals and other members of the élite to identify with the Cromwellian army group.

6

'Upon Appleton House,
to my Lord Fairfax'

When Thomas, third Baron Fairfax, resigned his position as commander in chief of the forces of the Commonwealth of England in
June 1650, he retired to his Yorkshire estates. How soon after that
date Andrew Marvell was employed as tutor to Mary Fairfax, born
1638, is unknown. But 'Upon Appleton House, to my Lord Fairfax'
is usually dated between June 1650 and 21 February 1653, when
Milton wrote to John Bradshaw, President of the Council of State,

there will be with you to morrow upon some occasion of business a
Gentleman whose name is Mr. Marvile; a man whom both by report,
& the converse I have had with him, of singular desert for the State to make
use of; who alsoe offers himselfe, if there be any imployment for him. His
father was the Minister of Hull and he hath spent foure yeares abroad
in Holland, France, Italy & Spaine, to very good purpose, as I beleeve,
& the gaineing of those 4 languages; besides he is a scholler & well read
in the Latin and Greeke authors, & noe doubt of an approved conversation
for he com's now lately out of the house of the Lord Fairefax who was
Generall, where he was intrusted to give some instructions in the Languages
to the Lady his Daughter.[1]

The mention of Andrew Marvell's father had its political resonance.
'Hull, the first city to oppose Charles I in the civil war had, Hackett
thought, been corrupted by its lecturers, one of whom was Andrew
Marvell, father of the poet.'[2]

There is no reason not to assume that Marvell wrote 'Upon
Appleton House' while employed as a tutor there. Indeed, his praise
of Mary Fairfax's accomplishments in Stanza lxxxix is a praise that
alludes to his 'instructions in the Languages':

---

[1] Milton to Bradshaw, Public Record Office SP 18/33, 75. J. Milton French, *Life
Records of John Milton* (New Brunswick, 1954), iii. 322–4. Marvell was not
appointed, but in 1657 he became Latin Secretary to the Council of State.
[2] J. Hackett, *Scrinia Reserata* (1693), ii. 186, cited in Christopher Hill, *Society
and Puritanism in Pre-Revolutionary England* (London, 1969), p. 107.

> For *She*, to higher Beauties rais'd,
> Disdains to be for lesser prais'd.
> *She* counts her Beauty to converse
> In all the Languages as *hers*;
> Nor yet in those *her self* imploves
> But for the *Wisdome*, not the *Noyse*;
> Nor yet that *Wisdome* would affect;
> But as 'tis *Heavens Dialect*.

(lxxxix. 705–12)[3]

Mary wants to be praised not for physical beauty but for the 'higher Beauties' of her intelligence, and linguistic skills; and it is not merely being able to 'converse / In all the Languages as *hers*' that is important to her, but that she knows the languages in order to read wisdom written in them. And this puritan, spiritual attitude to learning as instrument is mutated yet again into a further spiritual puritanism. She is not interested in wisdom as such; she does not affect knowledge as an accomplishment except in so far as it is heavenly knowledge, morally and spiritually elevating knowledge.

In praising Mary's linguistic skills, and in doing so taking the opportunity to indicate to Lord Fairfax how well the tutor has fulfilled his task, Marvell is being quite specific about the circumstances of his own presence at Appleton House. But there is no equivalent specificity about the circumstances of Fairfax's presence in the poem. The details of Fairfax's retirement are significantly absent. Fairfax himself, indeed, is never the highlighted subject; his presence is recorded by the reaction of the house:

> Yet thus the laden House does sweat,
> And scarce indures the *Master* great:
> But where he comes the swelling Hall
> Stirs and the Square grows Spherical;
> More by his *Magnitude* distrest
> Then he is by its straitness prest:
> And too officiously it slights
> That in it self which him delights.

(vii. 49–56)

Fairfax's 'magnitude' is recorded. He is a 'great' man. But why he should take up rural retirement at the age of thirty-eight, resigning

---

[3] Cœlia in Marvell's 'To his worthy Friend Doctor Witty upon his Translation of the Popular Errors' may be another representation of Mary as student of languages.

command of the army to his lieutenant-general Oliver Cromwell, aged fifty-one, is not specified. The circumstances, as we have seen, were highly political. His nineteenth-century biographer, C. R. Markham, writes:

The invitation to Charles by the Scots, and his arrival in Scotland, led to the resignation of Lord Fairfax. On May 31, 1650, Cromwell returned from Ireland, and on June 24 the Council of State debated the question of invading Scotland. It was supposed that the Scots, with their new King, intended to invade England, and it was suggested, in Council, that it would be wiser to carry the war into the enemy's country than to wait till this invasion took place. It was finally resolved to make war upon Scotland, but Fairfax demurred to the justice of such a measure, and hesitated to conduct a campaign which appeared to him to be unjustifiable. He said that if the Scots invaded England, he was ready to lay down his life in opposing them, but he refused to march into Scotland and make war upon a people between whom and the English there still existed a Solemn League and Covenant. Ludlow and others of the Council laboured hard to overcome his scruples, but unsuccessfully.[4]

Though 'Cromwell urged every argument he could think of',[5] Fairfax refused to agree to the invasion, and rather than participate, resigned. Maurice Ashley remarks:

Undoubtedly there were members of the new governing classes who now wanted Lord Fairfax to be superseded by Cromwell. Since 1649 Fairfax had never concealed his Royalist and Presbyterian sympathies, although he himself was neither a Royalist nor a Presbyterian. While Cromwell was away rumours were heard of plans to give him the command against the Scots and to retain Fairfax in a more or less honorary capacity. Though tongues were wagging freely, it is not known exactly what went on in the Council of State.[6]

But Marvell not only avoids speculation on the hidden manœuvres, he avoids mention of any of the circumstances. Most accounts of Fairfax's resignation relate it to his unhappiness not only at the proposed campaign against the Scots, but at the execution of Charles I eighteen months earlier.[7]

Discussing the various factions emerging in the army and parliament, Fairfax later explained:

[4] Clements R. Markham, *A Life of the Great Lord Fairfax* (London, 1870), p. 359.   [5] Ibid., p. 360.
[6] Maurice Ashley, *The Greatness of Oliver Cromwell* (New York, 1962), p. 243.
[7] See Fairfax, *Short Memorials*, p. 121 (quoted *supra* p. 132).

I was much troubled to see things in this Condition, and rather desired to be a Sufferer than a Commander: But before I laid down my Commission, I thought fit to consult some Friends, rather than gratify my private Reason and Desires, especially having receiv'd it from a Publick Authority, which might justly expect to have notice before I laid it down.

This was the Cause of my continuing in the Army longer than I would have done, which did indeed preserve the Parliament for some time from those Violences that it afterwards suffer'd from these Disturbers.[8]

Lady Fairfax's outburst at the trial of King Charles was well known:

When the name of her husband was called, Lady Fairfax . . . rose, and, addressing the court in a loud voice, declared that the Lord Fairfax was not there in person, that he would never sit among them, and that they did him wrong to name him as a sitting commissioner.

Afterwards, when the President interrupted the King while he was speaking, and required his answer to the charge exhibited in the name of the Commons of England, assembled in Parliament and the good people of England, Lady Fairfax again interrupted the proceedings . . . and cried out, 'It is a lie—not half the people. Where are they and their consents? Oliver Cromwell is a traitor.'[9]

Later commentators had no hesitation in ascribing Fairfax's resignation to political disillusion. Richard Baxter wrote: 'The Lord Fairfax now laid down his commission and would have no more of the honour of being Cromwell's instrument or mask, when he saw that he must buy it at so dear a rate'.[10] Though there were those who saw it as a betrayal: 'it could not have been done more spightfully and ruinously to the whole parliamentary interest . . . ', wrote Lucy Hutchinson of the resignation, ' . . . whereby he then died to all his former glory, and became the monument of his own name, which every day wore out.'[11]

Fairfax's dilemmas and the reasons for his resignation from army command were inexpressible. They were widely speculated on, but they were a dangerous area for a young man 'of singular desert for the State to make use of'. And Fairfax himself is barely present in the

[8] *Short Memorials of Thomas Lord Fairfax written by Himself* (London, 1699), p. 105.

[9] Markham, *Life of Fairfax*, p. 349. Markham discusses the variant accounts of Lady Fairfax's interjections.

[10] *The Autobiography of Richard Baxter*, abridged by J. M. Lloyd Thomas, ed. N. H. Keeble (London, 1974), p. 66.

[11] Lucy Hutchinson, *Memoirs of the Life of Colonel Hutchinson*, p. 278.

poem. Annabel Patterson remarks: 'If the man of conscience, letters, and wisdom does not appear in these poems, the modesty topos protects us from the inference that he does not exist; and by this happy notion Marvell himself is protected from affirming qualities of which, perhaps, he might have had some doubt'.[12] But the issue is less any possible doubts Marvell might have had, than the impossibility of appearing to celebrate Fairfax in a way that might seem to support his opposition to the Scots campaign at a time when the campaign was being fought, or in singling him out as a potential focus of opposition to Cromwell's command.

Fairfax had announced the grounds of his refusal to undertake the campaign against Scotland to the Council of State committee:

'What my conscience yields unto as just and lawful', he concluded, 'I shall follow, and what seems to me otherwise I will not do. My conscience is not satisfied, and therefore I must desire to be excused.'[13]

This stress on conscience finds its place in the poem.

> For he did, with his utmost Skill
> *Ambition* weed, but *Conscience* till.
> *Conscience*, that Heaven-nursed Plant,
> Which most our Earthly Gardens want.
> A prickling leaf it bears, and such
> As that which shrinks at ev'ry touch;
> But *Flowrs* eternal, and divine,
> That in the Crowns of Saints do shine.
>
> (xlv. 353–60)

The allusion to the grounds of Fairfax's resignation is specific. Yet the allusion is carefully depoliticized, deliberately generalized, and abstracted from any specific, contemporary signification. Conscience is presented in the abstract, unrelated to any circumstance or issue. Fairfax is allowed praise for an undeniable spiritual virtue; but the material circumstances in which he exercised that conscience are excluded from mention. Politics are displaced into emblematic gardening.

Conscience is cultivated, ambition weeded out; the particular policy disputes (trial of the King, execution of the King, war against

---

[12] Annabel M. Patterson, *Marvell and the Civic Crown* (Princeton, 1978), p. 98.
[13] Markham, *Life of Fairfax*, p. 360.

Scotland) in which Fairfax found himself in opposition to the majority of the Council of State, are collapsed into the abstract moral trope of removing ambition. Marvell is concerned not to resurrect old issues, nor to reopen the recent past at a time when war has broken out again. He finds a way of praising Fairfax's moral integrity without arguing that Fairfax had advocated the wrong, or the right, measures. The stanza preceding the cultivation of conscience has often been read as a rebuke to Fairfax for resigning, or as an expression of regret for his withdrawal.

> And yet there walks one on the Sod
> Who had it pleased him and *God*,
> Might once have made our Gardens spring
> Fresh as his own and flourishing.
> But he preferr'd to the *Cinque Ports*
> These five imaginary Forts:
> And, in those half-dry Trenches, spann'd
> Pow'r which the Ocean might command.
>
> (xliv. 345–52)

But for a hired tutor to presume to offer advice to the former lord-general of a victorious army is inconceivable. Twentieth-century commentators unconsciously write as if Marvell's twentieth-century repute as a great poet, admired by T. S. Eliot, was a repute known to his contemporaries.[14] In the 1650s he was in no position to offer advice or rebukes to a former lord-general.

And there is no evidence that Fairfax might in fact 'have made our Gardens spring / Fresh as his own and flourishing'. Fairfax himself clearly saw that any power he might attain was conditional on his fulfilling the designs of those who backed him. Writing of the declaration of war against Scotland he remarks in *Short Memorials*:

All this I saw with grief and sorrow, and though I had as much the Love of the Army as ever, and was with great importunity solicited by that

---

[14] Lawrence Hyman, 'Politics and Poetry in Andrew Marvell', *PMLA* 73 (1958), 475–9, writes of 'Marvell's impatience with Fairfax's retirement from the world . . . he is attacking the whole idea of withdrawal from action'. Harry Berger, Jr., 'Marvell's "Upon Appleton House": An Interpretation', *Southern Review* (Adelaide), 1 (1965), 7–32, writes: 'One feels a bare hint of censure: perhaps instead of peaceably playing war in his garden Fairfax should have remained in public life and militarily resisted further Parliamentarian aggression'.

remaining Parliament and Soldiers, to continue my Command; and though I might, so long as I acted their Designs, have attained to what height of Power, and other Advantages I pleas'd; yet by the mercies and goodness of God, I did, so long as I continued in the Army, oppose all those Ways in their Councils, and when I could do no more, I then declined their Actions: Though I did not resign my Commission which I had from the Parliament, till the remaining part of it took it from me.[15]

His lack of political ambitions and skills is something on which historians are agreed. 'He had no talents for intrigue', Johnson writes in the introduction to the *Fairfax Correspondence*.[16] And Markham sums him up as

A consummate general, a cultivated gentleman, the very soul of honour and straightforward dealing, he yet had no talent for politics. The wordy contention and finesse of a statesman's life were distasteful to him, and to engage in any intrigue or in any business which was not open as noonday was to him an impossibility![17]

Moreover, the young man who had just penned a tribute to Cromwell's success in the Irish campaign and was shortly to offer himself to the Council of State would scarcely have been expressing regret that Fairfax had resigned from public office. The tone is one of tribute to Fairfax's abilities, but acceptance that it did *not* please him and God that Fairfax should 'have made our Gardens spring / Fresh as his own and flourishing'. The possibility is a past possibility, a might-have-been; to raise it serves to pay elegant tribute to Fairfax's past eminence; and Fairfax's cultivation of conscience and weeding-out of ambition is what is emphasized. The personal, moral qualities displace any dangerous political speculations. The expectations of the retirement poem, the stress on the cultivation of private morality away from the public political sphere, are expectations happily accepted here.

Instead of politics Marvell offers patriotism at this point:

> Oh Thou, that dear and happy Isle
> The Garden of the World ere while,

---

[15] Fairfax, *Short Memorials*, pp. 127–8.
[16] *The Fairfax Correspondence: Memoirs of the Reign of Charles I* ed. George W. Johnson (London, 1848), i. ciii.
[17] Markham, *Life of Fairfax*, p. 285.

> Thou *Paradise* of four Seas,
> Which *Heaven* planted us to please . . .
>   (xli. 321–4)

A number of commentators have remarked on the echoes of John of Gaunt's speech in Shakespeare's *Richard II*, 'This other Eden, demi-paradise' (II. i. 42).[18] But while echoing the generalized patriotism, Marvell excludes that other garden metaphor in *Richard II*, where the political corruptions are spelled out.

> Go thou, and like an executioner
> Cut off the heads of too fast growing sprays,
> That look too lofty in our commonwealth:
> All must be even in our government.
>   (III. iv. 33–6)

The description of a garden readily invited political analogies:

> Why should we, in the compass of a pale,
> Keep law and form and due proportion,
> Showing, as in a model, our firm estate,
> When our sea-walled garden, the whole land,
> Is full of weeds, her fairest flowers chok'd up,
> Her fruit-trees all unprun'd, her hedges ruin'd,
> Her knots disordered, and her wholesome herbs
> Swarming with caterpillars?
>   (III. iv. 40–7)

If Marvell's 'Paradise of four Seas' echoes John of Gaunt, then this other passage cannot but have been in his mind; but it is repressed, the metaphors too dangerous. The caterpillars are displaced to the other end of the poem and on to the poet, not the state:

> The Oak-Leaves me embroyder all,
> Between which Caterpillars crawl.
>   (lxxiv. 587–8)

The poem's title, 'Upon Appleton House, to my Lord Fairfax', indicates both the tribute to Fairfax and the focus on the house. A

---

[18] C. A. Patrides, ' 'Till Prepared for Longer Flight', in *Approaches to Marvell*, pp. 37–8. The myth is explored in Josephine Waters Bennett, 'Britain Among the Fortunate Isles', *Studies in Philology*, 53 (1956), 114–40. Peter Ure, ed., *Richard II* (The Arden Shakespeare) (Cambridge, Mass., 1956). All quotations from this edition.

poem about Fairfax would be too difficult at this political point; but the genre of the country-house poem[19] readily allowed the tribute to the owner to emerge through the account of the house and estates. As Raymond Williams indicates, the genre functions 'to ratify and bless the country landowner, or, by a characteristic reification, his house'.[20]

The use of the country-house poem genre, then, can be seen in part here as a strategy, a way of dealing with Fairfax by implication and allusion. But it is not the sole strategy; Don Cameron Allen goes too far in claiming that 'the poem is really not about the house' when he indicates its other concerns: 'It is about the actual house, the actual gardens, fields, meadows, streams, and wood. It is about the house of Fairfax in past, present, and future. It is about the house of flesh, the body and mind of man.'[21] This is all true; but Appleton House, the buildings and grounds, is primary. Appleton House houses the house of Fairfax, but the poem is not called 'upon the House of Fairfax'. The ambiguities of house as family line are present, but secondary. The characteristic reification that allows the owner to be praised by an account of the material property is the expression of a habit of mind that privileges material property. The country-house genre of poems is analogous to the related cult of 'paintings of buildings — buildings not considered as ideal works of architecture, as in the work of some early Renaissance artists — but buildings as a feature of landed property'.[22]

The history of the building allows the history of the Fairfaxes to be looked at. But out of the whole range of possible family history, the item that Marvell chooses is the account of the immurement of Isabel Thwaites in the nunnery at Nun Appleton, by her guardian, Lady Anna Langton, the prioress, her rescue by William Fairfax, the acquisition of the nunnery after the Reformation by the Fairfaxes, and the use of the nunnery buildings and stone as the 'quarry' from which Appleton House was built.

---

[19] G. R. Hibbard, 'The Country House Poem of the Seventeenth Century', *JWCI* 19 (1956), 159–74. 'Pretty well the last of the line is Marvell's *Upon Appleton House*', writes Alastair Fowler, *Conceitful Thought* (Edinburgh, 1975), p. 116.

[20] Raymond Williams, *The Country and the City* (St Albans, 1975), p. 45.

[21] Don Cameron Allen, *Image and Meaning: Metaphoric Traditions in Renaissance Poetry* (Baltimore, 1968), p. 117.

[22] John Berger, *Ways of Seeing* (Harmondsworth, 1972), p. 100.

The nunnery episode allows the Lord-General's dilemma of conscience to be dramatized, but carefully distanced from any contemporary application. There is an analogy between his dilemmas of conscience and those of his great-great-great-grandfather William Fairfax; but there is no obvious analogy in their historical situations. A shared delicacy of conscience is stressed but it does not seem possible to decode the nunnery episode into some specific seventeenth-century confrontation. The dilemma is carefully generalized:

> What should he do? He would respect
> Religion, but not Right neglect:
> For first Religion taught him Right
> And dazled not but clear'd his sight.
> Sometimes resolv'd his Sword he draws
> But reverenceth then the Laws:
> For Justice still that Courage led
> First from a Judge, then Souldier bred.
>
> (xxix. 225–32)

In the end William Fairfax used force and stormed the nunnery; after the scrupulous agonies of conscience he is able to act in a forceful fashion when necessary. The Lord-General's military successes are by implication validated.

William Fairfax's use of force is presented as justified because it is in accord with the historical process. When the prioress refuses to hand over Isabel, Marvell phrases the issue 'Yet, against Fate, his Spouse they kept / And the great Race would intercept' (xxxi. 247–8). It is fate that Isabel should be released to marry William Fairfax; and out of that union ultimately comes the Lord-General, champion of the Puritan army. And William's act is of course an act of revolutionary Protestantism, rescuing from the Catholics a woman whose descendants will be champions of Protestant reform. In Stanza xxxiii, as the numerological significance underlines, he is a type of Christ arising from the grave.

But not only does William Fairfax get Isabel, he also gets the nunnery:

> Thenceforth (as when th'Inchantment ends
> The Castle vanishes or rends)
> The wasting Cloister with the rest
> Was in one instant dispossest.

> At the demolishing, this Seat
> To *Fairfax* fell as by Escheat.
> And what both *Nuns* and *Founders* will'd
> 'Tis likely better thus fulfill'd.
>
> For if the Virgin prov'd not theirs,
> The *Cloyster* yet remained hers.
> Though many a *Nun* there made her Vow
> 'Twas no *Religious House* till now.
>
> (xxxiv–xxxv. 269–80)

William Fairfax married Isabel Thwaites in 1518. The nunneries were dissolved by decrees of Henry VIII in 1542. The timespan of twenty-four years is contracted to 'one instant' in Marvell's poem. The stress on the instantaneous ending of enchantment glides over a quarter of a century; it was dying, 'wasting', when attacked, anyway. William's attack on the nunnery is in accord with the historical process; slightly ahead of time, a Puritan 'forward youth', but the twenty-four years are made to look like a moment. And the acquisition of the nunnery is justified by the piety of the Fairfax family: ' 'Twas no *Religious House* till now'.

The collapsing of twenty-four years into 'one instant' is a strategy of legitimizing William's onslaught on the nunnery, integrating his action with this historical process. Beneath the burlesque account of the nuns' battle with their invader, and the militant Protestant satiric account of sensual misbehaviour in the nunnery, is an anxious need to defend the land-grab.

Some twenty-five years later Marvell was to touch on the topic in his *Account of the Growth of Popery and Arbitrary Government in England* (1677):

The Lands that were formerly given to superstitious Uses, having first been applied to the publick Revenue, and afterwards by several Alienations and Contracts distributed into private possession, the alteration of Religion would necessarily introduce a change of Property. *Nullum tempus occurit ecclesiae*, it would make a general Earth-quake over the Nation, and even now the Romish Clergy on the other side of the Water snuff up the savoury Odour of so many rich Abbies and Monasteries that belonged to their Predecessors. Hereby no considerable Estate in England but must have a piece torn out of it upon the Title of Piety, and the rest subject to be wholly forefeited upon the Account of Heresie. Another Chimney-Money of the old Peter-Pence must again be paid as Tribute to the Pope, beside that which is established on His Majesty; and the People, instead of those moderate Tythes that are with too much difficulty paid to their Protestant Pastors, will be exposed to all the exactions of the court of Rome, and a thousand Artifices by which in former times they were used to drain away the Wealth of ours more than any other Nation. So that in conclusion there is no Englishman that hath a Soul, a Body or an Estate to save, that Loves either God, his King or his Country, but is by all those Tenures bound, to the best of his Power and Knowledge, to maintain the Established Protestant Religion.[23]

Marvell's explicit account of the property aspects of the preservation of English Protestantism illuminates the politics of the nunnery episode of 'Upon Appleton House'. The two issues are inextricably involved; only through the appropriation of the nunnery can it become a true religious house; the acquisition of the nunnery by William Fairfax is not only a just reward for his religious correctness in attacking it and rescuing Isabel, twenty-four years in advance of the general dissolution of the monasteries; it is also a necessity of the establishment of true religion that the Catholic property should be taken over. The same sort of thinking lay behind the Irish campaign, seizing the land of papists and putting it to profitable Protestant uses.

Marvell is concerned to sanctify property here, to legitimize the estates of the Fairfaxes which in part were acquired from the dissolution of Nun Appleton. By stressing the godliness of the Fairfax household he is claiming that it is performing a more godly function than the earlier nunnery, and possibly fulfilling better the intention of the original founder: 'And what both *Nuns* and *Founders* will'd / 'Tis likely better thus fulfill'd' (xxxiv. 275–6).

The need to justify the appropriation of the former nunnery suggests an anxiety. There was criticism from both the right and the left, from the conservative and the revolutionary. Robert Herrick in 'A Panegerick to Sir Lewis Pemberton' praises Pemberton for having 'No *Planke* from *Hallowed* Altar' (127) incorporated into the fabric of his house:

> Safe stand thy Walls, and Thee, and so both will,
>   Since neithers height was rais'd by th'ill
> Of others; since no Stud, no Stone, no Piece,
>   Was rear'd up by the Poore-mans fleece:

[23] *State Tracts* (1693), p. 73, quoted in Christopher Hill, *Puritanism and Revolution* (London, 1958) pp. 47–8.

No Widowes Tenement was rackt to guild
    Or fret they Seeling, or to build
A *Sweating-Closset*, to annoint the silke-
    soft-skin, or bath in *Asses milke*:
No *Orphans* pittance, left him, serv'd to set
    The Pillars up of *lasting Jet*,
For which their cryes might beate against thine eares,
    Or in the dampe Jet read their Teares.
No *Planke* from *Hallowed* Altar, do's appeale
    To yond' *Star-chamber*, or do's seale
A curse to Thee, or Thine; but all things even
    Make for thy peace, and pace to heaven.

(115–30)[24]

Gerrard Winstanley's *The Law of Freedom in a Platform* (1652) codified the radical programme put forward in Digger tracts of the preceding three years, and offered a communist threat to the beneficiaries of the Reformation land-grab. Defining 'the particular work of a Parliament', Winstanley wrote:

First, as a tender father, a Parliament is to empower officers and give out orders for the free planting and reaping of the commonwealth's land, that all who have been oppressed and kept from the free use thereof by conquerors, kings and their tyrant laws may now be set at liberty to plant in freedom for food and raiment; and are to be a protection to them who labour the earth, and a punisher of them who are idle. But some may say, 'What is that I call commonwealth's land?'

I answer, all that land which hath been withheld from the inhabitants by the conqueror or tyrant kings, and is now recovered out of the hands of that oppression by the joint assistance of the persons and purses of the commoners of the land; for this land is the price of their blood. It is their birthright to them and their posterity, and ought not to be converted into particular hands again by the laws of a free commonwealth.

And in particular, this land is all abbey lands, formerly recovered out of the hands of the pope's power by the blood of the commoners of England, though the kings withheld their rights herein from them.

So likewise all crown lands, bishops' lands, with all parks, forests, chases, now of late recovered out of the hands of the kingly tyrants, who have set lords of manors and task-masters over the commoners to withhold the free use of the land from them.

So likewise all the commons and waste lands, which are called commons because the poor was to have part therein: but this is withheld from the commoners, either by Lords of manors requiring quit rents and overseeing

---

[24] *The Poems of Robert Herrick*, ed. L. C. Martin (Oxford, 1965), p. 149.

the poor so narrowly that none dare build him a house upon this common land, or plant thereupon without his leave, but must pay him rent, fines and heriots and homage, as unto a conqueror; or else the benefit of this common land is taken away from the younger brethren by rich landlords and freeholders, who overstock the commons with sheep and cattle, so that the poor in many places are not able to keep a cow unless they steal the grass for her.[25]

Winstanley had attempted the practical implementation of his vision. On 1 April 1649 he and a group of fellow-radicals occupied and proceeded to dig, 'plant and manure the waste land upon George Hill in the Parish of Walton in the Country of Surrey', declaring their aims in *The True Leveller's Standard Advanced: Or, The State of Community opened, and Presented to the Sons of Men.*[26] They were called Diggers because of their cultivation of this patch of waste land, where they established a co-operative settlement. Other groups sprang up elsewhere in England, and the beginnings of a ground-roots communism were established. Needless to say they were suppressed, their crops destroyed, their housing demolished, and their leaders harassed, and in the end the movement collapsed. But for a year or more they presented a radical challenge to Parliament: not in any strength or influence they could muster, but in the positive revolutionary example that they presented.

G. P. Gooch remarks that:

It would be easy to exaggerate the importance of the little colony of Diggers on St. George's Hill. The greater number of them, beyond all doubt, had no other views than were common to the Franconian and Thuringian peasants of 1525, or those who followed the standard of Ket in 1549. On the other hand, it would be difficult to overestimate the significance of their spokesman in the history of thought. Alone of his English contemporaries, he recognised the well-being of the proletariat as constituting the criterion not only of political but of social and economic conditions. Determining that their rights were not secured in the actual state of society, he proceeded to develop a complete scheme of socialism.[27]

The Diggers came to the notice of Fairfax.

---

[25] Gerrard Winstanley, *The Law of Freedom and Other Writings*, ed. Christopher Hill (Harmondsworth, 1973), pp. 339–40.

[26] Ibid., p. 75.

[27] G. P. Gooch, *English Democratic Ideas in the Seventeenth Century* (1898) (New York, 1959), pp. 190–1.

On April 16, the Council of State received the following intelligence. 'On Sunday sennight last, there was one Everard, once of the army but cashiered, who termeth himself a prophet, and four more came to St. George's Hill in Surrey and began to dig, and sowed the ground with parsnips, carrots and beans. On Monday following they were there again, being increased in their number. On Friday they came again, twenty or thirty, and wrought all day at digging. They do threaten to pull down and level all park pales and lay open and intend to plant them. They give out that they will be four or five thousand within ten days, and threaten the neighbouring people they will make them all come up to the hills and work'. The letter was at once forwarded by Bradshaw to Fairfax, with a request that he should send some horse to disperse the disorderly and tumultuous people. A force was at once dispatched, and three days later Fairfax was informed that the affair was not worth notice.[28]

And finally Fairfax and Winstanley came face to face.

On 20 April two of the principal Diggers, Everard and Winstanley, were brought before the Commander-in-Chief. They kept on their hats in Fairfax's presence, the traditional symbolic refusal to recognize social superiority and political authority . . .

Their intention, they told the general, was to cultivate the waste lands as a communal group: they would 'meddle only with what was common and untilled'. Any rights in the commons claimed by lords of manors, Winstanley later explained, had been 'cut off with the King's head' . . . They hoped that before long the poor everywhere would follow their example, and that property-owners would voluntarily surrender their estates and join in communal production . . .

Fairfax thought Everard was mad, and refused to take the incident seriously. He visited the colony at the end of May and had an amicable exchange with Winstanley, in which the latter repeated his assurance that the Diggers had no intention of using force.[29]

Not only did Winstanley encounter Fairfax face to face, he also addressed publications to him. In August 1649 he wrote *A Watch-Word to the City of London, and the Army*:

Therefore in the light of reason and equity, and in the light of the National Covenant which Parliament and people have taken with joint consent: all such prerogative customs, which by experience we have found to burden the nation, ought to be cast out with the kingly office, and the land of England now ought to be a free land and a common treasury to all her children, otherwise it cannot properly be called a commonwealth.

[28] Ibid., p. 181.   [29] Hill, *Law of Freedom*, pp. 27–8.

Therefore we justify our act of digging upon that hill, to make the earth a common treasury. First, because the earth was made by Almighty God to be a common treasury of livelihood for whole mankind in all his branches, without respect of persons; and that not any one according to the Word of God (which is love), the pure law of righteousness, ought to be lord or landlord over another, but whole mankind was made equal and knit into one body by one spirit of love, which is Christ in you the hope of glory . . .[30]

Winstanley and his group called themselves 'The true levellers', though they were generally referred to as 'Diggers'. The 'levellers' Marvell refers to in Stanza lvii are most likely to be this group, though Fairfax had also encountered the radical group in the army called 'Levellers' and together with Cromwell savagely suppressed the movement. The Levellers always denied that their intention was 'levelling'; the name was given them by their political opponents. As they declared in *A Manifestation from Lieutenant Col. John Lilburn, Mr. William Walwyn, Mr. Thomas Prince, and Mr. Richard Overton, (Now Prisoners in the Tower of London) And others, commonly (though unjustly) Styled Levellers* (1649):

First, Then it will be requisite that we express our selves concerning Levelling, for which we suppose is commonly meant an equalling of mens estates, and taking away the proper right and Title that every man has to what is his own. This we have formerly declared against, particularly in our petition of the 11 of Sept. so do we again professe that to attempt an inducing the same is most injurious, unlesse there did precede an universall assent thereunto from all and every one of the People.[31]

'Unless there did precede an universall assent' perhaps seemed disingenuous to the property-owners, even though the *Manifestation* went on to reiterate:

We profess therefore that we never had it in our thoughts to Level mens estates, it being the utmost of our aime that the Common-wealth be reduced to such a passe that every man may with as much security as may be enjoy his propriety.[32]

---

[30] Ibid., p. 133.

[31] Don M. Wolfe, ed., *Leveller Manifestoes of the Puritan Revolution* (New York, 1944), p. 390.

[32] Ibid., p. 391. Levelling was also proclaimed by the Ranters; see Abiezer Coppe, *A Fiery Flying Roll* (1649), in Nigel Smith, ed., *A Collection of Ranter Writings from the Seventeenth Century* (London, 1983), pp. 87–9.

The radical proposal for the redistribution of land involved not only the lands that could have been made available to the commoners by the dissolution of the abbeys and nunneries at the Reformation, but also the lands that could have been made available in the sequestration of Crown lands, bishops' lands, and lands confiscated from royalists by the Commonwealth, and also the traditional common-lands.

Markham stressed that Fairfax 'retired with clean hands. He might have obtained any grants of land he pleased for the asking; but he had no money or land but what he inherited from his father'.[33] Parliament awarded him part of the Duke of Buckingham's confiscated property, but Fairfax held it in trust and Buckingham regained it by his marriage with Mary Fairfax in 1657; Fairfax received the seigniory of the Isle of Man in October 1651 from Parliament, but he ensured that the rents continued to be paid to the Countess of Derby and 'the countess confessed she had never received her rents with such regularity from her own agents'.[34] So Fairfax made sure the rents were paid on time. The big landowners maintained solidarity across supposed political lines. None of the details of Fairfax's receipt of confiscated property is present in the poem; though the ultimate fate of Mary's moral education, cementing a property union with the Duke of Buckingham, can hardly be excluded.

The issue of common rights certainly enters the poem at the end of the mowing scene. The commoners are allowed to graze on the meadows once they are mown. Some residual, eroded rights remain.[35]

> This *Scene* again withdrawing brings
> A new and Empty Face of things;
> A levell'd space, as smooth and plain,
> As Clothes for *Lilly* stretch to stain.
> The World when first created sure
> Was such a Table rase and pure.
> Or rather such is the *Toril*
> Ere the Bulls enter at Madril.

---

[33] Markham, *Life of Fairfax*, p. 364.   [34] Ibid., p. 365.

[35] James Turner, *The Politics of Landscape: Rural Scenery and Society in English Poetry 1630–1660* (Oxford, 1979), p. 146: 'The enclosure of common land may be alleviated by open days; at Appleton House, between the mowing and the floating of the meadows . . . Marvell hints that the usual problems of enclosure and oppression have been solved by generous compromise—"Levellers" are no threat'.

> For to this naked equal Flat,
> Which *Levellers* take Pattern at,
> The Villagers in common chase
> Their Cattle, which it closer rase;
> And what below the Sith increast
> Is pincht yet nearer by the Beast.
> Such, in the painted World, appear'd
> *Davenant* with th'Universal Heard.
>
> (lvi–lvii. 441–56)

There is no disguising Marvell's distaste for the Levellers, for the levelling intentions of the radicals. He presents a vision of levelling down to destruction: this is the field after the hay has been mown, the field now flat, the cattle chewing the stubble even lower; it is 'naked', 'flat'; the cattle 'closer rase' it, it is 'pincht'. The connotations are all reductive, negative, mean. As Donald Friedman puts it, 'Marvell charges them with wanting to cut society down to the lowest level of spurious equality rather than lead it to the heights of civilisation that can be marked out only by the extraordinary personality'.[36] This was the propertied classes' view of those radicals they called Levellers. 'After 1653, if not earlier, almost all trends of opinion among the propertied class combined to denounce Levellers and levelling', Hill records.[37] 'The Beast' evokes the many-headed beast, the image of the multitude, the common people as seen from a ruling-class perspective.[38] 'Universal Heard' is usually glossed as an allusion to Davenant's *Gondibert*. But 'universal' recurs in the Leveller *Manifestation*, together with the other key term, 'naked':

the things we promote, are not good onely in appearance, but sensibly so: not moulded nor contrived by the subtill or politick Principles of the World,

---

[36] Donald M. Friedman, *Marvell's Pastoral Art* (Berkeley, 1970), pp. 204–5.

[37] Christopher Hill, *The World Turned Upside Down* (Harmondsworth, 1975), p. 345. Hill notes that Cromwell 'lumped Levellers and True Levellers together as "a despicable and contemptible generation of men," "persons differing little from beasts"', ibid., p. 122. Don Cameron Allen suggests, in *Image and Meaning*, p. 139, that Marvell 'probably did not distinguish between the aims of the two groups', Levellers and Diggers. Hill suggests Marvell 'probably deliberately confused' the Levellers 'with the communistic Diggers'; 'Milton and Marvell' in C. A. Patrides, ed., *Approaches to Marvell*, p. 16.

[38] Cf. C. A. Patrides, ' "The Beast with Many Heads", Renaissance Views on the Multitude', *Shakespeare Quarterly*, 16, (1965), 241–6; Christopher Hill, 'The Many Headed Monster', in *Change and Continuity in Seventeenth Century England* (London, 1974) pp. 181–204.

but plainly produced and nakedly sent, without any insinuating arts, relying wholly upon the apparent and universal beleefe they carry in themselves.[39]

And the *Manifestation* goes on to deny that the Levellers aimed at power for themselves or intended to achieve it by 'strength, or a forcible obstruction'; rather they were 'naked and defenceless'. It may be that Marvell had this Leveller tract in mind; or that 'naked' and 'universal' shared with 'equal' and 'in common' the resonance of a Leveller idiom. The 'universal herd' may also suggest another accusation the Levellers denied in the *'Manifestation*, 'that we are indeed for no government, but a Popular confusion'.[40] And it is tempting to read in the image of the 'green Sea' (xlix. 390) of the mowing-field a reference to the Levellers' insignia of sea-green ribbons: 'My Brethren of the Sea Green Order' as Richard Overton addresses them in *The Baiting of the Great Bull of Bashan* (1649),[41] a pamphlet whose title might be in part evoked in the comparison to the '*Toril* / Ere the Bulls enter at Madril' (lvi. 447–8) of 'the naked equal Flat' (lvii. 449).

While the sensual corruption of the Roman Catholic nunnery presents one antithesis to the life-style of Appleton House, the Levellers' vision presents another. Between sensuous excess and the 'naked equal Flat', Appleton House is represented as a virtuous middle way. Legouis glosses the mention of the Levellers as 'purely humorous'.[42] It may well be humorous, designed to provoke an approving reaction of 'Well, we finished off the Leveller mutineers at Burford, didn't we?' or 'Winstanley and his true Levellers didn't last more than a year, did they?' But the humour requires an awareness of the political threat to property and hierarchy that was raised by the Levellers and Diggers. 'Between 1646 and 1649, the revolution became an open class conflict, of which the Levellers were the spokesmen. It was a conflict between rich and poor, strong and weak, rulers and ruled, those who eat their bread in the sweat of other men's brows and those who laboured for their living with their own hands and sold the fruits of their labour.'[43]

[39] *Leveller Manifestoes*, p. 392.   [40] Ibid., p. 390.
[41] A. L. Morton, ed., *Freedom in Arms: A Selection of Leveller Writings* (London, 1975), p. 287.   [42] *Poems and Letters of Andrew Marvell*, i. 287.
[43] Brian Manning, *The English People and the English Revolution*, p. 307. Fairfax's active role in suppressing the Levellers is stressed by John Wilson in *Fairfax* (London, 1985), pp. 125–7, 155–7.

The Levellers are introduced into the poem when the villagers drive their cattle on to the mown field. The political threat organized by the Levellers is identified with the villagers. The villagers, the mowers, are a distant, unknown, and threatening force for Marvell. The qualities of country labourers are not qualities presented for admiration.[44]

This is demonstrated clearly enough in the very opening of the poem. Admiring Fairfax's modesty and humility in living in a moderately sized house, Marvell moralizes:

> Height with a certain Grace does bend
> But low Things clownishly ascend.
>
> (viii, 59–60)

It is gracious when the elevated humbly stoop, but when the low try to rise above their proper station, it is clownish; and 'clownish' carries here its basic meaning of countryman; the idiotic, clumsy, comic behaviour of the rural labourer, seen from a ruling-class perspective. In this poem celebrating retirement to a country life, the word for the authentic countryman is used in a pejorative sense.

But of course the poem is not celebrating country life from the standpoint of the rural worker any more than it is celebrating a house of the sort occupied by a rural worker. James Turner remarks in *The Politics of Landscape*:

It takes some effort to appreciate what has been censored from the ideal landscape. There is virtually no mention of land-clearance, tree-felling, pruning, chopping, digging, hoeing, weeding, branding, gelding, slaughtering, salting, tanning, brewing, boiling, smelting, forging, milling, thatching, fencing and hurdle-making, hedging, road-mending and haulage. Almost everything which anybody *does* in the countryside is taboo.[45]

In 'Upon Appleton House' the rural labourers are significantly seen in some productive activity. Raymond Williams comments on this,

---

[44] Though William Empson, in 'Natural Magic and Populism in Marvell's Poetry', in R. L. Brett, ed., *Andrew Marvell: Essays on the Tercentenary of His Death* (Oxford, 1979), pp. 48–9 sees Marvell as 'regarding a mower with (necessarily distant) yearning . . . It is the poet who is in love with Damon'.

[45] Turner, *The Politics of Landscape*, p. 165. He is developing a point made by Raymond Williams, *The Country and The City*, p. 45 (quoted *supra*, p. 26). Cf. 'Millet and the Peasant' in John Berger, *About Looking* (London, 1982), pp. 69–70.

The magical country, yielding of itself, is now seen as a working landscape filled with figures: the mowers and the haymakers, the 'Villagers in common' coming to graze their cattle on the mown meadows, the winter flooding of the river pastures. All these are seen, but in a figure: the conscious look at a passing scene: the explicit detached view of landscape.[46]

As Williams indicates, the working labourers are present and active in Marvell's country-house poem. They are doing the haymaking. But the interest is not in the details of their labour or in their social relationships. Marvell's interest in the mowing scenes is in their artistic and emblematic significance. The metaphors are of a masque:

> No Scene that turns with Engines strange
> Does oftner then these Meadows change
>
> (xlix. 385-6)

Or they are from the visual arts and optics:

> They seem within the polisht Grass
> A Landskip drawn in Looking-Glass
> And shrunk in the huge Pasture show
> As Spots, so shap'd on Faces do.
> Such Fleas, ere they approach the Eye,
> In Multiplying Glasses lye.
>
> (lviii. 457-62)

These are the villagers, associated with Levellers in the previous stanza, now compared to fleas or to spots on faces. Again there is a pejorative note; we cannot imagine Fairfax or his daughter described as fleas or spots. Fairfax, we have already seen in Stanza vii has 'magnitude': he does not shrink like Milton's fallen angels entering Pandaemonium in order to get in; the house expands around him. It is only the lower orders who are treated in this reductive way. For all Marvell's introducing rural labour, his interest is not in the labourers themselves, but what they can be transmuted into, what they can be presented as representing. The mown field 'seemeth':

---

[46] Williams, *The Country and the City*, p. 74.

> A Camp of Battail newly fought:
> Where, as the Meads with Hay, the Plain
> Lyes quilted ore with Bodies slain:
> The Women that with forks it fling,
> Do represent the Pillaging.
>
> (liii. 420–4)

The stress on representation, the invitation to allegorical interpretation, informs the entire mowing sequence. The undoubted identification of the mowing-field with a battle-field encourages the reader to see an allusion to the battles of the Civil War.[47] But while a general reference is apparent, attempts to make specific identification are always thwarted. The very opening of the sequence would seem to invite interpretation.

> And now to the Abbyss I pass
> Of that unfathomable Grass,
> Where Men like Grashoppers appear,
> But Grashoppers are Gyants there:
> They, in there squeking Laugh, contemn
> Us as we walk more low then them:
> And, from the Precipices tall
> Of the green spir's to us do call.
>
> (xlvii. 369–76)

Commentators are agreed that there is an allusion to Numbers 13[48] where Moses sent a ruler from every tribe of Israel 'to spy out the land of Canaan' which the Lord had told Moses 'I give unto the children of Israel'. But though they discovered the land that flowed with milk and honey, they reported:

---

[47] John Dixon Hunt, *Andrew Marvell: His Life and Writings* (London, 1978), p. 109: 'it seems perfectly plausible to read allusions to contemporary politics in various passages' but 'Nun Appleton generally distances and diminishes the outer world'. Cf. Ann Evans Berthoff, *The Resolved Soul: A Study of Marvell's Major Poems* (Princeton, 1970), p. 175: 'The best argument against the labored allegorization of the harvest/battle is that we do not need it and that, if allowed, it disrupts the poem'. Robert Wilcher, *Andrew Marvell* (Cambridge, 1985), p. 156: 'it is an impoverishment of the meadow sequence to reduce it to "an allegorical masque" of recent English history . . . More important than any specific contemporary allusion is the overwhelming impression of disorder created by the break-down of stable relationships between perceiver and perceived, language and reality, poet and poem.'

[48] Joan Grundy, 'Marvell's Grasshoppers', *N & Q*, NS 4 (1957), 142.

Nevertheless, the people be strong that dwell in the land, and the cities are walled, and very great: and moreover we saw the Children of Anak there

and they claimed:

We be not able to go up against the people; for they are stronger than we.

And they brought up an evil report of the land which they had searched unto the children of Israel, saying, The land, through which we have gone to search it, is a land that eateth up the inhabitants thereof; and all the people that we saw in it are men of a great stature.

And there we saw giants, the sons of Anak, which come of the giants: and we were in our own sight as grasshoppers, and so we were in their sight.

It was a Biblical episode used in the Leveller propaganda. In the third and final *Agreement of the People* setting out the Leveller programme, the 'Preparative' concludes:

We have if we look with the eyes of frailty, enemies like the sons of *Anak*, but if with the eyes of faith and confidence in a righteous God and a just cause, we see more with us then against us.[49]

The 'Preparative' to the *Agreement of the People* was signed by Lilburn, Walwyn, Prince, and Overton 'From our causelesse captivity in the Tower of *London, May* 1 1649'.[50] Their use of the Numbers passage is clear enough: it is only a failure of nerve that makes us think we cannot possess the destined promised land. That general meaning may be there in Marvell's allusion, without the specific resonance of the Levellers' radical programme.

Attempts at a more specific interpretation seem unconvincing. Don Cameron Allen offered:

Perhaps we must think of these grasshoppers, as Lovelace does, as soldiers and as kingly ones. It is not by chance that the mowers follow them, destroying their food and refuge, and laying the fields more bare than ever . . . The reign of the royal grasshoppers is short as the day, for their human counterparts, the parliamentary mowers, dramatically 'enter next' and take their place in the masque. They are the 'Israelites', God's chosen wasters who, after the plagues of frogs, lice, flies and grasshoppers were ended, spoiled their Egyptian masters. One member of their party, the shepherdess Thestylis, now a cruel *vivandière*, is pointed out for our careful contemplation.[51]

---

[49] *Agreement of the Free People of England, Leveller Manifestoes*, p. 401.
[50] Ibid.   [51] Allen, *Image and Meaning*, pp. 134–5.

For this interpretation Allen draws on another Biblical grasshopper reference in Nahum 3: 17: 'Thy crowned are as the locusts, and thy captains as the great grasshoppers, which camp in the hedges in the cold day, but when the sun ariseth they flee away, and their place is not known where they are.' And he goes on to suggest a specific interpretation of the slaughtered rail on which Thestylis so eagerly lights.

The history of Fairfax's horror at the King's execution (the slaughtered rail?) and his refusal to attack Scotland (the quick rail?) is possibly given a share in this poetic masque.

It is clear that the rails have political meaning, and that they also contain a lesson for both Fairfax and Marvell. As far as I know, the bird appears in these verses for the first time in a poetic context; but Marvell certainly knew that the 'rallus crex' was known to the Italians as 're di quaglie' and to the French as 'roi des cailles'. The bird is the king of quail, though not a quail itself; hence God, who sent the quails to the hungry Israelites, now rains kings into the laps of the British Jews. The bird is also neutral. It is sometimes a wading bird and sometimes it comes to the fields and lives with the quails. It is difficult to classify.[52]

But only one English king has been executed, God hardly 'rains kings into the laps of the British Jews', and Charles was far from 'neutral'; it was his armies Fairfax's troops had been fighting. Moreover, as Wallace points out,[53] the rail is female.

Problems arise as soon as specific interpretations are pressed.[54] But there is no doubt about the violence of the mowers, their massacre of the grass, the killing of the rail.

> With whistling Sithe, and Elbow strong
> These Massacre the Grass along:
> While one, unknowing, carves the *Rail*
> Whose yet unfeather'd Quils her fail.

---

[52] Ibid., p. 137.

[53] John M. Wallace, *Destiny His Choice: the Loyalism of Andrew Marvell* (Cambridge, 1968) p. 248.

[54] See also the interpretation by Douglas Brooks-Davies in 'Marvell's Political Mysticism: Hermes and the Druids at *Appleton House*', *Studies in Mystical Literature*, 1 (1980), 97–119; 'The mowers, then, are an image of blood-guilty civil-war England in the form of the fallen Egyptians of the *Asclepian* Lament doing unworthy things. They are mistaken for Israelites because "in their actions they . . . seem to be men of another race" ' (p. 102). And Robert Cummings, 'The Forest Sequence in Marvell's *Upon Appleton House*: The Imaginative Contexts of a Poetic Episode', *Huntington Library Quarterly*, 47 (1984), 179–210.

> The Edge all bloody from its Breast
> He draws, and does his stroke detest;
> Fearing the Flesh untimely mow'd
> To him a Fate as black forebode.
>
> But bloody *Thestylis*, that waites
> To bring the mowing Camp their Cates,
> Greedy as Kites has trust it up,
> And forthwith means on it to sup:
> When on another quick She lights,
> And cryes, he call'd us *Israelites*;
> But now, to make his saying true,
> Rails rain for Quails, for Manna Dew.
>
> (1–li. 393–408)

To denote Thestylis as bloody, as 'Greedy as Kites', is to evoke some suggestion of blood-lust, cancelling the humane note of detestation that the mower has for 'his stroke', a stroke that was designed to 'massacre the grass' anyway.

There are military episodes throughout the poem,[55] but it is only in the mowing sequence that there is any bloodshed. And the actual detail of military conflict is displaced from the Lord-General himself on to his troops. The troops are represented by the villagers. This is accurate enough; the foot soldiers were the lower orders. The distasteful details of bloodshed are thus distanced from the Lord-General, who is left clean-handed and uncontaminated. The violence is all the work of others, the distantly viewed common people. The poetic strategy is the same as that employed in 'An Horatian Ode', where Cromwell is the flame of heaven, and the 'armed Bands' are the ones with 'bloody hands' (ii. 55–6).

The rural labourers are introduced into the poem, then, not primarily to make any point about the positive aspects of rural life. The mowing scene is not like the mowing scene in *Anna Karenina*, where Tolstoy is drawing out life-enhancing qualities from the productive

---

[55] Marston Moor was only 10 miles from Appleton House, which was surrounded by battle sites. See the map of the Yorkshire Campaigns in Wilson, *Fairfax*, p. 25. 'Fairfax's career clearly prompted the use of military terms employed in the subsequent description of Fairfax himself and his estate (stanzas xxxvi–xlvi). However, these terms were also surely intended to provoke association with the traditional picture of the true Christian as a soldier armed with weapons of his faith': Maren-Sofie Røstvig, 'Upon Appleton House' in *The Happy Man* (Oslo, 1962), revised in *Marvell: Modern Judgements*, ed. Michael Wilding (London, 1969), p. 221. See also James Turner, 'Marvell's Warlike Studies', *Essays in Criticism*, 28 (1978), 288–301.

activity; rather it is an episode that invites analogies to be drawn with the events of the wider political world. 'Upon Appleton House' is often placed in the category of retirement poems; but this episode, which might have been central to a vision of rural retirement, serves in fact to allude to public events. And they are events that see a threat in the mowers, the rural labourers; that present them as participants in military massacre from which Fairfax is carefully excluded; and that see the possibility of threatening Leveller action.

To attempt to trace point by point analogies with contemporary political and military events in the mowing episode leads to inevitable contradictions. It is as if Marvell, while introducing a general context inviting analogies, is blocking any specific decoding. An unspecific military coloration was unexceptionable; covert allusions to Charles or to Cromwell would be dangerous. Fairfax was being watched carefully by Thurloe's agents for fear he should make any pact with Charles II. To commemorate his past military successes might seem to be pushing him forward against Cromwell, politically unwise. But one thing that Cromwell and Fairfax and the Royalists were united in was opposition to radical tendencies emerging through the Levellers or Diggers. Nothing would be lost by endorsing ruling-class prejudices against the lower orders.

The country-house poem involved a celebration of the theme of rural retirement. But the very theme of retirement was problematic. Increasingly popular as a poetic subject in the seventeenth century, it was initially very much a Roman Catholic theme. The Polish poet Casimir, whose Latin poems were known throughout Europe, had revived the classical originals of Horace and given them new life.[56] But Casimir was a Catholic, and the Catholic connections of the retirement theme were unavoidable—the model of cloistered withdrawal from the world. Moreover, within England, retirement was a theme popular with poets of Royalist sympathies in the mid-century; since the Royalists were out of political office and influence, the theme of retirement was obviously an appropriate one. Marvell in writing about Fairfax's retirement has to discriminate it from the false retirements, the corrupt retirements.

---

[56] E. M. W. Tillyard, *Myth and the English Mind* (New York, 1962), pp. 68–70.

The nunnery episode fulfils an important function here. For what young Isabel is offered are the appeals of a totally unretired value-system. Friedman calls it the 'unworldly seclusion of a Catholic religious'.[57] But it is not a withdrawal from the worldly ambitions and corruptions outside that the nunnery offers, but a protected intensification of them. The sensuous richness of the life is stressed:

> So through the mortal fruit we boyl
> The Sugars uncorrupting Oyl:
> And that which perisht while we pull,
> Is thus preserved clear and full.
>
> For such indeed are all our Arts;
> Still handling Natures finest Parts.
> Flow'rs dress the Altars; for the Clothes
> The Sea-born Amber we compose;
> Balms for the griv'd we draw; and Pasts
> We mold, as Baits for curious tasts.
>
> (xxii–xxiii. 173–82)

There is the appeal of vanity—the possibility that Isabel will serve as a model for embroidered portraits of the Virgin Mary, and hence be disseminated and worshipped widely:

> Yet thus She you resembles much.
> Some of your Features, as we sow'd
> Through ev'ry *Shrine* should be bestow'd
>
> (xvii. 132–4)

And then there is the ultimate appeal of ambition, the possibility that Isabel might become Abbess:

> Our *Abbess* too, now far in Age
> Doth your succession near presage
> How soft the yoke on us would lye,
> Might such fair Hands as yours it tye!
>
> (xx. 157–60)

---

[57] Friedman, *Marvell's Pastoral Art*, p. 221. George de Forest Lord describes it as 'a perversion of the good life' in 'From Contemplation to Action: Marvell's Poetic Career', *Philological Quarterly*, 46 (1967), 207–24. J. Dixon Hunt remarks on the central theme of the 'proper occasion and uses of retreat and retirement', *Andrew Marvell*, p. 97.

It is an appeal firmly confronted elsewhere in the poem. Fairfax weeds out ambition and cultivates conscience (xlv). And Mary has been brought up

> In a *Domestick Heaven* nurst,
> Under the *Discipline* severe
> Of *Fairfax*, and the starry *Vere*.
>
> (lxxxvi. 722–4)

The stress on the religious discipline of the Fairfax household is there to enforce the idea of correct retirement. The retirement of the nunnery by contrast is indulgence:

> And, if our Rule seem strictly pend
> The Rule it self to you shall bend.
>
> (ii. 155–6)

This same lack of discipline characterizes that other retirement that succeeds the mowing episode:

> But I, retiring from the Flood
> Take Sanctuary in the Wood.
>
> (lxi. 481–2)

Here the poet indulges in a solitary retirement. The nunnery offered a social retirement, with all the lures of society, including sexuality:

> Each Night among us to your side
> Appoint a fresh and Virgin Bride.
>
> (xxiv. 185–6)

The poet pursues the opposite extreme:

> How safe, methinks, and strong, behind
> These Trees have I incamp'd my Mind;
> Where Beauty, aiming at the Heart,
> Bends in some Tree its useless Dart.
>
> (lxxvi. 601–4)

And the ecstatic indulgence is with nature:

> Bind me ye *Woodbines* in your 'twines
> Curle me about ye gadding *Vines*.
>
> (lxxvii. 609–10)

But this solitary retirement has to be rejected as much as the nunnery's retirement. When Mary appears, the poet and nature both regain a discipline:

> Hide trifling Youth thy Pleasures slight.
>
>   (lxxxii. 652)

> See how loose Nature, in respect
> To her, it self doth recollect
>
>   (lxxxiii. 657–8)

Whatever their other functions, the nunnery and the wood episodes serve to define Fairfax's retirement. They are rejected counter-retirements: neither of them represents the virtues of the family. The implicit stress is on Fairfax's withdrawing from the public world and creating the proper environment for his only child, Mary.

Having defined Fairfax's true, moral, Puritan retirement in contrast with the types of corrupt or false retirement, Marvell is then left with the problem of whether retirement is in fact possible. What is so noticeable about 'Upon Appleton House' is how the images of retirement are constantly intruded upon by images of war and politics. The nuns 'in shining Armour white, / Like *Virgin Amazons* do fight' (xiv. 105–6), they 'lye as chast in Bed, / As Pearls together billeted' (xxiv. 189–90). And when William Fairfax attacks the nunnery by force, they respond in kind.

> Some to the Breach against their Foes
> Their *Wooden Saints* in vain oppose
> Another bolder stands at push
> With their old *Holy-Water Brush*.
> While the disjointed *Abbess* threads
> The gingling Chain-shot of her *Beads*.
> But their lowd'st Cannon were their Lungs;
> And sharpest Weapons were their Tongues.
>
>   (xxxii. 249–56)

It is a burlesque battle, drawing on traditions not only of Protestant anti-Catholic satire, such as we find in Milton's burlesque treatment of 'eremits and Friers' in *Paradise Lost* (iii. 474–97) but also of satire on women ('sharpest Weapons were their Tongues'). The nunnery episode is followed immediately by the description of the Gardens laid out 'in the just Figure of a Fort' (xxxvi. 286). Again the note has its comic aspect, but military images are sustained throughout the episode culminating in 'th'invisible *Artilery*' that 'seems / To point' at Cawood Castle (xlvi. 362-4).

We have already discussed the mowing sequence with its imagery of 'a Camp of Battail' (liii. 420). The Sanctuary in the Wood that follows it, 'this yet green, yet growing Ark' has its creatures 'in Armies, not in Paires' (lxi. 482, 488) and we are told that of its trees 'many fell in War' (lxii. 493). The imagery is sustained in the poet's celebration of his secure retreat:

> How safe, methinks, and strong behind
> These Trees have I incamp'd my Mind;
> Where Beauty, aiming at the Heart,
> Bends in some Tree its useless Dart;
> And where the World no certain Shot
> Can make, or me it toucheth not.
> But I on it securely play,
> And gaul its Horsemen all the Day.
>
> (lxxxvi. 601-8)

Even Mary Fairfax's entrance provokes the warlike note:

> *Blest Nymph*! that could so soon prevent
> Those *Trains* by Youth against thee meant;
> Tears (watry Shot that pierce the Mind;)
> And *Sighs* (Loves Cannon charg'd with Wind;)
> *True Praise* (That breaks through all defence;)
> And *feign'd complying Innocence*;
> But knowing where this *Ambush* lay,
> She scap'd the safe, but roughest Way.
>
> (lxxxx. 713-20)

That a poem addressed to a former Lord-General should be redolent of military reference is appropriate; there is an expected wit in ringing the changes on possible military analogies. But are they also to be read as a comment on the impossibility of retirement? Fairfax has withdrawn to his rural estates, but the war cannot be excluded. The war was indeed still going on; the campaign against the Scots begun in 1650 escalated into a further outbreak of civil war, and 'Even Fairfax lost his doubts now that England had been invaded; he organized the Yorkshire militia. Charles' advance on London was checked, and he was shepherded south-west to Worcester.'[58] The

---

[58] Christopher Hill, *God's Englishman: Oliver Cromwell and the English Revolution* (Harmondsworth, 1972), p. 124.

Scots and Royalists were not finally defeated till Cromwell won 'Worcester's laureate wreath' with the battle of 3 September 1651. The peaceful retreat of Appleton House was a retreat within a larger context of military activity, and Fairfax's withdrawal from engagement in that activity was something that could not but have been talked about and speculated upon, and yet could hardly be talked about in any public way.

It is characteristic of Marvell's poetry that retirement should be intruded upon. His only whole-hearted advocacy of retirement is in his version of a chorus from Seneca's *Thyestes* (391–403) which Wyatt amongst others had translated:

> Climb at *Court* for me that will
> Tottering favors Pinacle;
> All I seek is to lye still.
>
> (1–3)

Significantly this is a translation of another writer's work. In his own poems retirement is a vulnerable, temporary state. In the 'Horatian Ode',

> So restless *Cromwel* could not cease
> In the inglorious Arts of Peace
>
> (9–10)

In 'The Garden', 'th' industrious Bee', image of organized social living, intrudes and 'Computes its time' (69–70). So in 'Upon Appleton House' the nuns' cloistered retirement is broken in upon, just as the poet's retirement is intruded upon by Maria. And though the poem opened extolling the virtues of humility as shown in Fairfax's modest dwelling, humility is still no protection from the violence of war. As Marvell moralizes about the rails in the mowing episode,

> Unhappy Birds! what does it boot
> To build below the Grasses Root;
> When Lowness is unsafe as Hight,
> And Chance o'retakes what scapeth spight?
>
> (lii. 409–12)

The rail, like the faun in 'The Nymph Complaining,' is killed for all its non-involvement. The message seems to be that in wartime the innocent non-partisans get massacred as readily as those directly involved. The only advice is the pragmatic:

Or sooner hatch or higher build:
The Mower now commands the Field.

(liii. 417–18)

How are we to interpret these reflections on the vulnerability of retirement? Rather than seeing them as a rebuke or a regret for Fairfax's decision, perhaps we can interpret them as questioning whether Fairfax in fact has retired. If everything in his grounds and estates evokes images of war, does this perhaps suggest that he is still potentially considering military strategies? The critical consensus has been to interpret 'Upon Appleton House' from the historical perspective of the twentieth century. But to resituate the poem in the early 1650s is to see it addressed not to a Fairfax who withdrew from public life and handed over to Cromwell, but to a Fairfax who has withdrawn from the Scots campaign but who, in his late thirties, is still a significant potential military force. It is clear to us now that Fairfax retired, but it was not clear in the 1650s that he would not participate again. The military intrusions into scenes of retirement, the haunting political allusions to Levellers or the traitor worm felling the oak tree (lxx. 554) make better sense as questions than as statements. The attempts to provide a coherent explication of the poem have generally failed. Yet those critics who have tried have been able to provide provocative local insights. Rather than looking for a clear 'answer' to the poem, it is better to see it as offering a series of questions, a series of themes for meditation and speculation; with the largest speculation of all asking what the significantly absent Lord Fairfax is planning. Is it permanent retirement or a temporary marshalling of forces? His nephew, Brian Fairfax, wrote in the epistle dedicatory to the *Short Memorials of Thomas Lord Fairfax*:

The retired part of his Life gave him greater Satisfaction than all his former Victories, when he lived quietly at his own House at *Nun-Appleton* in *Yorkshire*; always earnestly wishing and praying for the Restitution of the Royal Family, and fully resolved to lay hold on the first good Opportunity to contribute his part towards it; which made him always lookt upon with a jealous eye by the Usurpers of that time.[59]

The possibility of Fairfax's declaring for Charles II was a real one. M. A. Gibb writes: 'more than once reports reached Secretary Thurloe

---

[59] Fairfax, *Short Memorials*, p. vii.

that Lord Fairfax's name was connected with royalist plots. How much truth lay in such reports it is impossible to estimate.'[60] In 1655 'wild rumours reached the King . . . that Fairfax had five thousand men behind him and had declared for Charles . . . all untrue'.[61] In 1658 Fairfax was reported to have said 'that he knew not but he might chuse by his old commission as generall to appeare in armes on behalf of the people of these nations'.[62] When Fairfax did ultimately act, his intervention was crucial. An account of his support of General Monck in the handwriting of his nephew Brian Fairfax is preserved in the *Fairfax Correspondence*.

Declaring for General Monk, then in Scotland, at his earnest request, against Lambert's army, which pressed hard upon him as he lay at Coldstream, whither my Lord Fairfax sent me his cousin, Brian Fairfax, with a verbal answer to his letter, brought by Sir Thomas Clargis, that he would appear at the head of what forces he could raise in Yorkshire the 1st of January, 1659, which he did to so good effect, that in three day's time (the report of my Lord Fairfax opposing them being spread about Lambert's army) the Irish brigade, consisting of twelve hundred horses, deserted him, and sent to offer their service to my Lord Fairfax, and several foot regiments at the same time declared for their old general, Fairfax: and in five days Lambert himself, with ten men, stole away from his own army.[63]

Markham comments on the episode:

Had the general remained neutral at Nunappleton, Lambert with his superior force, would probably have defeated Monk. Had he joined Lambert, Monk's soldiers would have come over to their old commander, just as Lambert's did. In either case the course of events would have been changed. The overthrow of the Committee of Safety, and the assembling of a free Parliament which recalled Charles, is due directly to the action taken by Lord Fairfax. He it was who, whether for good or for evil, restored the monarchy.[64]

And it was Fairfax who led the commission of six peers and twelve members of the House of Commons that conveyed the invitation to

---

[60] M. A. Gibb, *The Lord General: A Life of Thomas Fairfax*, London, 1938, p. 236. See Markham, *Life of Fairfax*, p. 370.
[61] Antonia Fraser, *King Charles II* (London, 1979), p. 142.
[62] David Underdown, *Royalist Conspiracy in England 1649-60* (New Haven, 1960), p. 225. See also pp. 39, 118-20, 138, 198, 224-5.
[63] *Fairfax Correspondence*, i. cx-cxi.
[64] Markham, *Life of Fairfax*, p. 382.

Charles at The Hague to return to England.[65] Hill writes, 'His role had been more decisive in making the restoration possible than that of anyone but Monck'.[66]

At the beginning of the poem is the image of the tortoise:

> The low roof'd Tortoises do dwell
> In cases fit of Tortoise-shell.
>
> (ii. 13–14)

It is there again in the concluding stanza:

> How *Tortoise like*, but not so slow,
> These rational *Amphibii* go.
>
> (lxxxxvii. 773–4)

The tortoise has its military connotations—it was the name of a tactical formation. But it carries too the suggestions of hidden politics. 'The tortoise is found in the emblem books as a symbol of the self-contained man and hence may be associated with the politic man; it is also commonly used as an emblem of Sloth . . . '[67] In Ben Jonson's *Volpone*, Sir Politic Would-be after he has been told that 'a spy set on you'

> has made relation to the Senate,
> That you professed to him to have a plot
> To sell the state of Venice to the Turk
>
> (V iv. 35–8)[68]

hides inside his 'most politic tortoise' (V. iv. 79). Ian Donaldson glosses the tortoise as a 'device' of triple significance: first it is an emblem of 'policy' 'safe so long as it remains within its shell, vulnerable as soon as it ventures any part of its body outside'; secondly it is an emblem of silence, as the tortoise was sometimes supposed to be tongueless; and thirdly, it is a symbol of keeping to one's home.[69]

---

[65] Ibid., p. 384.

[66] Christopher Hill, *The Collected Essays of Christopher Hill*, (Brighton, 1985) i. 164.

[67] R. E. R. Madelaine, 'Parasites and "Politicians": Some Comic Stage Images in *Volpone*', *Aumla*, 58 (1982), 176.

[68] G. A. Wilkes, ed., *The Complete Plays of Ben Jonson* (Oxford, 1982), vol. iii.

[69] Ian Donaldson, 'Jonson's Tortoise', *RES*, NS 19 (1968), pp. 162–6. John Creaser, 'The Popularity of Jonson's Tortoise', *RES*, NS 28 (1976), 38–46. William D. McGaw, 'Marvell's "Salmon-Fishers"—A Contemporary Joke', *ELN* 13 (1976), 177–80.

The associations are appropriate for the withdrawn former Lord-General, who may be self-contained, or slothful, or biding his political time. It is a fitting, framing image for this most enigmatic poem of this most enigmatic of poets, this 'notable English Italo-Machavillian' as a Royalist informer described Marvell in Saumur in 1656.[70]

[70] Letter of James Scudamore to Sir Richard Browne, 15 August 1656, British Library Add. MS 15858, fo. 135. Facsimile in Hilton Kelliher, *Andrew Marvell Poet & Politician* (London, 1978), pp. 61–2.

7

The Last of the Epics:
The Rejection of the Heroic
in Hudibras *and* Paradise Lost

With the English Civil Wars, the forward youth who would write
an epic poem was presented with first-hand material for his Muse.
The images of martial valour, the scenes of military glory, were
played out before his eyes, providing ready themes for the epic poem
England's literature awaited.

But the realities of civil war were less glorious than the literary
images of heroic grandeur. Although past civil wars had later found
epic treatment, the contemporary slaughter of fellow-countrymen
could have little appeal. The two most famous heroic poems of the
Restoration concerned themselves with questioning the very idea of
military glory; these two epics questioned the basic assumptions of
traditional epic.[1] That they should ask such questions at such a time
suggests that their authors had been reconsidering the heroic epics
and romances of the past in the light of the tragic experience of civil
war. The epic found itself transformed in England into the burlesque
epic of Samuel Butler's *Hudibras* (Parts i, 1663; ii, 1664; iii, 1678)
and the Christian epic of John Milton's *Paradise Lost* (1667).

---

[1] On the theme of the rejection of epic values, see John M. Steadman, *Milton and
the Renaissance Hero* (Oxford, 1967). This theme is also discussed in T. J. B. Spencer,
'*Paradise Lost*: The Anti-Epic', in *Approaches to Paradise Lost*, ed. C. A. Patrides
(London, 1968), pp. 81–98. The studies of Davis P. Harding and Arnold Stein cited
below support this general argument. John Wilders in his edition of *Hudibras* (Oxford,
1967) notes that 'in *Hudibras* both epic and romance are parodied indiscriminately'
(p. xxxiv). As Steadman points out, 'Renaissance heroic tradition comprised the
romance as well as the epic. . . . Literary frontiers had yet to be definitively drawn,
and the question of their demarcation was provoking acrimonious debate among such
theorists as Pigna and Giraldi, Tasso and Scaliger . . . Thus, for many critics, the
epic tradition embraced the romance tradition almost in its entirety' (Steadman, op.
cit., pp. 109, 110). In attacking the values of the heroic tradition it is appropriate
that Milton and Butler should refer both to epic and to romance.

Remarking on Garrick's brilliance as an actor, Hannah More once wrote: 'I should have thought it as possible for Milton to have written *Hudibras*, and Butler *Paradise Lost*, as for one man to have played Hamlet and Drugger with such excellence'.[2] I have no intention of implying here that Butler and Milton might have exchanged works.[3] Milton's note on 'The Verse' with its rejection of 'the jingling sound of like endings' could hardly find a more extreme anti-type than Butler's burlesque rhyme. These metrical extremes clearly enough express the extremes of tone, of decorum. But I want to suggest that these extremes find common middle-ground in the heroic tradition that both poems are reacting against, and that their grounds of rejection are similar.

For both poems include explicit rejections of the heroic code. Milton's is well known and often commented on. It finds its major expression in the invocation to Book ix when he announces he is about to deal with the Fall.

> . . . sad task, yet argument
> Not less but more heroic than the wrath
> Of stern Achilles on his foe pursued
> Thrice fugitive about Troy wall; or rage
> Of Turnus for Lavinia disespoused,
> Or Neptune's ire or Juno's, that so long
> Perplexed the Greek and Cytherea's son;
> If answerable style I can obtain
> Of my celestial patroness, who deigns
> Her nightly visitation unimplored,

[2] Quoted in Austin Dobson, *Eighteenth Century Vignettes: Third Series* (London, 1923), p. 19.

[3] Butler has an attack on Milton in 'Fragments of an Intended Second Part of the Foregoing Satire' [i.e., 'Satire upon the Imperfection and Abuse of Human Learning'], ii. 141–52. Butler satirizes Milton's emphasis on his opponent's errors of Latin style rather than his concern with the theme of regicide in his controversy with Salmasius. (In Butler's *Poetical Works*, ed. G. Gilfillan [Edinburgh, 1854], ii. 235; and *Milton: The Critical Heritage*, ed. J. T. Shawcross [London, 1970], p. 76.)

William Somervile attempted a burlesque juncture of the two styles in a brief poem 'Hudibras *and* Milton *reconciled*' (in his *Occasional Poems, Translations, Fables, Tables* etc. [London, 1727], pp. 93–6). The poet writing random octosyllabics of scatological analogies to the difficulty of writing poetry is disturbed, at one in the morning, by a Miltonic, blank-verse thunderstorm; and then returning to octo-syllabics,

> I piss'd, thrice shook my giddy Head,
> Let a great F**t, and went to Bed.

For a discussion of Butler as a satirist, see Ian Jack, *Augustan Satire* (Oxford, 1952).

And dictates to me slumbering, or inspires
Easy my unpremeditated verse:
Since first this subject for heroic song
Pleased me long choosing, and beginning late;
Not sedulous by nature to indite
Wars, hitherto the only argument
Heroic deemed, chief mastery to dissect
With long and tedious havoc fabled knights
In battles feigned; the better fortitude
Of patience and heroic martyrdom
Unsung . . .

(ix. 13–33)

Gradually Milton's critique of the old military heroism and his rejection of it for the new Christian heroism of 'patience and heroic martyrdom' has been recognized by the critics. We do not now need to worry about whether Satan is really the 'hero' of *Paradise Lost*; he *is* the hero in the tradition of classical, pagan, military heroes — but in Milton's views such 'great Conquerors' were 'Destroyers rightlier called and plagues of men' (xi. 697). The rejection of 'wars, hitherto the only argument / Heroic deemed' (ix. 28–9) is repeated in the account of the giants when Adam is shown:

Cities of men with lofty gates and towers,
Concourse in arms, fierce faces threatening war,
Giants of mighty bone, and bold emprise;
Part wield their arms, part curb the foaming steed . . .

(xi. 640–3)

The consciously inflated manner, the vocabulary of Spenser, and the Latinate 'part . . . part . . . ' construction echoing Virgil, establish the epic note. Then we see the heroes in action, seeking forage and driving

Ewes and their bleating lambs over the plain,
Their booty; scarce with life the shepherds fly,
But call in aid, which makes a bloody fray;
With cruel tournament the squadrons join;
Where cattle pastured late, now scattered lies
With carcasses and arms the ensanguined field
Deserted: others to a city strong
Lay siege, encamped; by battery, scale, and mine,
Assaulting; others from the wall defend

With dart and javelin, stones and sulphurous fire;
On each hand slaughter and gigantic deeds.

(xi. 649–59)

It is a sophisticated passage in its interplay of noble terminology and brutal action. The 'ewes and their bleating lambs' represent not only the slaughter of animals to feed the marauding army but also the loss of the shepherds' livelihood and also, metaphorically, the mothers and children suffering before the army, just as we see the shepherds flee. The pastoral 'where cattle pastured' is superseded by 'the ensanguined field'; and the cattle, awaiting their later slaughter unawares, their later shift into carcasses, are identified with the slaughtered men whose carcasses we see: men are driven as beasts to the slaughter in this world. The most striking phrase is the collocation of 'slaughter and gigantic deeds', insisting on their identity and making us aware of the nature of the actions denoted by such heroic, endorsive phrases as 'gigantic deeds'. Michael interprets the episode to Adam:

> Such were these giants, men of high renown;
> For in those days might only shall be admired,
> And valour and heroic virtue called;
> To overcome in battle, and subdue
> Nations, and bring home spoils with infinite
> Manslaughter, shall be held the highest pitch
> Of human glory, and for glory done
> Of triumph, to be styled great conquerors,
> Patrons of mankind, gods, and sons of gods,
> Destroyers rightlier called and plagues of men.

(xi. 688–97)

Butler's rejections of the heroic ethos is expressed throughout *Hudibras*, though never in such sustained passages. The most explicit statement occurs in the description of Talgol, the butcher, whose military prowess is associated with his civilian occupation. The same language is applicable to both his activities, and the descriptions of him are skilfully ambiguous. Butler may equally well be talking about his peacetime trade as a butcher or his military skill: that we cannot distinguish which, makes its simple, telling moral point:

> Yet *Talgol* was of Courage stout,
> And vanquish'd oftner then he fought:
> Inur'd to labour, sweat, and toyl,
> And, like a Champion, shone with Oyl.

Right many a Widow his keen blade,
And many Fatherless, had made.
He many a Bore and huge *Dun Cow*
Did, like another *Guy*, o'erthrow.
But *Guy* with him in fight compar'd,
Had like the Bore or Dun Cow far'd.
With greater Troops of Sheep h'had fought
Then *Ajax*, or bold *Don Quixot*: . . .

For he was of that noble Trade
That *Demi-Gods* and *Heroes* made,
Slaughter, and knocking on the head;
The Trade to which they all were bred;
And is, like others, glorious when
'Tis great and large, but base if mean.
The former rides in Triumph for it;
The later in a two-wheel'd Chariot,
For daring to profane a thing
So sacred, with vile bungleing.

(I. ii. 299–310, 321–30)[4]

Like Milton, Butler gets his effects by interweaving the elevated terms
of militarism's social acceptance—'noble', 'glorious', 'sacred'—with
the reductive language of the brutal action—'knocking on the head',
'trade', 'slaughter'. Both insist on the analogy of 'heroism' with the
'slaughter' of animals. But Butler's most telling stroke is his indication
of how murder when performed on a large scale becomes sacred.
Civilian murderers go to the gallows not for taking human life but
for taking insufficient life, for failing to perform the rite with full
military amplitude.

And Butler had an attack on the martial heroism of traditional
epic in his own voice, paralleling Milton's invocation to Book ix,
with his opening of the second canto of Book i:

There was an ancient sage *Philosopher*,
That had read *Alexander Ross* over,
And swore the world, as he could prove,
Was made of *Fighting* and of *Love*:
Just so *Romances* are, for what else
Is in them all, but *Love* and *Battels*?

---

[4] All quotations from *Hudibras* are from the text of John Wilders (Oxford,
1967). References to 'Grey' are to the two-volume edition of Zachary Grey (Cambridge,
1744).

> O'th' first of these w' have no great matter
> To treat of, but a world o'th' later:
> In which to doe the Injur'd Right
> We mean, in what concerns just fight.
> Certes our Authors are to blame,
> For to make some well-sounding name
> A Pattern fit for modern Knights,
> To copy out in Frays and Fights,
> (Like those that a whole street do raze,
> To build a Palace in the place.)
> They never care how many others
> They kill, without regard of mothers,
> Or wives, or children, so they can
> Make up some fierce, dead-doing man,
> Compos'd of many ingredient Valours,
> Just like the Manhood of nine Taylors.
> So a wild *Tartar* when he spies
> A man that's handsome, valiant, wise,
> If he can kill him, thinks t'inherit
> His Wit, his Beauty, and his Spirit:
> As if just so much he enjoy'd
> As in another is destroy'd.
> For when a Giant's slain in fight,
> And mow'd orethwart, or cleft downright,
> It is a heavy case, no doubt,
> A man should have his Brains beat out,
> Because he's tall, and has large Bones;
> As men kill Beavers for their stones.

(I ii. 1–34)

The satiric note is dropped here for a direct statement. Burlesque rhyme, and the reductive images, remain; but they remain to reinforce the bitterness of the attack, are used to deflate the idea of the Romance glorification of battles, of 'Wars hitherto the only argument / Heroic deemed'.

The dramatic enactment of the inadequacy of military heroism, its wrongness, and the reasons for its inadequacy and wrongness, is in *Paradise Lost* the war in Heaven. Satan shows his evil throughout the poem; but his attack on mankind is by 'false guile' (iii. 92); his use of *force* occurs in the war. For a long time the episode of the war in heaven worried commentators and critics for its absurdity, its lack of the proper dignity of the military encounters of the great epics. Count Pococurante complained in Voltaire's *Candide* (1759), that Milton 'has so little humour as to imitate in all seriousness

Ariosto's comic invention of firearms and make the devils fire cannons in Heaven!' But it was not until Arnold Stein's critical study *Answerable Style* of 1953 that it was accepted that Milton *was* being sardonically humorous, that the war was absurd. Even though the good angels had moral right on their side they could not achieve anything by military means; to enforce 'spiritual laws by carnal power . . . / On every conscience' (xii. 521–2) is wrong; it is what the corrupt church authorities try to do, Michael tells Adam. And looking back to the Civil Wars, is this not what the Saints attempted to do? Do we not see here Milton the old revolutionary looking back on his past involvements, meditating on why the Revolution with right on its side failed? His friend Andrew Marvell looked back similarly on the Revolution and remarked in *The Rehearsal Transpros'd*, 'I think the cause was too good to have been fought for.'[5] There was nothing wrong with the cause; but the use of military means to impose it was wrong; militarism is the code of the devil. War, Satan tells Michael during the war in heaven, is:

> The strife which thou call'st evil, but we style
> The strife of glory.
>
> (vi. 289–90)

Stein, in his analysis of this episode, has indicated how 'the invention of artillery is an attempt to usurp ultimate moral might by means of matter'.[6] Satan is attempting to usurp God's moral authority by means of force. The 'confusion of spirit and matter' here is indicative of Satan's own mental and moral confusion. It is for just such confusions that Butler derides Hudibras and his fellow-Presbyterians:

> For his *Religion* it was fit
> To match his Learning and his Wit:
> 'Twas *Presbyterian* true blew,
> For he was of that stubborn Crew
> Of Errant Saints, whom all men grant
> To be the true Church *Militant*:
> Such as do build their Faith upon
> The holy Text of *Pike* and *Gun*;

---

[5] Andrew Marvell, *The Rehearsal Transpros'd*, ed. D. I. B. Smith (Oxford, 1971), p. 135.

[6] Arnold Stein, *Answerable Style* (Minneapolis, 1953), p. 37.

Decide all Controversies by
Infallible Artillery;
And prove their Doctrine Orthodox
By Apostolick *Blows* and *Knocks*;
Call Fire and Sword and Desolation,
A *godly-thorough-Reformation* . . .

(I. i. 187–200)

The ironic collocations of 'Infallible Artillery' and of 'Apostolick *Blows* and *Knocks*' express succinctly the moral confusions that we see enacted by Satan in the war.

Rejecting then a certain code of behaviour, Milton and Butler are led to question the literary forms that ennoble that code. Butler wrote in his Note-books, 'Heroicall Poetry handle's the slightest, and most Impertinent Follys in the world in a formall Serious and unnaturall way: And Comedy and Burlesque the most Serious in a Frolique and Gay humor which has always been found the more apt to instruct, and instill those Truths with Delight into men, which they would not indure to heare of any other way.'[7] Both Milton and Butler recognize the ethical importance of literature and both are concerned that the false ethic of military heroism should no longer be spread. The original ethical impulse of the epic no longer remains, Butler believes: both the message and the medium are unacceptable. The old impulse must deliver its new message through new forms: and he describes the new form oddly in terms of the old knight-errant going forth: 'A Satyr is a kinde of Knight Errant that goe's upon Adventures, to Relieve the Distressed Damsel Virtue, and Redeeme Honor out of Inchanted Castles, And opprest Truth, and Reason out of the Captivity of Gyants or Magitians'.[8] The old heroic code, then, is to be extirpated and superseded by the new heroism of satire.

Milton's rejection of the traditional heroic, his identification of the 'destroyers' with Satan the destroyer, his giving Satan the heroic accoutrements, have often enough been remarked and documented.[9] His size, his strength, his shield, his spear—all these have their Homeric and Virgilian counterparts. At the same time Satan's

---

[7] Samuel Butler, *Characters and Passages from Note-books*, ed. A. R. Waller (Cambridge, 1908), p. 278.   [8] Ibid., p. 469.
[9] See, for instance, John M. Steadman, *Milton and the Renaissance Hero*; Davis P. Harding, *The Club of Hercules: Studies in the Classical Background of 'Paradise Lost'* (Urbana, 1962); Michael Wilding, *Milton's 'Paradise Lost'* (Sydney, 1969).

corruption, degradation, and evil are emphasized in his shield, compared to a spotty moon, in the fading glory of his appearance, in the comparison of him and his followers with Eastern tyrants and barbarian hordes. From the beginning of the poem Satan is both the traditional hero and the embodiment of evil: and the two qualities are shown to be inseparable in him and in all heroes. Military valour results inevitably in destruction: 'For only in destroying I find ease' (ix. 129).

The cruel destruction men wreak on each other in the world is clearly enough seen to result from the Fall; the military heroic is the direct result of the evil of Satan, himself embodying that heroism. Images of waste and destruction abound—the military devils are like locusts, barbarians, heroes of epic and romance. They perform the actions of classical heroic warriors; they even sing commemorations of their heroic deeds, archetypal or prototypical epic poems. They engage in the heroic games beloved of the epic as they wait for Satan to return from his mission to earth.

> Part on the plain, or in the air sublime
> Upon the wing, or in swift race contend,
> As at the Olympian games or Pythian fields;
> Part curb their fiery steeds, or shun the goal
> With rapid wheels, or fronted brigades form.
> As when to warn proud cities war appears
> Waged in the troubled sky, and armies rush
> To battle in the clouds, before each van
> Prick forth the airy knights, and couch their spears
> Till thickest legions close; with feats of arms
> From either end of heaven the welkin burns.
> Others with vast Typhoean rage more fell
> Rend up both rocks and hills, and ride the air
> In whirlwind; hell scarce holds the wild uproar.
> As when Alcides from Oechalia crowned
> With conquest, felt the envenomed robe, and tore
> Through pain up by the roots Thessalian pines,
> And Lichas from the top of Oeta threw
> Into the Euboic sea. Others more mild,
> Retreated in a silent valley, sing
> With notes angelical to many a harp
> Their own heroic deeds and hapless fall
> By doom of battle; and complain that fate
> Free virtue should enthral to force or chance.
> Their song was partial, but the harmony

> (What could it less when spirits immortal sing?)
> Suspended hell, and took with ravishment
> The thronging audience.

> (ii. 528–55)

Their achieved aim is the destruction of humankind, the reduction
of the richness of Paradise to

> an island salt and bare
> The haunt of seals and orcs, and sea-mews' clang.

> (xi. 834–5)

This satanic poem runs throughout *Paradise Lost*. Its literary modes
and the world view it assumes are given expression by Satan in
his soliloquies: 'chance' and 'fate' as Dennis Burden demonstrates,
become the recurrent and contradictory terms in which the fallen
angels see the universe, in opposition to the Christian poem's thesis
of God's *providence*. Not only do the fallen angels act like epic
heroes; their poets, as Burden stresses, are epic poets and tragic
poets.[10] In attacking the military ethic Milton is also attacking the
literary mode commemorating it; the two are inseparable. Toland
in his *Life of John Milton* quotes a letter of Milton's to Lady
Ranelagh's son in 1656:

As for what you write to me, that you are so much pleas'd with *Oxford*,
you cannot persuade me the more that you receiv'd any Improvement there,
or art becom a bit the wiser, unless you shew me som other Reasons for
it. Thos Victories of Princes which you extol, and such other things, wherin
Force has the greatest share, I would not have you too much admire,
especially now being a Hearer of Philosophers: where's the wonder if in the
Country of Rams there grow strong Horns, which are able to batter Towns
and Cities with such violence? But learn thou from thy Childhood to discern
and judg of great Examples, not from Violence and Force, but by Justice
and Temperance.[11]

Butler's rejection of the heroic is achieved by a quite different
procedure from Milton's. Hudibras and Ralph are supremely incompetent. Hudibras has the will to destroy, of course: at the end of
the battle in the second canto of the first book, Hudibras:

[10] Dennis H. Burden, *The Logical Epic* (London, 1967), p. 59.
[11] John Toland, *The Life of John Milton* (1698) in Helen Darbishire, ed., *The
Early Lives of Milton* (London, 1965), p. 176.

> star'd about, and seeing none
> Of all his foes remain but one,
> He snatch'd his weapon that lay near him,
> And from the ground began to rear him;
> Vowing to make *Crowdero* pay
> For all the rest that ran away.
>
> (I. ii. 1025–30)

Ralph prevents him, but the will was there.

Whether, even so, Hudibras could have killed Crowdero is doubtful. Butler heaps ridicule on his competence as a warrior, and on his physical qualities. Satan's size is emphasized by Milton; he transcends the dimensions of any conventional hero:

> he above the rest
> In shape and gesture proudly eminent
> Stood like a tower . . .
>
> (i. 589–91)

Quite the reverse is Hudibras, with neither the size nor the phallic symbolism of Satan. The Lady calls him 'a *Roan-Guelding*, twelve hands high' (ii. i. 694). For this non-equestrian age Zachary Grey's note provides a gloss: 'This is very satyrical upon the poor Knight, if we consider the signification of That Name; and from what the Widow says, we may infer, the Knight's Stature, was but Four foot high'.[12] Hogarth's engravings portray Hudibras as a hump-backed dwarf. When Hudibras approaches battle Butler comments:

> For as our modern wits behold,
> Mounted a Pick-back on the Old,
> Much further off; much further he
> Rais'd on his aged Beast could see:
> Yet not sufficient to descry
> All postures of the enemy.
>
> (I. ii. 71–6)

Perched on his horse, his vision is still circumscribed—unlike Satan's. Milton's description of the towering Satan is an echo of a description of Turnus in the *Aeneid*:

---

[12] *Hudibras*, ed. Zachary Grey (Cambridge, 1744), i. 339 n.

> . . . inter primos praestanti corpore Turnus
> vertitur arma tenens et toto vertice supra est
>
> (vii. 783-4)

That it is of Turnus, not Aeneas, qualifies the endorsive nature of
the allusion, of course; but it still allows Satan to be a dignified hero,
ennobled by a literary tradition. By contrast the Virgilian allusion
used to characterize Hudibras is applied in a wholly belittling way:

> For as *Aeneas* bore his Sire
> Upon his shoulders through the fire:
> Our Knight did bear no less a Pack
> Of his own Buttocks on his back;
> Which now had almost got the upper-
> Hand of his Head, for want of Crupper.
> To poize this equally, he bore
> A *Paunch* of the same bulk before:
>
> (I. i. 287-94)

Sir Philip Sidney had cited the episode in *A Defence of Poetry*:
'Who readeth Aeneas carrying old Anchises on his back, that wisheth
not it were his fortune to perform so excellent an act?'[13] Butler's
response is one of derision. His hero is so degraded that he reduces
even the most ennobling of classical touchstones to the grotesque
and contemptible.

Milton treats Satan in this way when he has finished with him.
After the Fall, when the notes change to tragic and the emphasis is
shifted on to 'the better fortitude / Of Patience and Heroic Martyrdom'
in Christ and Adam, then Satan's heroism is reduced to a tawdry
thing. He shares Hudibras's shiftiness and evasiveness when, after
Eve has eaten the apple, he 'slunk' away. And derision is heaped
on him upon his return to Hell:

> So having said, a while he stood, expecting
> Their universal shout and high applause
> To fill his ear, when contrary he hears
> On all sides, from innumerable tongues
> A dismal universal hiss, the sound
> Of public scorn . . .
>
> (x. 504-9)

---

[13] J. A. Van Dorsten, ed., *Sidney: A Defence of Poetry* (Oxford, 1966), p. 41.

This contemptuously comic treatment of the hero as he and his audience are turned to serpents is most unheroic. But it is similar to the treatment meted out to Hudibras. And there is a Hudibrastic note earlier in *Paradise Lost* in the description of the Paradise of Fools. The pilgrims wandering there find that:

> And now Saint Peter at heaven's wicket seems
> To wait them with his keys, and now at foot
> Of heaven's ascent they lift their feet, when lo
> A violent cross wind from either coast
> Blows them transverse ten thousand leagues awry
> Into the devious air; then might ye see
> Cowls, hoods and habits with their wearers tossed
> And fluttered into rags, then relics, beads,
> Indulgences, dispenses, pardons, bulls,
> The sport of winds: all these upwhirled aloft
> Fly o'er the backside of the world far off . . .
>
> (iii. 484–94)

The 'backside' is a familiar part of the Hudibrastic burlesque note and the banana-skin action is like Hudibras mounting his horse. This passage is related to the anti-heroic theme, for at the Paradise of Fools the first arrivals were the warriors of Book xi:

> First from the ancient world those Giants came
> With many a vain exploit, though then renowned . . .
>
> (iii. 464–5)

Such burlesque action is the basis of *Hudibras*, though rare in *Paradise Lost*. But occasionally, amidst being hailed with cudgel-blows and rotten eggs, Hudibras ventures a rare, traditionally heroic action, suitably described:

> He drew up all his force into
> One Body, and that into one Blow.
> But *Talgol* wisely avoided it
> By cunning sleight; for had it hit,
> The Upper part of him the Blow
> Had slit, as sure as that below.
>
> (I. ii. 819–24)

Had he hit—but of course he misses. In the next battle he ventures a similar blow of which Montague Bacon, quoted in Zachary Grey's

additional *Notes to Hudibras* (1752),[14] remarked, 'This is very like
Milton', quoting,

> Together both with next to almighty arm,
> Uplifted imminent one stroke they aimed
> That might determine, and not need repeat
>
> (vi. 316–18)

The passage in *Hudibras* referred to is this:

> The *Knight* with one dead-doing blow
> Resolving to decide the fight,
> And she with quick and cunning slight
> Avoiding it, the force and weight
> He charg'd upon it was so great,
> As almost sway'd him to the ground.
> No sooner she th' advantage found,
> But in she flew, and seconding
> With home-made thrust the heavy swing,
> She laid him flat upon his side . . .
>
> (I. iii. 844–53)

Certainly the opening two lines are heroic in a way comparable
with Milton's account. But in context the heroic is tarnished with
absurdity: for the blow is a failure, overtopples Hudibras, and causes
his defeat. Moreover he is attacking a woman, a most unheroic,
unchivalrous action. Before this final blow we have seen how he:

> rain'd a storm
> Of blows so terrible and thick,
> As if he meant to hash her quick.
>
> (I. iii. 836–8)

Grey cited a parallel to this description from the *Faerie Queene*. As
with the heroic note above, such a parallel serves only to contrast
the heroic with the actualities of the situation—Hudibras's attack
on a woman. This reflects ill enough on our hero and on heroism;
worse though is the fact that he is *defeated* by a woman. He is both
cruel and unchivalrous, and weak and incompetent.

Although incompetence and absurdity characterize Hudibras and
Ralph, the moral outrage of Milton's account of the wrongness of

---

[14] Zachary Grey, *Notes to Hudibras* (London, 1752), p. 31. I have normalized
the quotation from *Paradise Lost* to Fowler's text.

traditional heroic values is present just as strongly in *Hudibras*. We
do not need Sir Roger L'Estrange's unconvincing *Key to Hudibras*
(1715) to be reminded that contemporary readers read *Hudibras*
in the full context of the Civil Wars and the Regicide. Hudibras
and Ralph are buffoons and 'bumkins'; at the same time they are
figures from a recent, all-too-real political experience. The reader,
laughing at the fight over the bear, would remember without mirth
the bloodshed of Worcester, or Dunbar. Hudibras on horseback
provokes Butler's comment:

> So have I seen with armed heel,
> A Wight bestride a *Common-weal*;
> While still the more he kick'd and spurr'd,
> The less the sullen Jade has stirr'd.
>
> (I. i. 917–20)

Hudibras hiding under a table to avoid capture by the tormenting
devils at the Lady's house is dragged out from his security in a way
recalling a famous incident in the Civil Wars:

> And as another of the same
> Degree, and Party, in Arms, and Fame,
> That in the same Cause, had ingag'd,
> And War with equal conduct wag'd,
> By vent'ring only but to thrust
> His Head, a Span beyond his Post:
> B'a *Gen'ral* of the *Cavalliers*
> Was drag'd, through a window by th'Ears:
> So he was serv'd in his Redoubt,
> And by the other end pull'd out.
>
> (III. i. 1137–46)

These detailed allusions to events of the Civil War spread of course
throughout the poem, while the second canto of Book iii is unconcerned with the adventures of Hudibras and Ralph and consists of
a long digression about the end of the Interregnum.

The hideousness of civil war was vividly present for both Milton
and Butler. Milton's theme, though precluding a specific treatment
of recent British history, dealt with the archetypal civil war that Satan
provoked in heaven. Michael rebukes him:

> how hast thou disturbed
> Heaven's blessed peace, and into nature brought
> Misery, uncreated till the crime
> Of thy rebellion?
>
> (vi. 266–9)

Yet after the abortive rebellion, at least the devils can manage to live in peace—so different from the multiplications of divisions that occurred in Britain. The poet's own voice utters a cry of anguish in his description of Hell:

> O shame to men! Devil with devil damned
> Firm concord holds, men only disagree
> Of creatures rational, though under hope
> Of heavenly grace: and God proclaiming peace,
> Yet live in hatred, enmity and strife
> Among themselves, and levy cruel wars
> Wasting the earth, each other to destroy;
> As if (which might induce us to accord)
> Man had not hellish foes enough besides,
> That day and night for his destruction wait.
>
> (ii. 496–505)

Hudibras himself utters a similar plea against dissension in his first speech in the poem:

> There is a *Machiavilian* Plot,
> (Though ev'ry *nare olfact* it not)
> A deep design in't, to divide
> The well-affected that confide,
> By setting Brother against Brother,
> To claw and curry one another.
> Have we not enemies *plus satis*,
> That *Cane et anque perjus* hate us?
> And shall we turn our fangs and claws
> Upon our own selves, without cause?
>
> (I. i. 735–44)

We might recall Cromwell's remark in 1649: 'There is more cause of danger from disunion among ourselves than by anything from our enemies'.[15] It was a sad irony that Milton should lament over man's inability to agree, while describing the devils who, though initiators

---

[15] Christopher Hill, *God's Englishman: Oliver Cromwell and the English Revolution* (Harmondsworth, 1972), p. 103.

of discord, at least held agreement amongst themselves. But Butler's irony is more bitter still; for Hudibras who makes this plea for concord is (in Butler's view) the poem's representative of one of the major causes of faction, one of the Presbyterians largely responsible for the Civil War. Declaiming against the conflict of a bear-baiting, Hudibras is oblivious of the larger conflict he is participant in. Indeed the suppression of bear-baiting was one of the Cromwellian actions against the old order. A note in Grey's edition records how 'some of Colonel *Cromwell's* Forces coming by accident unto *Uppingham* Town in *Rutland* on the *Lord's Day*, found these Bears playing there in the usual manner: and in the height of their sport, caused them to be seiz'd upon, tied to a tree and shot'.[16] Whatever the developing complexities of irony that opened in the knight's speech, the sad question, 'Have we not enemies *plus satis*?' stands, like Milton's 'as if . . . Man had not hellish foes enough besides' (ii. 503–4), as a desperate, haunting lament.

What both *Paradise Lost* and *Hudibras* remarkably have in common are heroes of appalling degradation. We have already seen their commitment to violence. Their utter dishonesty must also be stressed — a quality so basic to both of them that it can easily be missed as not worthy of comment. Satan's dishonest rigging of the debate, his lying comment on his return to Hell that Night and Chaos 'fiercely opposed / My journey strange'(x. 478–9), and his lies to Eve, pretending to be a serpent, pretending to have eaten the apple himself; these are central to his character. His deceitfulness is utter: he deceives Uriel, 'the sharpest sighted spirit of all in heaven' (iii. 691), with a show of sincerity, and Milton comments:

> So spake the false dissembler unperceived;
> For neither man nor angel can discern
> Hypocrisy, the only evil that walks
> Invisible, except to God alone . . .
>
> (iii. 681–4)

These qualities are fully shared by Hudibras who lies to the Lady that he has undergone punishment, and pours forth hypocritical professions of his love for her.[17]

---

[16] Grey, *Hudibras*, i. 78.
[17] E. C. Baldwin in 'A Suggestion for a New Edition of Butler's *Hudibras*', *PMLA* 26 (1911), 528–48, sees hypocrisy as the central topic of the poem. Butler 'scourged

Corrupt from the outset, Satan and Hudibras are both heroes who yet degenerate into greater corruption. From his original heroic speeches (which none the less from the beginning provide clear evidence of his corruption) Satan follows a progressively downward course. His moments of nobility become fewer. He bravely sets off alone to Earth (though to do so he has to fix the debate) and we soon see him in the postures of a heroic confrontation for single combat: but his antagonist is his own son whom he fails to recognize and the posture issues in no fight. After the first two books he is reduced to using a series of degrading disguises, and he achieves his destruction of man not by heroic grandeur but by singling out a woman alone and lying to her. Hudibras's similar unchivalrous attack on a woman (and his worse defeat at her hands) has been noted. And Hudibras's knight-errantry is diverted from its public concerns in Part One to besieging the Widow to gain her property at the poem's end — a similar decline from truly heroic and romantic pretentions. From the speeches Hudibras began with in Canto One, speeches that bear at least some relationship to heroic utterance, he has degenerated to mere quarrels with Ralph, to logic-chopping, to the tortuous justification of lying:

> Is't not *Ridiculous*, and *Nonsence*,
> A *Saint* should be a slave to *Conscience?*
>
> (II. ii. 247–8)

Just as Satan, the warrior-hero, is reduced to deceit, to lies, to speeches rather than action, so Hudibras, the so-called knight, engages in no action in Part Three; heroic combat gives way to argument and lies. And like Satan, the lies are to the woman. From the beginning, of course, Hudibras has preferred words to deeds: but action has been forced on him by the bear-baiting crowd who respond to his harangue with blows. By the poem's end he is, like Satan, utterly discredited as a hero. For a second time he is defeated by a woman when the Widow traps and exposes him and foils his attempt to marry her. Satan likewise is rewarded for attacking a woman by receiving his defeat ultimately from the woman.

hypocrisy of every form . . . ' (p. 531); 'that the *Hudibras* is a satire upon hypocrisy exemplified in typical representatives of the society of the seventeenth century, rather than merely an attack upon an already vanquished political party, is clearly shown by even a casual reading of the Characters' (p. 533).

> Between thee and the woman I will put
> Enmity, and between thine and her seed;
> Her seed shall bruise thy head, thou bruise his heel.
>   So spake this oracle, then verified
> When Jesus son of Mary second Eve,
> Saw Satan fall like lightning down from heaven,
> Prince of the air; then rising from his grave
> Spoiled principalities and powers, triumphed
> In open show, and with ascension bright
> Captivity led captive through the air
> The realm it self of Satan long usurped,
> Whom he shall tread at last under our feet;
> Even he who now foretold his fatal bruise . . .
>
> (x. 179–91)

The final failure of both Hudibras and Satan singles them out from the ranks of other heroes. We must not forget that at the end of *Paradise Lost* Satan has not effected any successful revenge on God but has succeeded only in heaping worse punishment on his own head. Hudibras similarly has utterly failed to impose his puritanical discipline on the bear-baiting or the skimmington, has left Sidrophel not (as he thinks) dead but perfectly well, and has failed to win the Lady.

It is important to note that for all their rejection of the traditional heroic ethos both Milton and Butler judge their heroes from that ethos as well as from their other value-schemes. Although concerned to dismiss the heroic code Butler and Milton are concerned to show how their 'heroes' fail both by that code and by their own more humane one. Attacking women, being defeated by women, failing in their quests—these are all offences under the old code. Hudibras goes to great lengths to avoid the pain of the beating he has vowed to undergo. Vows should mean everything and pain nothing to the proper hero, of course. But neither Satan nor Hudibras is a proper hero. We are left wondering whether it is likely that the great figures hallowed in literature were either.

The hero of the epic poem traditionally provided an ideal of behaviour. This presented problems for early critics of *Paradise Lost*, for how could Satan be such a hero? By a terrible irony, though, he is: Satan, for fallen man, is indeed the ideal of behaviour, the model observed. This hero is not someone who ought to be, but someone who regrettably is, admired. The qualities most admired in the world are Satan's qualities: we see him compared with military heroes, adventurous seafarers, scientific inventors, classical orators. And so it becomes Milton's concern to show the evil of those qualities— to show how bravery or eloquence can so readily be used for evil ends. He underlines the false-heroic by creating the Christian heroes Christ and Adam. This new heroism, 'the better fortitude', supersedes the old.

Butler's method is less complex by far. He simply inverts the traditional heroic. The old hero was everything admirable: Hudibras is everything contemptible. There is no fear that the reader will admire him or Ralph. The danger is, of course, that Hudibras will be seen as contemptible only in his incompetence in fulfilling the heroic code, in having a rusty sword rather than a bloodstained one. Butler, however, avoids this danger. He avoids it partly by allowing no positives to creep in at all: there is no 'good hero', either of the supersessive sort (Christ or Adam), or of a traditional sort. Butler's new knight-errant is satire itself. Amongst the cast of the poem the hopelessness of Hudibras and Ralph is the total picture; their opposition, whether the crowd, Sidrophel, or Whackum, is equally disreputable. (The Lady alone is exempted from this degradation; but she represents nothing positive herself.) Implicitly, everyone in the civil wars was the same. It is important to note that, although Butler was hailed by the Royalists at the Restoration and has always been seen as a partisan writer, he does not introduce a 'good Royalist' to set against Hudibras and Ralph or the crowd. There is not much evidence that he had time for either side: his views on the Restoration court are as contemptuous as his views on the Cromwellian Commonwealth.

Not only are no positives allowed in, Butler also devalues both his epic hero and the epic conventions. Milton was concerned to surpass pagan epic: he summoned the 'heavenly Muse' (i. 6). He will 'soar / Above the Aonian mount' (i. 14–15), Mount Helicon; he replaces the pagan mount of the Muses with three Biblical mountains, Oreb, Sinai, and Sion Hill: three to one. And having shown the Bible richer in places of inspiration than the classical world, he then emphasizes that the Christian muse does not depend on the superstitions of place at all but flourishes in 'the upright heart and pure' (i. 18)—it is above geographical restriction.[18]

---

[18] See David Daiches, 'The Opening of *Paradise Lost*', in *The Living Milton*, ed. Frank Kermode (London, 1960), p. 63.

Butler observes the conventions too and invokes a muse—though somewhat grudgingly:

> We should, as learned Poets use,
> Invoke th'assistance of some Muse;
> However Criticks count it sillier
> Then Juglers talking t'a Familiar.
> We think 'tis no great matter which:
> They'r all alike: yet we shall pitch
> On one that fits our purpose most,
> Whom therefore thus do we accost.
>
> Thou that with Ale, or viler Liquors,
> Didst inspire *Withers*, *Pryn*, and *Vickars*,
> And force them, though it were in spight
> Of nature and their stars, to write;
> Who, as we find in sullen Writs,
> And cross-grain'd Works of modern wits,
> With Vanity, Opinion, Want,
> The wonder of the Ignorant,
> The praises of the Author, penn'd
> By himself, or wit-ensuring friend,
> The Itch of Picture in the Front,
> With Bays, and wicked Rhyme upon't,
> All that is left o'th' forked Hill
> To make men scribble without skill,
> Canst make a Poet, spight of fate,
> And teach all people to translate;
> Though out of Languages in which
> They understand no part of speech:
> Assist me but this once, I 'mplore,
> And I shall trouble thee no more.

(I. i. 631–58)

While Milton is trying to elevate and Christianize the muse Butler is deliberately reducing it to the lowest: he introduces it late, complains at the necessity, casts doubt on its value, reduces it to charlatanism with the mention of 'Juglers', and puts its power down to ale. The twin peaks of Parnassus are degraded to the image of serpent duplicity, 'th' forked Hill'.

Butler's particular degradations of his chosen form show his intention at its clearest. Instead of Virgil's '*Arma virumque* . . . ', instead of the nobility of Milton's 'Of man's first disobedience, and the fruit / Of that forbidden tree . . . ' (i. 1–2), Butler opens:

> When *Civil Dudgeon* first grew high,
> And men fell out they knew not why;
> When hard words, *Jealousies* and *Fears*,
> Set Folks together by the ears,
> And made them fight, like mad or drunk,
> For Dame *Religion* as for Punk . . .
>
> (I. i. 1–6)

The vocabulary destroys any dignity. Noble combat is 'Dudgeon', it is motiveless, causeless; the issues are no more significant than petty quarrels. In the revised text of the poem 'Dudgeon' is replaced by 'Fury', ennobling the opening at the expense of this contemptuous note, but the analogy of fighting for religion 'as for Punk' remains to reduce the combat to the most vulgar and trivial. Grey's edition notes: 'Sir *John Suckling* has express'd this Thought a little more decently, in the *Tragedy* of *Brennoralt*.'

> *Religion now is a young Mistress here,*
> *For which each Man will fight, and die at least;*
> *Let it alone awhile, and 'twill become*
> *A kind of married Wife, People will be*
> *Content to live with it in quietness.*[19]

But Butler's indecency is crucial, for in this conflict there was no decency. The poet is concerned to show the degradation of the times, to show that there is no place for the noble here. Such set pieces of epic poetry as the description of dawn are reduced to the contemptible in *Hudibras*. Milton still retains an epic dignity:

> Now Morn her rosy steps in the eastern clime
> Advancing, sowed the earth with orient pearl . . .
>
> (v. 1–2)

Not so Butler:

> The Sun had long since in the Lap
> Of *Thetis*, taken out his *Nap*,
> And like a *Lobster* boyl'd, the *Morn*
> From *black* to *red* began to turn.
>
> (II. ii. 29–32)

The intervening deities, those stock characters in epic, provided a problem for the seventeenth-century poet. Both Milton and Butler

---

[19] Grey, *Hudibras*, i. 2 n.

reject the traditional use of them. Milton reduces and Christianizes them by making their role to some degree the allowable but limited role of the angels, guarding Eden at night, expelling Satan, and instructing Adam. Butler dismisses them even more fully from his epic. He rationalizes, trivializes, and vulgarizes divine intervention; when Hudibras is about to shoot Talgol:

> . . . *Pallas* came in shape of Rust
> And 'twixt the Spring and Hammer thrust
> Her *Gorgon*-shield, which made the Cock
> Stand stiff as if 'twere turn'd t'a stock.
>
> (I. ii. 781–4)

With the absurdity of the modern hero, Hudibras, and the reduction of the epic set-pieces to the trivial or vulgar, critical attention is readily directed towards the traditional epic heroes. Butler looks afresh at events of the past the muse has celebrated and doubts their nobility. When Orsin throws a stone at Hudibras the action seems most unheroic. But Butler draws a classical parallel. This is not, however, to ennoble Orsin but to reduce the past to the same vulgar level. The stone is 'not so huge a one / As that which *Diomed* did maul / *Æneas* on the Bum withall' (I. iii. 492–4). The Homeric heroes may have been bigger and better than the moderns and thrown larger stones; but 'maul' and 'Bum' put them in their proper context. Similarly the siege of Troy is reduced to: ' . . . when the restless *Greeks* sate down / So many years before *Troy* Town (I. ii. 424–5). The reduction of besiege to 'sat down', and the ironic juxtaposition to it of 'restless', economically make their point.

Amongst these deviations from the expected practice of epic and romance, perhaps the most remarkable feature shared by *Paradise Lost* and *Hudibras* is their lack of action. The major activity in *Paradise Lost* occurs in the war in Heaven—and that is told in retrospect, the result already determined, and told with a satirical note. At its high point the war becomes comic, absurd. The puns with which Satan introduces his cannon, set the tone:

> Vanguard, to right and left the front unfold;
> That all may see who hate us, how we seek
> Peace and composure, and with open breast
> Stand ready to receive them, if they like
> Our overture, and turn not back perverse;
> But that I doubt, however witness heaven,

Heaven witness thou anon, while we discharge
Freely our part; ye who appointed stand
Do as you have in charge, and briefly touch
What we propound, and loud that all may hear.

(vi. 558–67)

And Satan and Belial continue to pun on 'open front / And breast' (vi. 610–11) and 'terms of weight, / Of hard contents' (vi. 621–2), until the angels, prompted by rage, hurl back mountains. This 'scoffing in ambiguous words' (vi. 568) and the absurd conclusion which takes to parodic excess the traditional heroic 'vast Typhoean rage' by which the devils in hell 'rend up both rocks and hills (ii. 539–40) for diversion 'So hills amid the air encountered hills / Hurled to and fro with jaculation dire, / That under ground they fought in dismal shade' (vi. 664–6), are incidents worthy of *Hudibras*. Indeed, puns about cannon and breaches do occur in *Hudibras*: And *Cannons* shoot the higher pitches / The lower we let down their breeches . . . (II. i. 263–4).

The Angels' response to Satan's artillery with mother earth is paralleled in *Hudibras* when '*Colon* chusing out a stone, / Levell'd so right, it thumpt upon' Hudibras who was gripping his pistol (I. iii. 519 ff.). But to force particular parallels is not the point; it is the spirit behind the portrayals of military engagements which is significant. For, contrasted with the expected, traditional, epic note, there is a striking similarity of attitude to the military set-pieces.

The battle apart, there is little action in *Paradise Lost*. The story was so well known that there could be no surprise or suspense. There is little *narrative* interest. Adam and Eve can only wait, doing nothing except cultivate their garden. God's foreseeing the Fall prevents any surprise. Satan's preparation and carrying-out of his campaign is the main narrative impulse, but this is deliberately frustrated by our being shown God's prescience. When one of the characters of the poem is omniscient, the narrative can hardly provide a major impulse in the poem. When we reach the Fall the action takes only two lines.

Hudibras has even less coherent action than *Paradise Lost*. There is the first battle with the bear-baiting crowd, the second battle, the stocks; and the wooing of the Lady. The encounter with Sidrophel provides a diversion only tenuously related to the main narrative lines. But those narrative lines themselves are never fulfilled. Hudibras is diverted from his public duties to wooing the Lady, and a digression on the Interregnum disrupts for an entire canto the small amount of narrative impulse his wooing might have had. The incidents are few and the note is bathetic throughout. Hudibras does not win the Lady, he does not conquer the crowd but is put in the stocks by them, he does not kill Sidrophel. Sidrophel's excitement at the star of omen he detects epitomizes the bathetic mode of the poem's action and expectations; the star is in fact a child's kite.

Predominantly *Hudibras* is concerned with arguments, with incessant talking and quarrelling. Before the first incident Hudibras announces:

> now the Field is not far off,
> Where we must give the world a proof
> Of Deeds, not Words, and such as suit
> Another manner of Dispute.
>
> (I. i. 859–62)

But it is of the words that the reader remains most conscious:

> For *Rhetorick*, he could not ope
> His mouth, but out there flew a Trope
>
> (I. i. 81–2)

And the Lady recognizes Hudibras in the stocks; as she says,

> Not by your Individual Whiskers,
> But by your Dialect and Discourse; . . .
>
> (II. i. 155–6)

Similarly in *Paradise Lost* we remember the parliament of Hell, the debate in Heaven, the dialogue on astronomy, the argument between Adam and Eve about gardening alone, the serpent's rhetorical seduction, the long speeches of quarrel and reconciliation, the final books of instruction from Michael. Satan introduces his cannon with a punning attack of words, and Arnold Stein has noted the significance of the devils' being driven to Hell by verbal abuse 'When the fierce foe hung on our broken rear / Insulting' (ii. 78–9).[20]

Perhaps this can be related to the age. There were battles enough in the Civil War. But there were also floods of pamphlets, disputes,

---

[20] Stein, *Answerable Style*, p. 21.

controversies. After all, the winning side was Parliament—the forum for discussion, for speeches, for words. Milton's friend George Thomason collected some 20,000 publications from the years 1640-60. It is with such debates and disputes that both poems are mainly concerned. Milton's proclaimed intention to 'justify the ways of God to men' is an explicitly disputatious one, with centuries of argument behind it. And the debate in Hell has always and inevitably been seen in relationship to the political debates of the Interregnum. In *Hudibras*, indeed, that aspect bearing a particularly realistic relationship to the Interregnum is the argument between Independent and Presbyterian, the argument conducted with abstruse evidence and doubtful logic, full of shifts and dishonesties. Even in the stocks Hudibras and Ralph while away time not by planning how to escape (as Milton's devils do in Hell) but in further ideological dispute (like the philosophizing devils after the debate). Deeds give way to words in these two parliamentary epics.

We are familiar with the reaction of disillusion, with the rejection of the old ethos after the First World War, in the writing of Frederick Manning, R. C. Sherriff, Robert Graves, and in so many of the poets. It is likely that something similar happened after the Civil War. The case that Milton's disillusionment with his countrymen in the Interregnum and with the Restoration prevented his writing the planned patriotic epic has often been advanced. But the shift in *Paradise Lost* was not only away from the patriotic to the supranational but from the epic ethos to a new Christian epic, to 'patience and heroic martyrdom' (ix. 31-2), to the quietism and pacifism that many of the Puritans came to adopt.[21] He would not sing the praises of the old military heroic. Montague Bacon's 'Dissertation

---

[21] Milton's turning in *Paradise Lost* to the 'paradise within' has been often enough remarked—e.g. by E. M. W. Tillyard in *Milton* (London, 1930), pp. 292-3.

A distaste for war and military methods emerges strikingly in Milton's two sonnets to military commanders. He addresses Fairfax in 1648:

> O yet a nobler task awaits thy hand;
> For what can Warr but endless warr still breed,
> Till Truth and Right from Violence be freed;

and in 1652 he addresses Cromwell:

> yet much remaines
> To conquer still; peace hath her victories
> No less renownd than warr.   (9-11)

Upon Burlesque Poetry', included in Zachary Grey's additional *Notes to Hudibras* (1752), suggests an interesting parallelism of attitude between Milton and Butler. Discussing Butler's burlesque style he writes:

I am endeavouring to shew why He chose This Style—He who, as Mr. *Dryden* observes, was capable of Any.

I shall quote two unexceptionable Authors for this: In the first Place, *Milton*, who, in his History of the Times before the *Conquest*, says, That the Reason of his employing himself in Things so remote was, to chase out of his Thoughts the present Times, which were not worthy of his Pen: Their Actions, he says, were so *petty*, so beneath all History, that he could not bear to treat of them. Sir *William Temple* too says, That the publick Affairs before 1660 were so full of Madness, that he could not think of engaging in them.

Now, if, by the Testimony of these two Authors, which no Party will refuse upon this Occasion, the Times we are speaking of were so *petty*, so *beneath all History*, so full of Madness, were they not a fit Subject for a *Travestie*? Were they not the proper Object of Burlesque? Was it not a proper Burial for a Scene of *Pettiness*, *Putridness* Madness and Inconsistency?[22]

The times were too contemptible for heroic treatment. Butler wrote in his Note-books, 'if any man should but imitate what these Heroical Authors write in the Practice of his life and Conversation, he would become the most Ridiculous Person in the world, but this Age is far enough from that, for though none ever abounded more with those Images (as they call them) of Moral and Heroicall Virtues, there was never any so opposite to them all in the mode and Customs of Life'.[23] Milton withdrew from the present into history, and later again into *Paradise Lost*, showing a better ethic than the one man had followed.

The critique of military heroism is one of the primary moral themes of *Paradise Lost*, relevant for all times. It also had, as George Williamson has pointed out, a specific contemporary relevance; Raphael's account of the war in heaven 'becomes a lesson not only for Adam . . . but also for the British, whom Milton thought too ready to resort to force'.[24] In his account of the Long Parliament in his *History of Britain* Milton spelled out his indictment of militarism:

[22] Grey, *Notes*, pp. 4–5.
[23] *Characters and Passages from Note-books*, p. 278.
[24] George Williamson, *Milton and Others* (London, 1965), p. 21.

For Britain (to speake a truth not oft spok'n) as it is a land fruitful enough of men stout and couragious in warr, so it is naturallie not over fertil of men able to govern justlie & prudently in peace; trusting onelie on thir Mother-witt, as most doo, & consider not that civilitie, prudence, love of the public more then of money or vaine honour are to this soile in a manner out-landish . . . Valiant indeed and prosperous to winn a field, but to know the end and reason of winning, unjudicious and unwise, in good or bad success alike unteachable.[25]

And in a letter to Henry Oldenburg of 20 December 1659, Milton wrote:

I am far from compiling a history of our political troubles, which you seem to urge; for they are worthier of silence than of publication. What we need is not one who can compile a history of our troubles but one who can happily end them.[26]

Butler dealt with the times—but dealt with them in their contemptibility. He offered no better ethos, but was concerned to show the absurdity of the existing one. Butler claimed, after all, that the basic incident of *Hudibras* was true: 'As for ye Story I had it from ye Knts owne Mouth, & is farr from being feign'd, yt it is upon Record, for there was a Svite of Law upon it betweene ye Knt, & ye Fidler, in wch ye Knt was overthrowne to his great shame, & discontent, for wch he left ye Countrey & came upt to Settle at London'.[27] If the event was true, that was comment enough on the degeneration of the times: that was one reason why the traditional heroic was no longer a possible form. Heroes were never of any real ethical worth according to Butler; but by the seventeenth century even the small distinction they had was lost: 'A Hero was nothing but a fellow of a greate Stature and strong Limbes, who was able to carry a heavier Load of Armes on his Back, and strike harder Blows, then those of a lesser Size; and therefor since the Invention of Guns came up; there can bee no true Hero in great Fights, for all mens Abilitys are so leveld by Gun-shot, that a Dwarf, may do as heroique Feats of Armes that way as a Gyant, and if he be a good markesman, be too hard for the stoutest Hector and Achilles too'.[28]

---

[25] *Digression* to *The History of Britain* in CPW v/1. 451.   [26] CPW vii. 515.

[27] See Ricardo Quintana, 'The Butler-Oxenden Correspondence', *MLN* 48 (1933), 1–11, 486.

[28] Samuel Butler, *Prose Observations*, ed. Hugh de Quehen (Oxford, 1979), p. 214.

The technological developments of the modern age have rendered the epic obsolete. Butler's insight prefigures Marx's questions:

Is Achilles possible side by side with powder and lead? Or is the *Iliad* at all compatible with the printing press and steam press? Do not singing and reciting and the muses necessarily go out of existence with the appearance of the printer's bar, and do not, therefore, disappear the prerequisites of epic poetry?[29]

Judged by the old code the present times are contemptible; but the old heroic code is, judged by the realities of the recent war, contemptible too. Milton and Butler seem to have been in accord on these positions.

An essential part of Milton's critique of the traditional heroic was the provision of an alternative. Christ provides the example for Adam to follow. In the concluding Books Michael offers Adam instruction. Is *Hudibras* in contrast utterly negative? In allowing Hudibras and Ralph no redeeming features and in introducing no acceptable new heroism, is Butler offering nothing?

In the public field he certainly offers nothing. Butler's view of the public world, Interregnum or Restoration, seems to have been one of sardonic despair. Hill writes: 'Like many later clever men whose ideals had turned sour, Butler proclaimed, a little prematurely, the end of ideology for everyone else too.'[30] Yet the final impression of *Hudibras* is not one of utter nihilism. For what comes through, despite Hudibras's maraudings, is an impression of the richness of everyday, private life, the rich texture of rural life. Where else in English literature of this period do we find so full an awareness of the nature of everyday life, of the popular diversions and amusements, of the rich store of proverbial wisdom, of the traditional balladry? Sir Philip Sidney praised *Chevy Chase*: Butler parodically borrows a couplet from it and is perhaps only the second to mention that famous ballad in a literary context.[31] Grey's notes show a whole range of popular ballads and ditties and stories to which Butler alludes. He alludes also to a huge wealth of popular amusements:

---

[29] Karl Marx, *A Contribution to a Critique of Political Economy* (London, 1971), p. 216.

[30] *The Collected Essays of Christopher Hill*, vol. 1. *Writing and Revolution in Seventeenth Century England* (Brighton, 1985), p. 39.

[31] *Sidney: A Defence of Poetry*, p. 46; *Hudibras*, I. iii. 95–6.

besides bear-baiting there are mentions of mountebanks, travelling monsters at fairs, football, kite-flying, whipping-tops, puppet-plays; such games as blindman's buff and ducks-and-drakes; such customs as the skimmington. There is the traditional lore and superstition about animals — hares changing sex, crows smelling powder, foxes weighing the geese they carry; and the continual animal imagery goes to establish a full, rich, rural England, a hinterland of reference behind the Hudibrastic absurdities. There are the traditional beliefs about astrology, witchcraft, and will-o'-the-wisps; and there are the innumerable proverbs. Especially noticeable are the foods — *Hudibras* is a culinary repository of the seventeenth century, the best indication of what was eaten — porridge, plum porridge, black puddings, mince-pies, custard, toasted cheese, lobster, bacon, leeks, onions, bread and cheese, white-pot, buttermilk, curds, ale.

In *The Pleasure of the Text* Roland Barthes remarks:

In an old text I have just read (an episode of ecclesiastical life cited by Stendhal) occurs a naming of foods: milk, buttered bread, cream cheese, preserves, Maltese oranges, sugared strawberries. Is this another pleasure of pure representation (experienced therefore solely by the greedy reader)? But I have no fondness for milk or so many sweets, and I do not project much of myself into the detail of these dishes.[32]

He identifies the pleasure arising from these detailed citations of food as combining 'two realisms . . . the intelligible of the "real"' and 'the hallucinatory tail of reality':

. . . astonishment that in 1791 one could eat 'a salad of oranges and rum', as one does in restaurants today: the onset of historical intelligibility and the persistence of the thing (orange, rum) in *being there*.[33]

And he asks:

Why do some people, including myself, enjoy in certain novels, biographies, and historical works the representation of the 'daily life' of an epoch, of a character? Why this curiosity about petty details: schedules, habits, meals, lodging, clothing, etc.? Is it the hallucinatory relish of 'reality' (the very materiality of '*that once existed*')? And is it not the fantasy itself which invokes the 'detail', the tiny private scene, in which I can easily take my place? Are there, in short, 'minor hysterics' (these very readers) who receive

[32] Roland Barthes, *The Pleasure of the Text* (New York, 1975), p. 45.
[33] Ibid., p. 46.

bliss from a singular theater: not one of grandeur but one of mediocrity (might there not be dreams, fantasies of mediocrity?)[34]

It is just this 'mediocrity', refocused as a positive, that Butler celebrates. The grandiose delusions of epic and romance are rejected in favour of an 'ordinary' reality, 'everyday' reality.

It is this everyday, rural England that Butler cumulatively establishes; and much of his hostility to the Puritans comes from their attempts to suppress and reform tradition, their dictatorship of foods:

> Quarrel with *minc'd Pies*, and disparage
> Their best and dearest friend, *Plum-porredge*;
> Fat *Pig* and *Goose* it self oppose,
> And blaspheme *Custard* thro' the *nose*
>
> (I. i. 225–8)

and their dictatorship of holidays:

> And some against th' *Ægyptian Bondage*,
> Of *Holy-days* . . .
>
> (III. ii. 285–6)

He is opposed both to the silliness of proscribing certain foods and to the limiting and narrowing of the richness of the traditional life.

Butler's positive values are only implicit. But it is this rich texture of rural life he draws on for his imagery, for the establishment of his world. It is the private, non-political, domestic life. Not the self-conscious Horatian retirement of Marvell and Cowley but the non-aristocratic, rural world of the small farmer, the private world of domesticity. Just as Milton's epic rejects the heroic grandeur of Satan's Hell in favour of the domestic simplicities of Adam and Eve, so Butler rejects the heroic values. Milton establishes Adam and Eve in a bliss of simplicity; in our first encounter with them we see them pick fruit and improvise drinking vessels:

> The savoury pulp they chew, and in the rind
> Still as they thirsted scoop the brimming stream.
>
> (iv. 335–6)

The famous comment 'No fear lest dinner cool' (v. 396) is a positive note in the establishment of this domestic simplicity. And although

---

[34] Ibid., p. 53.

the Fall has changed things considerably these private, domestic values remain with Adam and Eve. Michael tells Adam he will find 'a paradise within thee, happier far' (ii. 587). Paradise is to be sought privately, individually: it is not to be imposed on others by military tyranny or any other coercion but to be sought by the individual within him- or herself.

For both Milton and Butler, happiness came to be seen as residing not in military glory, noisy public splendour: nor in literary 'retirement'; but in the everyday, the domestic. The epic had to be wrenched from its old ethos for this view to be expressed. Nor did it revive again in England. Others wrote, or began, epics—Blackmore completed some fourteen. But none ever achieved the success, none ever achieved the vast readerships, of *Paradise Lost* and *Hudibras*. The two most popular, most read, epic poems in English both rejected the old epic values.

8

Paradise Lost:
The Parliament of Hell

It was William Blake who wrote, in *The Marriage of Heaven and Hell* (1793), 'The reason Milton wrote in fetters when he wrote of Angels & God, and at liberty when of Devils & Hell, is because he was a true Poet and of the Devil's party without knowing'.[1] This has become a basic comment for those who argue not only that Satan is the 'hero' of *Paradise Lost*, but that he also represents 'liberty', freedom, and opposition to tyranny. Since Milton was a propagandist for the rebels in the English Revolution, it is often assumed that he must have some sympathy for the rebels in *Paradise Lost*. Now I want to argue that this is too simple an assumption, though at the same time not an utterly absurd one; it is a case that at least tries to make sense of what we know of Milton the man, Milton the political activist, and his poem *Paradise Lost*. Most twentieth-century critics of *Paradise Lost*, with the exception of William Empson,[2] have rejected the interpretation that Milton was in sympathy with Satan because of their shared rebelliousness; and in rejecting that, these critics have rejected any attempt to make sense of Milton's political position in relation to the poem. Yet Blake's and Shelley's comments still have a wide popular currency. Shelley's remains the most succinct statement of the Satanic case:

Milton's poem contains within itself a philosophical refutation of that system of which, by a strange and natural antithesis, it has been a chief popular support. Nothing can exceed the energy and magnificence of the character of Satan as expressed in *Paradise Lost*. It is a mistake to suppose that he could ever have been intended for the popular personification of evil. Implacable hate, patient cunning, and a sleepless refinement of device to inflict the extremest anguish on an enemy, these things are evil; and, although

[1] William Blake, *The Marriage of Heaven and Hell*, Facsimile (London, 1975), p. 6. [2] William Empson, *Milton's God* (London, 1961).

venial in a slave are not to be forgiven in a tyrant; although redeemed by much that ennobles his defeat in one subdued are marked by all that dishonours his conquest in the victor. Milton's Devil as a moral being is far superior to his God, as one who perseveres in some purpose which he has conceived to be excellent in spite of adversity and torture is to one who in the cold security of undoubted triumph inflicts the most horrible revenge upon his enemy, not from any mistaken notion of inducing him to repent of a perseverance in enmity but with the alleged design of exasperating him to deserve new torments.[3]

The issues I want to raise now are whether Milton presents Satan as the champion of liberty and freedom. Both Blake and Shelley see the conflict between God and Satan in political terms: Blake writes of 'liberty' and 'the Devil's party', Shelley of God as a 'tyrant'.[4] I want to take another look at some of the political implications and issues of the opening books of *Paradise Lost*.

But before we look at the explicitly political materials of the poem, we need to consider the way in which Satan and the devils are presented. The underlying assumption of Shelley's case is that they are presented as consistently admirable and noble. This was a common assumption in the early nineteenth century: Burns called Milton's Satan 'my favourite hero'; Hazlitt, in his *Lectures on the English Poets* (1818), wrote of 'the daring ambition and fierce passions of Satan', and stated: 'Satan is the most heroic subject that ever was chosen for a poem'. 'Some people', he wrote 'may think [Milton] has carried his liberality too far, and injured the cause he professed to espouse by making him (i.e. Satan) the chief person in his poem. Considering the nature of his subject, he would be equally in danger of running into this fault from his faith in religion and his love of rebellion; and perhaps each of these motives had its full share in determining the choice of his subject.'[5] Baudelaire wrote in his *Intimate Journals* 'the most perfect type of manly beauty is Satan — as Milton saw him'.[6]

[3] *A Defence of Poetry* (1821) in *Shelley's Prose*, ed. David Lee Clark (Albuquerque, 1966), p. 290.

[4] Jackie diSalvo, *War of Titans: Blake's Critique of Milton and the Politics of Religion* (Pittsburgh, 1984).

[5] William Hazlitt, *Lectures on the English Poets* (London, 1911), p. 63.

[6] Charles Baudelaire, *Intimate Journals*, trans. Christopher Isherwood (San Francisco, 1983), p. 34.

Yet this assumption of Satan as being a sort of ideal hero is too simple. From the beginning the presentation of Satan is one that is far from straightforward. Certainly, when we encounter him in the opening books, he has heroic features: bravery, a sort of nobility, dignity; but these qualities are always qualified by others presenting him in a different light. The presentation of Satan is consistently ambiguous—something very appropriate for the father of lies: the uncertainty about him, the ambiguity of his presentation, half noble, half debased, is in itself representative of the indirectness, the untruthfulness, of evil: you just can't be sure. Satan has to be ambiguous: he has to seem virtuous, in order to be dishonest, in order appropriately to lie; if he were straightforwardly evil, then his evil would have been shown with honesty—which would be quite inappropriate. Then he would be straightforward, and not Satan.

So we are shown a Satan who is presented both as heroic and as ignoble, by imagery that at one moment amplifies him, and at another belittles him. The first mention of him is in the invocation to Book i:

> Who first seduced them to that foul revolt?
> The infernal serpent; he it was, whose guile
> Stirred up with envy and revenge, deceived
> The mother of mankind, what time his pride
> Had cast him out from heaven, with all his host
> Of rebel angels, by whose aid aspiring
> To set himself in glory above his peers,
> He trusted to have equalled the most high,
> If he opposed; and with ambitious aim
> Against the throne and monarchy of God
> Raised impious war in heaven and battle proud
> With vain attempt.
>
> (i. 33–44)

He is initially referred to with contempt as 'the infernal serpent', his name not given because of his unworthiness; the unworthiness is insisted upon by the explicit moral condemnation—'foul', 'impious'; his attributes are all contemptible — 'guile', 'envy', 'revenge'— and he revenges himself not on God but on a woman; worse, on a mother. His degradation is emphasized by the insistence on his defeat when the paragraph continues: 'Him the almighty power / Hurled headlong flaming . . . ' (i. 45–6). It is in defeat that he is first seen, and a deserved defeat for having been so stupid as to defy the *omnipotent*. His pride, too, is seen here as a corrupt quality: he was trying to raise himself above his equals, his 'peers', by creating 'impious' war; it is not presented as the worthy pride of a heroic warrior.

The political form in which this heroic militarism finds expression is monarchism. Satan's 'aspiring' / To set himself in glory above his peers' (i. 38–9) is the aspiration to monarchy that Milton described in *The Readie and Easie Way To Establish a Free Commonwealth* (1660) at the moment the achievements of the English Revolution crumbled before the Restoration. 'A free Commonwealth', he wrote, was

not only held by wisest men in all ages the noblest, the manliest, the equallest, the justest government, the most agreeable to all due libertie and proportiond equalitie, both humane, civil and Christian, most cherishing to vertue and true religion, but also (I may say it with greatest probabilitie) planely commended or rather enjoind by our Saviour himself, to all Christians, not without remarkable disallowance and the brand of *Gentilism* upon kingship. God in much displeasure gave a king to the *Israelites*, and imputed it a sin to them that they sought one: but Christ apparently forbids his disciples to admit of any such heathenish government: *the kings of the gentiles*, saith he, *exercise lordship over them; and they that exercise autoritie upon them, are call'd benefactors. But ye shall not be so: but he that is greatest among you, let him be as the younger; and he that is chief, as he that serveth.* The occasion of these his words, was the ambitious desire of *Zebede's* two sons to be exalted above their brethren in his kingdom, which they thought was to be ere long upon earth. That he speaks of civil government, is manifest by the former part of the comparison, which inferrs the other part to be alwaies in the same kinde. And what government comes neerer to this precept of Christ, then a free Commonwealth; wherin they who are greatest, are perpetual servants and drudges to the publick at thir own cost and charges, neglect thir own affairs; yet are not elevated above thir brethren, live soberly in thir families, walk the streets as other men, may be spoken to freely, familiarly, friendly, without adoration. Whereas a king must be ador'd like a Demigod, with a dissolute and haughtie court about him, of vast expence and luxurie, masks and revels . . .[7]

Satan's 'ambitious aim' is the same as 'the ambitious desire of Zebede's two sons to be exalted above their brethren'. Book ii opens with 'High on a throne of royal state . . . Satan exalted sat' (ii. 1–5), while Satan's heroic attribute of pride is firmly identified as 'monarchal pride' (ii. 428) in the course of the parliament.

[7] *CPW* vii. 359–60.

Amidst this complex of associations, Satan's pride is one of those crucially ambiguous qualities: it is both selfish and evil, yet it is also that quality necessary for the heroic warrior, the quality that makes him brave and courageous, that leads him to victory. So even when Satan is being morally condemned, there are implications also of his dignity, courage, and nobility. In this introductory account of him, he is not left simply degraded; we are reminded of his angelic qualities, his superhuman abilities. Being chained to the lake marks his defeat, but the description allows us to see that he was once an angel; the time he spends there is given to the human reader in human terms, but the human time-unit is used to emphasize that Satan is superhuman, immortal, different from the reader:

> Nine times the space that measures day and night
> To mortal men, he with his horrid crew
> Lay vanquished . . .
>
> (i. 50–2)

His first action is described in terms that insist on his being, even if fallen, still angelic: his sight is as keen as angels' still; he is not utterly defeated and degraded: 'At once as far as angels' ken he views' (i. 59). At the end of the paragraph (i. 82) we are given his name.

Satan's size, his strength, his heroic accoutrements of spear and shield, all have their Homeric or Virgilian or Spenserian counterparts; all are used for evil purposes, for destruction, for the corruptions of militarism. Similarly, his followers have their noble associations; but the followers, like Satan, are ambivalent, and are described, too, in degrading terms. When they rise from the lake (i. 338–60) they are described contemptuously as 'a pitchy cloud of locusts', then they are somewhat ennobled and raised from being insects to being barbarians, and finally they achieve the dignity of being more noble than earthly princes; while at the same time, of course, the association of earthly princes with the followers of Satan, an association reiterated throughout the poem, makes its moral comment on historical and contemporary politics: ' . . . godlike shapes and forms / Excelling human, princely dignities, / And powers that erst in heaven sat on thrones' (i. 358–60). Their association with other heroes of epic and romance is emphasized: they could not be surpassed:

> though all the Giant brood
> Of Phlegra with the heroic race were joined
> That fought at Thebes and Ilium, on each side
> Mixed with auxiliar gods; and what resounds
> In fable or romance of Uther's son
> Begirt with British and Armoric knights;
> And all who since, baptized or infidel
> Jousted in Aspramont or Montalban,
> Damasco, or Marocco, or Trebizond
> Or whom Biserta sent from Afric shore
> When Charlemain with all his peerage fell
> By Fontarabbia.

> (i. 576–87)

Critics have argued about passages like this with their lists of names of people and places, either in terms of their beautiful sound, or their irrelevance in using words for words' sake. But this is a passage relevant to the main argument of *Paradise Lost*: it firmly associates the devils with traditional heroic figures of epic and romance, and so builds up the case against the old heroic virtues, the military heroism that Milton rejects explicitly in the invocation to Book ix. They are shown with all the glorious nationalistic and literary associations, simultaneously with being shown as destructive, as barbarous, as a plague of locusts.

In the process of presenting the ambiguity of Satan and his followers Milton uses juxtapositions and transitions reminiscent of conjurors' tricks. As well as creating a comic or satiric, certainly an undignified, effect, this establishes Satan, like Comus, in that world of conjuring and magic so forcefully rejected by the Puritans. At the end of Book i the gigantic devils approach Pandaemonium, but in order to get into it they have to reduce their size:

> Behold a wonder! They but now who seemed
> In bigness to surpass Earth's giant sons
> Now less than smallest dwarfs, in narrow room
> Throng numberless . . .

> (i. 777–80)

They are described in their reduced form by the imagery of bees — imagery that has a noble epic tradition behind it, and that also suggests organized contemporary social living. Not only were the bees a model of political life in classical literature, but they offered a living model for anyone who cared to examine them in nature. Izaak Walton recorded in *The Compleat Angler* that there were people who 'have judged it worth their time and costs to make *Glass-hives*, and order them in such a manner as to see how *Bees* have bred and made their *Honeycombs*, and how they have obeyed their King, and governed their Commonwealth'.[8]

Walton's bees were of course a covert monarchical emblem. Fowler notes: 'In the *First Defence* Milton found it necessary to rebut Salmasius' argument that the loyalty of bees to their monarchs set an example to mankind'. The iconography of Royalism could lurk provocatively in many strange places under the Commonwealth. Milton, writing under the Restoration monarchy, uses the same icon negatively—identifying monarchical government quite clearly with Satan and his followers. The republican model was the ant. Milton wrote in *The Readie and Easie Way*:

Go to the Ant, thou sluggard, saith Solomon, *consider her waies, and be wise; which having no prince, ruler, or lord, provides her meat in the summer, and gathers her food in the harvest.* Which evidently shows us, that they who think the nation undon without a king, though they swell and look haughtie, have not so much true spirit and understanding in them as a Pismire.[9]

The bees prepare us for the political debate that will follow, insisting on our seeing in Hell and the devils an image of the fallen world; but the image at the same time reduces the devils to the insect triviality of the locusts they were compared with when Satan summoned them from the lake. When the grand debate begins in Book ii in all its pomp and glory, it has to be read with this reducing image of these minute insects counterpointing it. And the hissing noise the bees make looks forward to the hissing the devils make in that episode in Book x when they are all turned to serpents. At the end of Book i the devils assembling at Pandaemonium

> Thick swarmed, both on the ground and in the air,
> Brushed with the hiss of russling wings. As bees

[8] Izaak Walton and Charles Cotton, *The Compleat Angler*, p. 150. Cf. Charles Butler, *The Feminin' Monarchi', or the Histori of Bee's* (Oxford, 1634).

[9] *CPW* vii. 362.

> In spring time . . .
>   So thick the airy crowd
>   Swarmed and were straitened . . .
>   (i. 767–77)

The 'hissing' and 'thick swarming' are picked up in Book x:

>   dreadful was the din
>   Of hissing through the hall, thick swarming now . . .
>   (x. 521–2)

Their ignoble degradation in Book x is foretold in the language describing them at the end of Book i. Their vulnerability is expressed by the mention of the 'straw-built citadel' in which the bees they are compared to live; the devils, too, live in a fragile straw-built citadel. Such are all political structures to the committed revolutionary. Here the devils have become for their own convenience and by their own choice like hissing insects. God will make them hissing serpents literally in Book x, and with no choice or planned convenience on their part. At the state welcome for Satan's return from Earth, they are all suddenly turned by God into serpents. And this degradation is looked forward to in their transformation scene at the end of Book i. From the earliest, then, their grandeur and dignity are qualified.

They are qualified also by the sorts of images Milton uses to describe them. Reduced in size they now seem 'less than smallest dwarfs',

>   or faerie elves
>   Whose midnight revels, by a forest side
>   Or fountain some belated peasant sees,
>   Or dreams he sees . . .
>   (i. 781–4)

We are in the world of the *Maske*, with Comus's paganism and all that complex of associations. It is all thoroughly ambiguous, as always with the Satanic; it is unclear whether the belated peasant 'sees, / Or dreams he sees,' whether they are really there or not; as 'they on their mirth and dance / Intent, with jocund music charm his ear' (i. 786–7).

Charm carries the ambiguities further; is this an aesthetic response or the effect of magic? The fairies and elves are here like the pagan gods with which the devils elsewhere are identified as examples of delusion, false beliefs, and superstitions that lead man astray. And that idea looks forward to the image of the serpent as a will-o'-the-wisp when Satan is seducing Eve (ix. 633 ff.). Here too there is a night-wanderer, the 'belated peasant'.

But apart from this appropriateness, the image is again reducing the devils to ignobility, folklore, superstition—as well as reducing them physically. It is with the complexities of this group of images in mind that we must read the debate in Book ii. The glory of the debate of 'a thousand demi-gods on golden seats' (i. 796) has been thoroughly qualified.

The debate in Hell has continually been interpreted in political terms, and it seems unlikely that contemporary readers of *Paradise Lost* would not have looked for parallels with recent historical events. Later interpreters have frequently done so. Walter Bagehot in 1864 wrote:

Milton, though always a scholar by trade, though solitary in old age, was through life intent on great affairs, lived close to great scenes, watched a revolution, and if not an actor in it, was at least secretary to the actors. He was familiar—by daily experience and habitual sympathy—with the earnest debate of arduous questions, on which the life and death of the speakers certainly depended, on which the weal or woe of the country perhaps depended. He knew how profoundly the individual character of the speakers—their inner and real nature—modifies their opinion on such questions; he knew how surely that nature will appear in the expression of them. This great experience, fashioned by a fine imagination, gives to the debate of the Satanic Council in Pandemonium its reality and its life. It is a debate in the Long Parliament, and though the *theme* of *Paradise Lost* obliged Milton to side with the monarchical element in the universe, his old habits are often too much for him; and his real sympathy—the impetus and energy of his nature—side with the rebellious element.[10]

This is a very appealing interpretation. It is certainly an attempt to make sense of Milton's known political engagement, in the poem. But to accept Bagehot's account, the overall structure of the poem has to be shown as flawed; for in the context of *Paradise Lost*, it was Milton's intention to 'justify the ways of God to men', (i. 26) and to show the evil of Satan. If Satan represents both abhorred evil and the Cromwell Milton chose to work for, there is a disabling ambivalence in the poem.

[10] Walter Bagehot, *Literary Studies* (London, 1911), ii. 321.

Certainly the debate in Pandaemonium has reality and life. But is its conduct at all admirable? When we examine the parliament carefully, certain striking contradictions emerge. They cast doubt on the admirability of the whole enterprise; they also point to contradictions in our own parliamentary systems. In his early tracts, Milton extolled the idea of parliamentary government, of representative rule as against the autocratic or tyrannic rule of bishop and king:

There is no Civill *Goverment* that hath beene known . . . more divinely and harmoniously tun'd, more equally ballanc'd as it were by the hand and scale of Justice, then is the Common-wealth of *England*: where under a free, and untutor'd *Monarch*, the noblest, worthiest and most prudent men, with full approbation, and suffrage of the People have in their power the supreame, and finall determination of highest Affaires.[11]

Similarly he could describe parliament as 'so much united excellence . . . in one globe of brightnesse and efficacy, . . . encountring the dazzl'd resistance of tyranny'.[12] But the parliament of Hell is something different. It consists not of 'united excellence' but of united evil, gathered not into 'one globe of brightnesse' but into the darkness of Hell. It might be replied that this is to assume things not yet demonstrated in the poem: perhaps after all the devils are excellent, and God is the evil one. In the world of the poem this of course emerges as far from the case. From the beginning the corruption of this parliament is apparent; for it is not a parliament that has the 'final determination of highest affairs', or that confronts and challenges tyranny.

The essence of the parliament is that in any representative way it is unworkable. It is neither fully representative, nor efficient. The devils all swarm to the newly built Pandaemonium and, in order to be accommodated, reduce their size to 'less than smallest dwarfs'; it is a reduction that, for the reader, lessens their dignity too. But it still does not allow total representation, mass democracy, open decision-making. They stand around the hall of Pandaemonium:

> But far within
> And in their own dimensions like themselves
> The great seraphic lords and cherubim

[11] *Of Reformation* (1641), CPW i. 599.
[12] *An Apology Against a Pamphlet Call'd A Modest Confutation of the Animadversions upon the Remonstrant against Smectymnuus*, (1642), CPW i. 924.

> In close recess and secret conclave sat
> A thousand demi-gods on golden seats,
> Frequent and full.
>
> (i. 792–7)

This is not an egalitarian society. The majority are excluded and reduced; the loss of size enacts their loss of political force and voice. The ruling class remain their own size and confer in conditions of ostentatious display of wealth—'golden seats'. But this inner decision-making body of the élite has its own inadequacies. As Merritt Hughes wrote: 'The mere numbers of Satan's inner council of a "thousand Demi-Gods on golden seats" (i. 796) would have seemed to Milton to be a travesty of a responsible governing body',[13] and he quotes Milton's comment on the proposal in 1659 for a 'popular assembly upward of a thousand' people in number that the members would be

unweildie with thir own bulk, unable in so great a number to mature thir consultations as they ought, if any be allotted them, and that they meet not from so many parts remote to sit a whole year lieger in one place, only now and then to hold up a forrest of fingers, or to convey each man his bean or ballot into the box, without reason shew or common deliberation . . .[14]

In Hell, this is exactly what happens. There is a show of representation—but, in fact, only Satan, Moloch, Belial, Mammon, and Beelzebub speak. Since Satan is styled the monarch here—his throne is of 'royal state' (ii. 1) and his pride is 'monarchal' (ii. 428)— that means that, of the non-regal speakers in this parliament of a thousand, only four offer opinions. The Levellers had been aware of the dangers of too large a parliamentary membership. In *Foundations of Freedom*, the second *Agreement of the People* (1648), they had specified 'That the Representative of the whole Nation, shall consist of three hundred persons',[15] and in the third, *An Agreement of the Free People of England* (1649), they proposed 'a Representative of the people consisting of four hundred persons, but no more'.[16]

---

[13] Merritt Y. Hughes, 'Satan and the "Myth" of the Tyrant', in *Ten Perspectives on Milton* (New Haven, 1965), p. 187.
[14] *The Readie & Easie Way to Establish a Free Commonwealth*, 2nd edn. (1660), *CPW* vii. 441.
[15] Don M. Wolfe, ed., *Leveller Manifestoes of the Puritan Revolution*, p. 295.
[16] Ibid., p. 402.

The contradictions between the appearance of representation, and the realities are huge. But there are greater ones: for the whole debate has anyway been rigged beforehand. Moloch, Belial, and Mammon are allowed to speak, and then Beelzebub offers his plan, which had, however, been devised beforehand by the monarch, Satan:

> Thus Beelzebub
> Pleaded his devilish counsel, first devised
> By Satan, and in part proposed . . .
>
> (ii. 378–80)

The debate, therefore, has been mere window-dressing. Satan and Beelzebub had decided what to do beforehand; they go through the appearance of discussion, but there is no debate, no discussion. The speeches are all separate blocks of rhetoric—classic political speech-making—but there is no discussion, nothing emerges, nothing is evolved; the consultations are never matured. Quite the opposite is the discussion in Heaven between God and Christ (in Book iii), where God raises a possible way of dealing with man's sin, and Christ suggests an alternative, a modification. In Heaven there is an evolving dialectic. In Hell any chance of that is prevented—by the decision previously made by Satan and by the refusal to allow discussion. As soon as Satan has got what he wants—the assent of his assembly that he should go on a mission to the World—he swiftly puts an end to the debate, to stop any further discussion or any new ideas from developing:

> Thus saying rose
> The monarch, and prevented all reply,
> Prudent, lest from his resolution raised
> Others among the chief might offer now
> (Certain to be refused) what erst they feared;
> And so refused might in opinion stand
> His rivals, winning cheap the high repute
> Which he through hazard huge must earn. But they
> Dreaded not more the adventure than his voice
> Forbidding . . .
>
> (ii. 466–75)

The autocratic, tyrannical nature of Satan is firmly delineated here. This is the model for how parliamentary assemblies should not be. When it ends

> Towards him they bend
> With awful reverence prone; and as a god
> Extol him equal to the highest in heaven . . .
>
>   (ii. 477–9)

It is a mark of their degradation. As Milton wrote in *The Readie and Easie Way to Establish a Free Commonwealth*:

Certainly then that people must needs be madd or strangely infatuated, that build the chief hope of thir common happiness or safetie on a single person; who if he happen to be good, can do no more than another man, if to be bad, hath in his hands to do more evil without check, then millions of other men. The happiness of a nation must needs be firmest and certainest in a full and free Councel of their own electing, where no single person, but reason only swayes. And what madness is it, for them who might manage nobly their own affairs themselves, sluggishly and weakly to devolve all on a single person; and more like boyes under age then men, to committ all to his patronage and disposal, who neither can perform what he undertakes, and yet for undertaking it, though royally paid, will not be thir servant, but thir lord?[17]

And he goes on to make it quite clear that a parliament under monarchy is an illusory parliament:

And doubtless, no Parlament will be ever able under royaltie to free the people from slavery: and when they go about it, will finde it a laborious task; and when they have don all, they can, be forc'd to leave the contest endless between prerogative and petition of right, till only dooms-day end it . . .[18]

The reason is enacted in the parliament of Hell. Under a monarchy it is always the case that parliament

shall be call'd, by the kings good will and utmost endeavour, as seldome as may be; and then for his own ends: for it will soon return to that, let no man hope otherwise, whatever law or provision be made to the contrarie. For it is only the kings right, he will say, to call a Parlament; and this he will do most commonly about his own affairs rather then the kingdom's, as will appear planely so soon as they are call'd.[19]

If there is major disagreement, 'the Parlament shall be soon dissolvd'.[20] So it is when Satan dissolves his parliament, in order to prevent competition to himself, he is emphatically described as 'the monarch' (ii. 467). The whole parliament has been called to ratify Satan's

---

[17] *CPW* vii. 361–2.   [18] Ibid., p. 366.
[19] Ibid., p. 375.   [20] Ibid., p. 376.

decision about his own business, his individualist revenge. It is
summarily dissolved when Satan has achieved what he wants. As
Milton noted, the word 'parlament' was 'signifying but the *parlie*
of our Commons with thir *Norman* king when he pleasd to call
them . . . '[21]

The Levellers' third *Agreement* made another provision for a
proper parliamentary government. Parliament, it declared,

shall continue their Session day by day without intermission for four
monthes at the least; and after that shall be at Liberty to adjourn from
two monthes to two monthes, as they shall see cause untill their yeer be
expired . . .[22]

Satan's parliament is indeed a short parliament; it lasts not for four
months at the least, but for four speakers, before Satan concludes
the proceedings. The whole debate is disposed of in a day and
nothing else is discussed. The absence of any other business or
issues is an unstressed absence, but it is important. Satan summons
parliament for the single purpose of endorsement of his foreign
campaign, not for any domestic issues within Hell. Charles I, having
ruled without Parliament for twelve years, was forced to summon
it as a result of his military campaign against the Scots in which he
had been defeated—just as Satan had been defeated in his military
campaign against God in Heaven: 'Thus they their doubtful consultations dark / Ended rejoicing in their matchless chief . . . '(ii. 486–7).
The consultations are dark because they take place in Hell, which
is without light and which is appropriately dark for its moral
benightedness; but the darkness refers also to the secrecy, the closed
conclave they met in. When God the Father discussed the fate of man
with Christ, there is no formal assembly, no pompous Pandaemonium
with its golden seats; he simply speaks to Christ, and 'Thus while
God spake, ambrosial fragrance filled / All heaven, and the blessed
spirits elect / Sense of new joy ineffable diffused . . . ' (iii. 135–7),
and it slowly emerges that this is a debate open to all Heaven. It is
not held formally, not held secretly. When God asks who will die on
behalf of man, every member of heaven hears: 'He asked, but all the
heavenly choir stood mute, / And silence was in heaven . . . ' (iii.
217–18): and when the debate is concluded:

[21] Ibid., p. 373.   [22] *Leveller Manifestoes*, p. 404.

> No sooner had the almighty ceased, but all
> The multitude of angels with a shout
> Loud as from numbers without number, sweet
> As from blest voices, uttering joy, heaven rung
> With jubilee, and loud hosannas filled
> The eternal regions . . .
>
> (iii. 344–9)

I do not wish to imply that Heaven is a democracy; in Milton's system it is quite clearly a monarchy; but for him it was the only monarchy justified. In contrast, Satan's system is like earthly monarchies—indefensible, because the ruler is not omnipotent—and Satan refuses to allow proper parliamentary government. Satan's system requires secrecy, autocratically reached decisions, and fear: its consultative structures are mere false show. The power of the debate, of course, lies in Milton's creation of the archetypal political figures, and of the archetypal political rhetoric. The archetypal quality is demonstrable in the responses of later critics: in the way different generations of critics interpret the characters and attitudes of the main speakers in accord with their own times. Bagehot again is a typical example. He writes:

Satan who presides over and manipulates the assembly—Moloch . . . who wants to fight again; Belial, 'the man of the world', who does not want to fight any more; Mammon, who is for commencing an industrial career; Beelzebub, the official statesman . . . who, at Satan's insistence, proposes the invasion of the earth—are as distinct as so many statues.[23]

The debate in Hell is one of the great set pieces of *Paradise Lost*. It is also fully functional. It sets the fall of man in a cosmic framework, makes it an event in the struggle between good and evil; and it shows the planning of evil from which God will produce further good. All this is shown, by the dramatization of the debate, in action. Evil is not merely described, but we hear the voices of evil, and see its proponents hatching it.

The heroic grandeur of the fallen angels is presented in the heroic grandeur of the verse, in the ideal political rhetoric. Mammon's classic statement for splendid isolation is a piece of brilliant political persuasion:

[23] Bagehot, *Literary Studies*, ii. 322.

> Let us not then pursue
> By force impossible, by leave obtained
> Unacceptable, though in heaven, our state
> Of splendid vassalage, but rather seek
> Our own good from ourselves, and from our own
> Live to ourselves, though in this vast recess,
> Free, and to none accountable, preferring
> Hard liberty before the easy yoke
> Of servile pomp.
>
> (ii. 249–57)

Cunningly, he emphasizes the 'impossible', the 'unacceptable'—the verse resting on these words to insist that the devils cannot return to Heaven; and the idea of their being in Heaven is dismissed in a throw-away parenthesis—'though in Heav'n'. He appeals to their egotism, as a politician appeals to a political nationalism—'*Our own* good from *our selves*, and from *our own*'. '*Our*' and '*own*' fill the whole line—placed in its beginning, middle, and end; it is an appeal to 'us'—national pride, national egotism; so that 'hard liberty' becomes not, as it might have been put, something unpleasant, but something worth striving for. Because it is 'hard', therefore it is good.

The sonorous speeches are carefully contrived. Their glorious sound is not there at the expense of any subtlety in the verse. The picture of the elder statesman Beelzebub is magnificently drawn:

> with grave
> Aspect he rose, and in his rising seemed
> A pillar of state; deep on his front engraven
> Deliberation sat and public care;
> And princely counsel in his face yet shone,
> Majestic though in ruin: sage he stood
> With Atlantean shoulders fit to bear
> The weight of mightiest monarchies . . .
>
> (ii. 300–7)

His fading glory is carefully evoked, supporting the picture of both fallen angel and ageing politician. Milton has conveyed his dignity and his impressive size simultaneously by the almost subliminal image of stone, of a state building, a carved façade, a monument. The impression is prepared for by 'pillar of state' which is used figuratively for his political status, but suggests, too, a column supporting a state building or parliament-house; and the image is reinforced by a pun on 'grave', with a suggestion of engraved, implying again stone-work, and with the architectural meaning of 'aspect'. Similarly 'ruin' hints at a ruined building as well as at his fading, battle-scarred appearance and—as always in Milton's use of the word in *Paradise Lost*—the Latin base-meaning of 'fall'. The whole picture is successful because of the way in which Milton has only sketched in, only lightly touched, these suggestions of a building. He excelled at the implicit image as well as at the more usual simile. And we might note the emphatic republican reminder that this devilish politician is the support of 'mightiest monarchies'.

The way in which Milton captures the notes of ideal parliamentary rhetoric, the way in which he neatly catches the various types of political character, has made the debate-scene justly admired. The political manipulations and corruptions of Satan and his followers are firmly established. Yet this negative analysis does not result in a negative analytical presentation; it is allied to a magnificent creativity of depiction, to a poetry justly admired for its positive richness and resonance. But the admiration has not always accompanied full understanding. Hazlitt, for instance, wrote:

The whole of the speeches and debates in Pandemonium are well worthy of the place and the occasion—with Gods for speakers, and angels and archangels for hearers. There is a decidedly manly tone in the arguments and sentiments, an eloquent dogmatism, as if each person spoke from thorough conviction; an excellence which Milton probably borrowed from his spirit of partisanship, or else his spirit of partisanship from the natural firmness and vigour of his mind.[24]

But this admirability has to be set in the context of the rigged debate, and in the context of the ideas advocated. The subject under discussion, the proposals made have to be taken account of when we admire the splendid rhetoric: the proposals to wage further war, to develop a materialistic technological society, to withdraw into 'ignoble ease and peaceful sloth', and finally to invade and destroy Paradise. The content of the debate is too easily forgotten in admiring the rhetoric: and Milton's point is that this fine achievement of humanity, elegant and persuasive speech-making, can so readily be used for corrupt purposes. That is why in Book ix when Satan is persuading Eve to eat the apple, he is compared with 'some orator

---

[24] Hazlitt, *Lectures*, p. 66.

renowned / In Athens or free Rome, where eloquence / Flourished, since mute' (ix 670-2). The qualities of eloquence and rhetoric used to establish 'free Rome' can all too readily be used against freedom, to destroy Adam and Eve and bind them to evil. Everything associated with Satan and his followers has this ambiguity—the rhetoric may be noble, yet it is used for evil: the Romantic critics admired Satan by recognizing only the ennobling qualities he had— and by ignoring the inseparable evil, ignobility, and corruption. The parliament in Hell has all the appearance of nobility and dignity in its fine rhetoric, its gilded seats: but it too, when we look at it carefully, is as ambiguous as everything else, and when we examine it, the glory gives way to its rather more dubious qualities. Satan praises classical rhetoric in his temptation of Christ in *Paradise Regained*:

> Thence to the famous orators repair,
> Those ancient, whose resistless eloquence
> Wielded at will that fierce democraty,
> Shook the Arsenal and fulmined over Greece,
> To Macedon, and Artaxerxes' throne . . .
>
> (iv. 267-71)

But Christ dismisses it:

> Their orators thou then extoll'st, as those
> The top of eloquence, statists indeed,
> And lovers of their country, as may seem;
> But herein to our prophets far beneath,
> As men divinely taught, and better teaching
> The solid rules of civil government
> In their majestic unaffected style
> Than all the oratory of Greece and Rome,
> In them is plainest taught, and easiest learnt,
> What makes a nation happy, and keeps it so,
> What ruins kingdoms, and lays cities flat;
> These only with our Law best form a king.
>
> (iv. 353-64)

It is important when reading Satan's speeches to remember his rhetorical skills, to think of him as a politician. He is not naïvely to be taken at his face-value; he is as much concealing as expressing his true thoughts and true character. In his public speeches he is putting up a public political front. Much of the attack on Milton's 'grand style' came from a perverse failure to recognize this. T. S. Eliot in his first essay on Milton criticized Satan's speech to the angels in Heaven:

Thus it is not so unfair, as it might at first appear, to say that Milton writes English like a dead language. The criticism has been made with regard to his involved syntax. But a tortuous style, when its peculiarity is aimed at precision (as with Henry James), is not necessarily a dead one; only when the complication is dictated by a demand of verbal music, instead of by any demand of sense.

> Thrones, dominations, princedoms, virtues, powers,
> If these magnific titles yet remain
> Not merely titular, since by decree
> Another now hath to himself engrossed
> All power, and us eclipsed under the name
> Of King anointed, for whom all this haste
> Of midnight march, and hurried meeting here,
> This only to consult how we may best
> With what may be devised of honours new
> Receive him coming to receive from us
> Knee-tribute yet unpaid, prostration vile,
> Too much to one, but double how endured,
> To one and to his image now proclaimed?
>
> (v. 772 ff.)

The complication of a Miltonic sentence is an active complication, a complication deliberately introduced into what was a previously simplified and abstract thought. The dark angel here is not *thinking* or conversing, but making a speech carefully prepared for him; and the arrangement is for the sake of musical value, not for significance. A straightforward utterance, as of a Homeric or Dantesque character, would make the speaker very much more real to us; but reality is no part of the intention. We have in fact to read such a passage not analytically, to get the poetic impression. I am not suggesting that Milton has no idea to convey, which he regards as important: only that the syntax is determined by the musical significance, by the auditory imagination, rather than by the attempt to follow actual speech or thought. It is at least more nearly possible to distinguish the pleasure which arises from the *noise*, from the pleasure due to other elements, than with the verse of Shakespeare, in which the auditory imagination and the imagination of the other senses are more nearly fused, and fused together with the thought. The result with Milton is, in one sense of the word, *rhetoric*.[25]

But of course Satan was making a speech; he was certainly neither thinking nor conversing, nor attempting to speak in a way allowing

[25] T. S. Eliot, *On Poetry and Poets* (London, 1957), p. 142.

his own thoughts to be followed. Satan was addressing the angels at a crucial political moment, inciting them to rebellion. His own thoughts, his own motives, anything personal, had to be subordinated and hidden; the intention is political manipulation, and the means used are rhetorical. To criticize rhetoric for being rhetoric seems misguided. Milton presents Satan exploiting the musical qualities of language to lull his followers into deception. It is a fine capturing of the politician's voice. Verbal trickery, rhetoric, aesthetic manipulation are a constant feature of Satan's political method. A. J. A. Waldock fittingly characterized Satan's display of oratory to Eve (ix. 700) as 'a feat not so much of logic as of legerdemain. It is crammed with specious argument, with sequences that look like syllogisms but stop before they have arrived, with stretches of reasoning that sound as if they are reaching a conclusion but do not quite reach it'.[26] And it is a basic critical method to separate the writer from the presented character. Satan's linguistic emptiness is not Milton's. Milton is presenting Satan for our assessment. When Eliot writes 'we have in fact to read such a passage not analytically, to get the poetic impression' he is falling into a Satanic trap; it is only by reading the passage analytically, placing it in its context, that we can see Satan's musical, rhetorical skills; and at the same time evaluate these skills and see their manipulative, deceitful nature. Milton brilliantly creates a rhetorical orotundity that is both impressive and yet also specious, deceptive, 'rhetorical' in the pejorative sense.

It is important to see Satan's part in the parliamentary debate in Hell clearly. He is not participating in free discussion: rather he is manipulating the whole parliamentary show. He is acting in all essentials as a monarch, as a tyrant. With his henchman, Beelzebub, he is running the society of Hell not by the principles of parliamentary liberty, but by means of a tyrannical power-group. And it is important not to be led from a dislike of Milton's God into assuming that his adversary Satan must automatically be good. Satan is undeniably tyrannical and dictatorial.

Critic after critic has remarked on the similarity of Satan's assembly of his troops to a fascist rally — Wilson Knight, Bush, Broadbent, Ricks:[27]

---

[26] A. J. A. Waldock, *Paradise Lost and Its Critics* (London, 1961), p. 36.

[27] See Douglas Bush, *Paradise Lost in Our Times* (Ithaca, 1945); G. Wilson Knight, *Chariot of Wrath* (London, 1942); Hughes, 'Satan and the "Myth"',

>   . . . and now
> Advanced in view, they stand, a horrid front
> Of dreadful length and dazzling arms, in guise
> Of warriors old with ordered spear and shield,
> Awaiting what command their mighty chief
> Had to impose; he through the armed files
> Darts his experienced eye, and soon traverse
> The whole battalion views, their order due,
> Their visages and stature as of gods,
> Their number last he sums. And now his heart
> Distends with pride, and hardening in his strength
> Glories . . .

>   (i. 562–73)

Earlier critics found different identifications—Coleridge saw in Satan a type of Napoleon. To make such specific identifications, tells us about the critics' political loyalties and hostilities; but the point to be made about Milton's Satan is that he is an archetypal tyrant, an autocratic, military monarch. To relate this archetype to the particular performers on the contemporary political stage is something Milton would have thought quite proper—Satan is the initiator of all evil: it was through Satan's destruction of Paradise that political organization became necessary—and became also inevitably corrupt. The primal evil of Satan finds its expression in part through later tyrants. However, to limit Satan to being the equivalent of a Napoleon or Hitler would obviously be too narrow an interpretation, and lest we forget it, unhistorical as well.

John Toland recognized the centrality of the political theme of *Paradise Lost* in his *Life of John Milton* (1698):

An Epic Poem is not a bare History delightfully related in harmonious Numbers, and artfully dispos'd; but it always contains, besides a general representation of Passions and Affection, Virtues and Vices, some peculiar Allegory or Moral . . . Nor was *Milton* behind any body in the choice or dignity of his Instruction; for to display the different Effects of Liberty and Tyranny, is the chief design of his *Paradise Lost*.[28]

Toland quotes the visionary conclusion to Milton's *Of Reformation* (1641) looking forward to Christ's 'shortly expected' Second Coming when he will 'put an end to all earthly *Tyrannies*, proclaiming thy

pp. 165–9; C. Ricks, ed., *Paradise Lost and Paradise Regained* (New York, 1968), p. xvii.   [28] Toland in Helen Darbishire, ed., *Early Lives of Milton*, p. 182.

universal and mild Monarchy thro Heaven and Earth'.[29] And Milton defines 'tyrant' in his *Tenure of Kings and Magistrates* (1649):

A Tyrant whether by wrong or by right comming to the Crown, is he who regarding neither Law nor the common good, reigns onely for himself and his faction.[30]

Presenting Satan as a tyrant allows Milton some important redefinitions. Frederic Jameson writes:

Milton's party need feel no guilt about the revolt against the king for a simple reason, that he is not really a king at all, but something quite different, namely a tyrant: and the latter is defined as himself being a rebel against God's law. Thus, not the regicides, but the king himself is the rebel, occupies the place of Satan: the thrust of the accusation is structurally reversed — I banish you! you are the only guilty party here.[31]

The opprobrium attached to 'rebels', 'revolutionaries', 'radicals' on earth is a projection by the tyrant and his party of the moral opprobrium that is properly and justly theirs. The Good Old Cause was not a rebellion but an attempt at restoring a just, divine condition, a true Restoration. Only five lines into the epic we read ' . . . till one greater man / Restore us, and regain the blissful seat' (i. 5–6). 'Restore', the vocabulary of the Stuart return of 1660, is a profoundly shocking and unexpected word to find from a revolutionary regicide. It has to be faltered over, our political attention engaged. Emphatically placed at the poem's opening invocation, it is a provocative reappropriation of true vocabulary. The 'blissful seat' to be restored to is the extreme opposite of that Satanic, Stuart 'restoration' of 1660.

One particular expression of Satan's tyranny in *Paradise Lost* is achieved through a succession of images relating him to Eastern tyrants. In *Eikonoklastes* Milton compared Charles I with the proverbial Turkish tyrant,[32] and it is by images from that area of association that Satan is presented. He is called the devil's 'great Sultan' (i. 348) and the description of his throne at the opening of

[29] Ibid., p. 183: *CPW* i. 616.

[30] *The Tenure of Kings and Magistrates*, *CPW* iii. 212.

[31] Frederic Jameson, 'Religion and Ideology' in Francis Barker et al. eds., *1642: Literature and Power in the Seventeenth Century* (Colchester, 1981), p. 329.

[32] Hughes, 'Satan and the "Myth"', p. 171.

Book ii firmly places him in the barbaric East, firmly monarchical and cruel:

> High on a throne of royal state, which far
> Outshone the wealth of Ormus and of Ind,
> Or where the gorgeous East with richest hand
> Showers on her kings barbaric pearl and gold,
> Satan exalted sat . . .
>
> (ii. 1–5)

When in Book iv he first sees Adam and Eve, he is presented clearly as the tyrannical monarch. His soliloquy is phrased in political terms:

> league with you I seek,
> And mutual amity so strait, so close,
> That I with you must dwell, or you with me
> Henceforth . . .
>
> (iv. 375–8)

He continues:

> hell shall unfold,
> To entertain you two, her widest gates,
> And send forth all her kings . . .
>
> (iv. 381–3)

The political organization of hell with its kings, and the political thinking of Satan with the 'league' he requires, lead on to his political justification for his action:

> And should I at your harmless innocence
> Melt, as I do, yet public reason just,
> Honour and empire with revenge enlarged,
> By conquering this new world, compels me now
> To do what else though damned I should abhor.
> So spake the fiend, and with necessity,
> The tyrant's plea, excused his devilish deeds.
>
> (iv. 388–94)

It is a crucial passage—Satan's first sight of Adam and Eve; and the first point in the poem at which Satan is explicitly called tyrannical. Hitherto we have been left to draw our own conclusions; but at this point his nature has become clear, at this point he can firmly be labelled. Alastair Fowler observes how appropriate Milton's presentation of Satan was to the contemporary restoration political situation: 'Satan is here cast in the role of a contemporary Machiavellian politician, excusing the evil means he resorts to by appeals to such values as "the common weal", "the good of the state", "policy" and *necessity*.[33] But this is not the comment exclusively or merely of a seventeenth-century Machiavellian; it is not limiting. Satan is presented as like political rulers from the classical past through the seventeenth century and to the present day. 'Public reason', 'honour and empire', and 'necessity' are the phrases used to justify evil. Whenever Milton writes of 'necessity', 'public reason', 'public good', or suchlike phrases, it is with the resonance of political manipulation and tyrannical corruption. So Dalila is persuaded by 'the magistrates / And princes of my country' (850–1) to betray Samson in *Samson Agonistes*:

> at length that grounded maxim
> So rife and celebrated in the mouths
> Of wisest men; that to the public good
> Private respects must yield; with grave authority
> Took full possession of me and prevailed;
> Virtue, as I thought, truth, duty so enjoining.
>
> (865–70)

Satan's attack on Adam and Eve, then, has its political dimension. Planned politically, by that parliamentary assembly, it is continued in this way by Satan's political language. What we are to note is the huge discrepancy between the political planning, organization, and theory of Satan's attack, and the political innocence of Adam and Eve. Adam and Eve are simply two people, the only two people, living in domestic harmony. With only two of them, no political organization is needed. There is no coercion or oppression. They exist in a state of simplicity and innocence, and this is intruded upon by a political force. The couplet: 'When Adam delved and Eve span / Who was then the gentleman?' dates from the Peasants' Revolt of 1381. It is the text behind Milton's great epic. Adam has the 'complete perfections' of natural man, the true dignity all mankind is born with, 'More solemn than the tedious pomp that waits / On Princes' (v. 354–5). C. S. Lewis repeated Walter Raleigh's remark that Adam 'goes to meet the archangel not so much like a host as like an ambassador' and goes on to refer to his 'kingly manner' and the

---

[33] John Carey and Alastair Fowler, *The Poems of John Milton* (London, 1968), p. 636 n.

'ceremonial' of his life with Eve.[34] But this is surely to misinterpret. All that ambassadorial, monarchical, political pomp and delusion is explicitly, emphatically, and unambiguously rejected by Milton in the account of Adam meeting Raphael:

> Mean while our primitive great sire, to meet
> His godlike guest, walks forth, without more train
> Accompanied than with his own complete
> Perfections, in himself was all his state,
> More solemn than the tedious pomp that waits
> On princes, when their rich retinue long
> Of horses led, and grooms besmeared with gold
> Dazzles the crowd, and sets them all agape.
>
> (v. 350–7)

When both have eaten the apple, their plight is described in political terms. As a result of the fall they have become political beings. Political—Satanic—language enters:

> They sat them down to weep, nor only tears
> Rained at their eyes, but high winds worse within
> Began to rise, high passions, anger, hate,
> Mistrust, suspicion, discord, and shook sore
> Their inward state of mind, calm region once
> And full of peace, now tossed and turbulent:
> For understanding ruled not, and the will
> Heard not her lore, both in subjection now
> To sensual appetite, who from beneath
> Usurping over sovereign reason claimed
> Superior sway . . .
>
> (ix. 1121–31)

The political metaphor is sustained. 'Their inward *state* of mind' by a significant ambiguity becomes not just an inward condition but a political state which has been subject to disruption. 'Understanding ruled not'; understanding and will are 'both in subjection now'; 'sensual appetite' has *usurped* 'over sovereign reason' and 'claimed / Superior sway'. The political results of the Fall are demonstrated here in the language. As Michael later says to Adam:

---

[34] C. S. Lewis, *A Preface to Paradise Lost* (London, 1960), p. 119.

> Since thy original lapse, true liberty
> Is lost, which always with right reason dwells
> Twinned, and from her hath no divided being:
> Reason in man obscured, or not obeyed,
> Immediately inordinate desires
> And upstart passions catch the government
> From reason, and to servitude reduce
> Man till then free. Therefore since he permits
> Within himself unworthy powers to reign
> Over free reason, God in judgment just
> Subjects him from without to violent lords;
> Who oft as undeservedly enthral
> His outward freedom; tyranny must be
> Though to the tyrant thereby no excuse.
>
> (xii. 83–96)

Tyranny is a consequence of Satan's successful temptation of Adam and Eve. Part of the knowledge achieved by eating the fruit of the tree, then, is a political knowledge. But there would have been no need for the knowledge had there been no Fall. In *The Tenure of Kings and Magistrates*, Milton offered an explanation for the growth of states and authorities:

No man who knows ought, can be so stupid to deny that all men naturally were born free, being the image and resemblance of God himself, and were by privilege above all the creatures, born to command and not to obey: and that they liv'd so. Till from the root of *Adam's* transgression, falling among themselves to doe wrong and violence, and foreseeing that such courses must needs tend to the destruction of them all, they agreed by common league to bind each other from mutual injury, and joyntly to defend themselves against any that gave disturbance or opposition to such agreement. Hence came Citties, Townes and Common-wealths. And because no faith in all was found sufficiently binding, they saw it needfull to ordaine som authoritie, that might restraine by force and punishment what was violated against peace and common right . . .[35]

It is as a direct consequence of the Fall that political, legal, and other authority systems were established. Hell, occupied by the fallen angels, had already established such structures: 'for orders and degrees / Jar not with liberty, but well consist' (v. 792–3), Satan declares.

[35] *CPW* iii. 198–9.

With its parliament, technology, and military might, Hell is an urban world, a political city. 'Pandaemonium, city and proud seat / Of Lucifer' (x. 424–5). In contrast, Paradise is an utterly rural world; it needs no government because man contains his own government within. Satan's invasion is the invasion of a sophisticated, technological, political state into an innocent, rural community; it both destroys the community and 'civilizes' it. It is the birth of the modern world.

9

Regaining the Radical Milton:
Paradise Lost, Paradise Regained,
and Samson Agonistes

During the 1930s, John Milton suffered the most sustained and most widespread attack ever mounted on his verse. The most influential of the critics involved were F. R. Leavis and T. S. Eliot—though Ezra Pound's more scattered pronouncements of twenty years earlier were also influential. The attack continued through the 1940s, was augmented by such new allies as A. J. A. Waldock, and continued through the 1950s by the followers of Dr Leavis, establishing itself as a new critical orthodoxy.[1] Leavis opened his chapter on Milton in *Revaluation* (1936): 'Milton's dislodgement, in the past decade, after his two centuries of predominance, was effected with remarkably little fuss'.

At the time these attacks seemed immensely radical. And they gained a large following from the radical young, who saw in Milton an image of all that was most oppressive, alien, and inflexible in English culture. Mark Pattison's unfortunate comment[2] that an appreciation of Milton was 'the last reward of consummated scholarship' indicates the sort of acceptance that Milton had among the conservative literary and academic establishment: Milton's verse was presented as the supreme example of the use of classical traditions in English verse: to appreciate him, you needed to have a thorough classical education. His choosing to write a poem on a religious theme also endeared him to those who saw in literature an aid to devotion—so we have such gems as John Wesley's abridgement of

---

[1] F. R. Leavis, *Revaluation* (London, 1936); *The Common Pursuit* (London, 1952); T. S. Eliot, *On Poetry and Poets* (London, 1957); id., ed., *The Literary Essays of Ezra Pound* (London, 1954); A. J. A. Waldock, *Paradise Lost and Its Critics* (London, 1961); John Peter, *A Critique of Paradise Lost* (London, 1960).

[2] Mark Pattison, *Milton*, (English Men of Letters) (London, 1879).

Paradise Lost (1763) and Sarah Siddons's prose paraphrase of it for children (1822).

It is amazing, now, that Pound, Eliot, and Leavis should ever have been associated with any stance thought to be radical. Their ensuing political record has placed them firmly with the conservative — even reactionary — forces of Western society. It was only because Milton had been placed in the pantheon of National Literary figures, and had come to be represented as the embodiment of the qualities of the establishment class — a classical education, a Christian theology, a cold, unapproachable demeanour — that any attack on him could be seen as radical. So William Morris in the height of his Marxist activities could write in a questionnaire in the *Pall Mall Gazette* (2 February 1886) that he hated Milton for his cold classicism and Puritanism.[3]

There was nothing radical in the attacks of Pound, Eliot and Leavis — in the sense in which we can call the revolutionary propagandist Milton radical. The conservative nature of their attack has in recent years become clear: it was a formalist attack, it was concerned not with Milton's ideas or themes, but with his language; their critical methodology was one that stressed a concentrated study of the words on the page, and the exclusion of biographical, historical, sociological, and political concerns. Eliot's essays on Milton and Marvell[4] were immensely influential through this century — yet one would never guess from either of them that both his subjects were active revolutionaries. Certainly the stress on Marvell as politician, which ran through practically all the eighteenth- and nineteenth-century references to him, had obscured his poetry. But Eliot put into the forefront a formalist emphasis on the language and structure of the poem that obscured the poetry in a different way — draining the works of Marvell and Milton of their political meanings.

After the American escalation of the Vietnam War, things became very different. One of the major responses to that military intervention was massive resistance to military conscription, massive opposition to the war itself. Suddenly the universities became politicized, since students were being drafted; connections between

---

[3] Jack Lindsay, *William Morris* (London, 1975), p. 298.
[4] T. S. Eliot's essay 'Andrew Marvell' (1921) is reprinted in *Selected Essays* (London, 1961), pp. 292–304.

the universities and the military were revealed; demonstrations within the universities and against traditional academic structures and habits of thought produced some academic reassessments. The idea of value-free methodologies was suddenly questioned widely and emphatically; a number of academics began to re-examine the methodologies they had unthinkingly applied over the years, to see what the meanings of those methodologies were—and if they were the meanings they wanted to disseminate. The formalist critical method, the American 'New Criticism', was not a value-free, irrelevance-free, essentialist study of 'the poem itself'—with the diversions of biography, history, and ideology removed so that the poem proper could be studied; rather it was a method that excluded the questioning and disturbing meanings of a literary work, and left a safe, untroubling analysis of technique divorced from meaning. The popularity of the New Criticism during the Cold War period, its popularity amongst conservative academics, was suddenly explained—indeed it was seen as something which *had* to be explained, and which could be explained in social and political terms: not as something separate from politics.

Other academic critics began that search for precedents for radical positions—looking to rediscover heroes of the past, sources in the past for current radical positions—just as Milton and others during the Civil War and Interregnum sought justification of their positions in the Anglo-Saxon records.

We are now in a position to rediscover Milton the radical. We are now in a position to approach Milton's work in its historical context of political and ecclesiastical revolution, to move beyond merely formalistic attacks. There is one other important gain, too, that has nothing to do with the post-Vietnam rethinking of our critical position. For years Eliot and Leavis had got away with their assertions about the nature of Milton's verse—'the inescapable monotony of the ritual', 'the pattern, the stylized gesture and movement [that] has no expressive work to do, but functions by rote, of its own momentum', 'the medium [that] calls pervasively for a kind of attention, compels an attitude towards itself, that is incompatible with sharp, concrete realisation', the way 'Milton forfeits all possibility of subtle or delicate life in his verse'. Then Christopher Ricks published *Milton's Grand Style* (Oxford, 1963)—a brilliant study that looked at the verse from just those formalist assumptions of Eliot and Leavis, but that looked more intelligently, more sensitively, without the predisposed hostility, and demonstrated its amazing sensitivity and subtlety.

The Leavis–Eliot case about Milton's style, then, has been convincingly and finally answered—by Ricks, and by various other American critics, some of whom he drew on, such as Cleanth Brooks, Isabel MacCaffrey, Jackson Cope, and W. C. B. Watkins. (Ricks's strength was his eclectic assembly of evidence—and his directing of it all to this particular formalist battle.) Now that we are confident that Milton wrote sensitively, subtly, and intelligently, we can begin to rediscover what he wrote *about*, and the stance he took.[5]

For his contemporaries Milton was notorious as someone who, quite unsolicited, wrote a pamphlet justifying the execution of Charles I; he was notorious as Cromwell's Secretary for Foreign Tongues in the Council of State, the chief apologist for the Commonwealth, the propagandist for the Republic whose works were addressed to Europe, where the Royalists lingered in exile. He was the lecher who had three wives; he was the libertine who wrote two pamphlets in favour of divorce; he was the libertarian who advocated freedom from censorship for the written word, and the hard-line revolutionary who advocated not extending such freedoms to Roman Catholics.[6] Both friends and enemies alike were well aware of his years as Secretary for Foreign Tongues. John Aubrey in his life of Milton records how during the years of the Commonwealth: 'the only inducement of severall foreigners that came over into England, was chiefly to see Oliver Protector, and Mr. John Milton; and would see the hous and chamber wher he was borne: He was much more admired abrode then at home'.[7]

---

[5] Christopher Ricks, *Milton's Grand Style* (Oxford, 1963); Isabel G. MacCaffrey, *Paradise Lost as 'Myth'* (Cambridge, Mass., 1959); Jackson I. Cope, *The Metaphoric Structure of Paradise Lost* (Baton Rouge, 1955); Cleanth Brooks, 'Milton and the New Criticism', *Sewanee Review*, 59 (1951), 3–22, reprinted in *A Shaping Joy* (London, 1971). Raymond Southall's Marxist approach in *Literature and the Rise of Capitalism* (London, 1973), pp. 113–33, works from the old Leavis–Eliot orthodoxy.

[6] On *Areopagitica* see John Illo, 'The Misreading of Milton' in Lee Baxandall, ed., *Radical Perspectives on the Arts* (Harmondsworth, 1972), pp. 178–92, and Michael Wilding, '*Areopagitica*: Freedom for the Sects', *Prose Studies*, 9 (1986), 1–38.

[7] *Aubrey's Brief Lives*, ed. Oliver Lawson Dick (Harmondsworth, 1962), p. 274.

Anthony à Wood expressed the conservative, Royalist attitude:

... the Rebellion thereupon breaking forth, *Milton* sided with the Faction, and being a man of parts, was therefore more capable than another of doing mischief, especially by his pen . . . at first we find him a Presbyterian and a most sharp and violent opposer of Prelacy, the established ecclesiastical Discipline and the orthodox Clergy . . . That shortly after he did set on foot and maintained very odd and novel Positions concerning Divorce, and then taking part with the Independents, he became a great Antimonarchist, a bitter Enemy to K.*Ch*. I. and at length arrived to that monstrous and unparallel'd height of profligate impudence, as in print to justify the most execrable Murder of him the best of Kings . . . Afterwards being made Latin Secretary to the Parliament, we find him a Commonwealths man, a hater of all things that looked towards a single person, a great reproacher of the Universities, scholastical degrees, decency and uniformity in the Church . . .[8]

At the Restoration his life was in danger. He was in danger from the law, and he was in danger from assassination. Summary revenge was likely from the Royalists. He went into hiding. His prose works *Eikonoklastes* and his *Defensio* against Salmasius were ordered to be burned by the common hangman; the Attorney General was instructed to instigate proceedings against him and an order was issued for his immediate arrest.

Then nothing happened. Milton's friends worked on behalf of him. Andrew Marvell 'acted vigorously in his behalf, and made a considerable party for him . . . '[9] though, since Marvell himself had worked for the Council of State, it is unlikely that he could do much, though now a Member of Parliament, alone. Still, he had not supported the regicides in print, like Milton. The Royalist poet and playwright Davenant is also supposed to have helped Milton, in return for Milton's protecting Davenant's life in 1650. In the end Milton escaped with his life. Several copies of his books were burned by the hangman. And in November 1660 he was arrested and jailed. But after discussion of his case in the Commons he was released, and Andrew Marvell again made a plea that the exorbitant fee of £150, to be paid to the Sergeant-at-Arms for his imprisonment, should be reduced. In December 1660 he was granted an official pardon.[10]

[8] Helen Darbishire, ed., *The Early Lives of Milton*, pp. 38–9.
[9] Edward Phillips, ibid., p. 74.
[10] W. R. Parker, *Milton* (Oxford, 1968), i. 571–6.

When he came to publish *Paradise Lost* seven years later he drew attention to that period.

> I sing with mortal voice, unchanged
> To hoarse or mute, though fallen on evil days,
> On evil days though fallen, and evil tongues;
> In darkness, and with dangers compassed round,
> And solitude.
>
> (vii. 24–8)

It is a small point—but it is an important one. It is a carefully placed reminder by Milton of his political commitment and of his judgement on the present times. Alastair Fowler notes in his edition of the poem that 'The obfuscated syntax conceals a topical allusion to Milton's dangerous situation during the persecutions that immediately followed the Restoration'.[11] The obfuscation was necessary—not only was Milton referring to his personal situation as a supporter of the regicides, he was also condemning the Restoration period as 'evil days' (he emphatically repeats the phrase), and he was also asserting that his voice had not changed; this voice of the republic asserts that he has not changed his position, he has not become silent, he has not become hoarse; he will continue to reassert his beliefs, and he is still able to.

It requires a careful reading to draw out these implications. But it is not an over-reading. To make such a reassertion Milton had to be oblique, careful. John Toland records in his *Life of John Milton* (1698) that *Paradise Lost* was nearly banned altogether by the censor:

I must not forget that we had like to be eternally depriv'd of this Treasure by the Ignorance or Malice of the Licenser; who, among other frivolous Exceptions, would needs suppress the whole Poem for Imaginary Treason in the following lines.

> . . . As, when the Sun new risen
> Looks thro the Horizontal misty Air
> Shorn of his Beams, or from behind the Moon
> In dim Eclipse disastrous Twilight sheds
> On half the Nations, and with fear of change
> Perplexes Monarchs.
>
> (i. 594–9)[12]

[11] John Carey and Alastair Fowler, *The Poems of John Milton* (London, 1968), p. 776 n.   [12] Darbishire, *Early Lives*, p. 180.

Anything that suggested that monarchs might get perplexed, anything that might reflect ill on monarchs in the work of this notorious supporter of the execution of the previous monarch, had to be looked at carefully. Even as late as 1681, twenty years after the Restoration, when Andrew Marvell's *Miscellaneous Poems* were published post-humously, three poems praising Cromwell were removed from the volume in the course of production. This was the climate of political paranoia, the context of fear and repression in which Milton was writing. And the censorship of his political prose tracts continued long after his death. In 1687 the auctioneer selling the library of the Earl of Anglesey who had just died,

> went to one of the Secretaries of State and Sir Roger L'Estrange, being much concerned because Anglesey 'by his place as a Privy Councillor might read such books as others might not, and . . . therefore he had submitted the catalogue to them'. Among the books L'Estrange did not allow to be sold were 'all Mr. Baxter's works and Milton's *Iconoclastes* in French'.[13]

Despite the dangers and the censorship Milton reasserted his views and replied to his detractors. Everyone has noticed how he stresses his blindness in the invocations to *Paradise Lost*:

> . . . but thou
> Revisit'st not these eyes, that roll in vain
> To find thy piercing ray, and find no dawn;
> So thick a drop serene hath quenched their orbs,
> Or dim suffusion veiled.
>
>   (iii. 22–6)

What the references to his blindness are stressing here, and in the invocation to Book vii, and in the reference to Siloa's book by which the blind man was healed in The Gospel according to St John in the invocation to Book i, is Milton the political propagandist, Milton the Cromwellian, the republican, the regicide. A contemporary reader could scarcely have been unaware of this. Parker in his biography of Milton records how, shortly after the Restoration,

> there was published in London a large sheet or placard entitled, *The Picture of the Good Old Cause drawn to the Life in the Effigies of Master Praise-God Barebone, with Several Examples of God's Judgements on some Eminent*

---

[13] Douglas R. Lacey, *Dissent and Parliamentary Politics in England 1661–89* (New Brunswick, 1969), p. 463 n.

Engagers against Kingly Government. Milton was the third of seven 'Examples of God's Judgements' . . . The placard pointed out that Milton had been 'struck totally blind' for writing the *Eikonaklastes* and the *Defensio* against Salmasius. His six companions in crime were all dead, most of them having been murdered. The significant fact about the sheet, of course, is its implication that God had anticipated the work of Parliament in these seven instances. Even John Garfield, the vindictive and unscrupulous reviewer of Jane's *Eikon Aklastos*, declared in his dedication to Charles II: 'I shall leave him under the rod of correction, wherewith God hath evidenced His particular judgement by striking him blind'. Royalists had long pronounced Milton's blindness an evidence of divine retaliation . . .[14]

Stressing his blindness, drawing attention to it, Milton is replying to his Royalist detractors. God has not punished him but rewarded him. He has lost his sight not as a punishment, but in order the better to receive inner illumination:

> So much the rather thou celestial Light
> Shine inward, and the mind through all her powers
> Irradiate, there plant eyes, all mist from thence
> Purge and disperse, that I may see and tell
> Of things invisible to mortal sight.
>
> (iii. 51–5)

The contrast between outward blindness and inner vision was, as numerous commentators have pointed out, a commonplace. Milton refers to: 'Blind Thamyris, and Blind Maeonides, / And Tiresias and Phineus prophets old' (iii. 35–6). But he is not merely placing himself in the tradition of the blind prophet-poet, as most commentators simply note. He is saying that by going blind while writing propaganda for the republic, he has been put in this category of prophet-poets with vision into God's ways; and to be put into that category is a selection conferred on few men, not a punishment.

Milton had written about his blindness earlier in the Latin *Pro Populo Anglicano Defensio Secunda*, the *Second Defence of the People of England*, in 1654. In this propaganda tract for the English Republic, Milton had replied to Royalist charges that he had been struck blind as a punishment:

Not blindness but the inability to endure blindness is a source of misery. Why should I not bear that which every man ought to prepare himself to

---

[14] Parker, *Milton*, i. 571.

bear with equanimity, if it befall him—that which I know may humanly befall any mortal and has indeed befallen certain men who are the most eminent and virtuous in all history? Or shall I recall those ancient bards and wise men of the most distant past, whose misfortune the gods, it is said, recompensed with far more potent gifts, and whom men treated with such respect that they preferred to blame the very gods than to impute blindness to them as a crime? The tradition about the seer Tiresias is well known. Concerning Phineus, Apollonius sang as follows in the Argonautica:

> Nor did he fear Jupiter himself,
> Revealing truly to men the divine purpose.
> Wherefore he gave him a prolonged old age,
> But deprived him of the sweet light of his eyes.

. . . As for what I have at any time written (since the royalists think that I am now undergoing this suffering as a penance, and they accordingly rejoice), I likewise call God witness that I have written nothing of such kind that I was not then and am not now convinced that it was right and true and pleasing to God. And I swear that my conduct was not influenced by ambition, gain, or glory, but solely by considerations of duty, honor, and devotion to my country. I did my utmost not only to free my country, but also to free the church.

. . . Then let those who slander the judgements of God cease to speak evil and invent empty tales about me. Let them be sure that I feel neither regret nor shame for my lot, that I stand unmoved and steady in my resolution, that I neither discern nor endure the anger of God, that in fact I know and recognize in the most momentous affairs his fatherly mercy and kindness towards me, and especially in this fact, that with his consolation strengthening my spirit I bow to his divine will, dwelling more often on what he has bestowed on me than on what he has denied.

. . . To be sure, we blind men are not the least of God's concerns, for the less able we are to perceive anything other than himself, the more mercifully and graciously does he deign to look upon us. Woe to him who mocks us, woe to him who injures us. He deserves to be cursed with a public malediction. Divine law and divine favor have rendered us not only safe from the injuries of men, but almost sacred, nor do those shadows around us seem to have been created so much by the dullness of our eyes as by the shade of angels' wings. And divine favor not infrequently is wont to lighten those shadows again, once made, by an inner and far more enduring light.[15]

Milton's comments on his blindness in the *Second Defence* provide a context in which to interpret the recurrent references to his blindness in *Paradise Lost* thirteen years later. He tells us that he went blind

---

[15] *A Second Defence of the English People* (1654), in *CPW*, IV part i, 584–90.

because he chose to write the first *Defence of the English People* against the advice of his doctors; he 'was offered a greater good at the price of a smaller evil: that I could at the cost of blindness alone fulfil the most honourable requirements of my duty'.

The direct connection of Milton's blindness and his radical propaganda is here spelled out—confirming our reading the blindness motif in *Paradise Lost* as reasserting his undaunted radicalism. The careful republican readers, the 'fit audience . . . though few' (vii. 31) would recognize the echoes. Not only is Milton reminding the reader of his blindness, the result of writing republican tracts, but he is asserting against the Royalists that his blindness was not a punishment but a reward, that he has been 'recompensed with gifts far preferable to eyesight', 'illumined by a far surpassing inner light'. Moreover he is repeating these claims made earlier in his notorious propaganda tract which had been publicly burned by the hangman in 1660. Resurrecting these particular arguments, Milton is in effect resurrecting the suppressed *Second Defence* in which they had earlier appeared. It is an oblique but telling gesture. In stressing his blindness, he is reasserting his radical beliefs; in asserting that his blindness has been compensated for by 'a far surpassing inner light', he is claiming that God has rewarded him for the radical political commitment, that God approves of revolutionary activity. His voice is indeed 'unchanged / To hoarse or mute' (vii. 24–5).

Andrew Marvell stressed this interpretation in the commendatory poem to the second edition of *Paradise Lost* (1674), writing:

> Where couldst thou words of such a compass find?
> Whence furnish such a vast expense of mind?
> Just heav'n thee, like Tiresias, to requite
> Rewards with prophecy thy loss of sight.
>
> (41–4)

Marvell well knew the significance of Milton's blindness. It was because of this 'condition' that Milton wrote to Bradshaw recommending that they employ Marvell if 'the Council shall think that I shall need any assistant in the performance of my place' in the letter of 1653 quoted earlier (p. 138). The Council appointed Philip Meadows as Milton's assistant. But in September 1657 Marvell was appointed Latin Secretary, working with Milton, whose duties by then had necessarily diminished due to the limitations his blindness had caused.[16]

Marvell, then, had direct personal knowledge of how Milton had gone blind while writing propaganda for the Commonwealth, and his statement that *'Just* heav'n' had *rewarded* Milton by making him, like Tiresias, gifted with prophecy for his loss of sight, is an unashamedly political assertion. Writing propaganda for the republic had been the right thing to do, because the way to achieve poetic-prophetic greatness is to become blind. Milton earned the reward of blindness by devoting those years of service to the revolution: the greatness of his poem is a validation of the rightness of devoting those years to the revolutionary cause. Milton's fellow-revolutionary and fellow-poet indicates in a commendatory poem how Milton's great poem is to be read; he confirms those meanings we have deduced from the poet's recurrent stress on his blindness.

The way in which Milton will 'see and tell / Of things invisible to mortal sight' is by the aid of the *inner light*: 'thou celestial Light / Shine inward'. The invocation to Book Three of *Paradise Lost* is a provocative reassertion of the Puritan doctrine of the inner light, the belief that God's word is available directly to every man, illuminating his life, his way. With the inner light, there is no need for bishops, rituals, churches, church hierarchies. It was a crucial doctrine in the religious conflicts leading to the Civil Wars—and it had clearly, too, its wider political implications. Each man can receive the word of God directly, and act as his inner light, his illuminated conscience, directs him; authorities hence become redundant and restrictive. Milton's contemporary, Samuel Butler, no lover of the Puritans, describes the Quaker as:

a Scoundrel Saint, of an Order without Founder, Vow, or Rule; for he will not swear, nor be tyed to any Thing, but his own Humour. He is the Link-Boy of the Sectaries, and talks much of his Light, but puts it under a Bushel, for nobody can see it but himself . . . He Vapours much of the Light within him, but no such Thing appears, unless he means as he is light-headed . . .

The political implications of the doctrine, with its inevitable rejection of hierarchies and church and social inequalities, were very apparent to Butler: 'His Church, or rather Chapel, is built upon a flat Sand,

---

[16] Parker, *Milton*, i. 425; ii. 1021–2; Pierre Legouis, *Andrew Marvell* (Oxford, 1965), pp. 93, 109.

without superior or inferior in it, and not upon a Rock, which is never found without great inequalities'.[17] The democratic, communistic, and egalitarian consequences of the concept of the inner light were frightening to the old order.

The primacy of the inner light is reasserted again in *Paradise Regained*. Milton has Christ reject the philosophic learning, of classical Greece which Satan offers him:

> . . . he who receives
> Light from above, from the fountain of light,
> No other doctrine needs, though granted true.
>
> (iv. 288–90)

Milton never renounced his belief in the inner light. The stress on the primacy of the individual conscience over the pressures of external authority, the stress on the accessibility to all men of 'the Spirit of god', he reasserts in one of the Archangel Michael's addresses to Adam. Having described the activities of the apostles, to whom God sent after the Crucifixion 'His Spirit within them' (xii. 488), Michael goes on to describe the corruptions of the church that followed. The clergy are stigmatized as 'wolves', a reassertion of Milton's revolutionary rhetoric, bearing a resonance for the 'fit audience' who recall the context of 'wolves' in his earlier work. It is a key word in his radical polemics.[18]

> . . . in their room, as they forewarn,
> Wolves shall succeed for teachers, grievous wolves,
> Who all the sacred mysteries of heaven
> To their own vile advantages shall turn
> Of lucre and ambition, and the truth
> With superstitions and traditions taint,
> Left only in those written records pure,
> Though not but by the Spirit understood.
> Then shall they seek to avail themselves of names,
> Places and titles, and with these to join
> Secular power, though feigning still to act
> By spiritual, to themselves appropriating
> The Spirit of God, promised alike and given

---

[17] Samuel Butler, *Characters and Passage from Notebooks*, pp. 149, 150.
[18] Don M. Wolfe, *Milton in the Puritan Revolution* (London, 1941), p. 109. See *supra*, p. 53.

> To all believers; and from that pretence,
> Spiritual laws by carnal power shall force
> On every conscience; laws which none shall find
> Left them enrolled, or what the Spirit within
> Shall on the heart engrave. What will they then
> But force the spirit of grace it self, and bind
> His consort liberty; what, but unbuild
> His living temples, built by faith to stand,
> Their own faith not another's: for on earth
> Who against faith and conscience can be heard
> Infallible? Yet many will presume:
> Whence heavy persecution shall arise
> On all who in the worship persevere
> Of spirit and truth . . .
>
> (xii. 507–33)

This is not an abstract statement nor a merely historical survey. Michael is showing Adam the future of the world, but this future is Milton's present—this is the contemporary, post-Restoration world he was living in. In these closing speeches of the poem, when Michael addresses Adam, the old political activist reasserts his convictions. Seven years after the Restoration he speaks out about the corruptions of church and state, the imposition of carnal power, physical force, on the individual conscience, the persecution of those who remain devoted to the spirit, rather than to the secular apparatus of church structures, the binding of liberty. And the reassertion is made by stating again the belief that God's spirit is accessible to all mankind, that formal church structures are not required. He had stated something of this at the very opening of his poem:

> O Spirit, that dost prefer
> Before all temples the upright heart and pure.
>
> (i. 17–18)

But the context there was such that this might on a careless reading seem simply a rejection of the temples of the pagan muses of classical epics, in favour of a Christian spirit for this new Christian epic. The possible ambiguity was something of a tactical necessity. But by the end of the poem, confident that the censors would not read that far, he is able to establish what he means by his doctrine of the inner light, in the full, explicit, ecclesiastical-political context.

Milton, then, continually draws attention to his past religio-political opinions and associations throughout the poem. When in the invocation to Book ix he tells us that in writing his epic he was 'long choosing, and beginning late' (26) it is best not to forget that one of the major reasons for his beginning late was his spending nearly twenty years in writing political propaganda; his contemporaries would not have forgotten that.

In this context the very idea of inspiration becomes problematical. The Muses are suddenly politicized. The poet's invocation to the Muses, the request for their inspiration and aid, are a traditional feature of classical poetry. But to see Milton's invocations as simply a formalistic following of classical literary patterns, is to reduce a crucial item of belief into an empty external ornament.

The idea that any individual can tune in directly to spirit, can perceive and receive and express the divine truth without any intermediary of church or state or educational authority, calls into question the necessity and validity of the authority-structures of church and state. Milton invokes the 'Heavenly Muse' in the invocation to Book i (i. 6); he opens Book iii:

> Hail, holy light, offspring of Heaven first-born
> Or of the Eternal Co-eternal beam,

identifying the holy Light with the heavenly Muse (iii. 19), and requesting that 'thou Celestial Light / Shine inward' (iii. 51–2). In Book vii he tentatively names the source of his inspiration:

> Descend from heaven Urania, by that name
> If rightly thou art calld, whose Voice divine
> Following, above the Olympian Hill I soar,
> Above the flight of Pegasean wing.
> The meaning, not the name I call: for thou
> Nor of the Muses nine, nor on the top
> Of old Olympus dwell'st, but heavenly born,
> Before the hills appeared, or fountain flowed,
> Thou with eternal Wisdom didst converse,
> Wisdom thy sister, and with her didst play
> In presence of the almighty Father, pleased
> With thy celestial Song.
>
> (vii. 1–12)

The correct naming is unimportant—the muse may or may not be called Urania. The important thing is 'the meaning': he is invoking the original muse, the muse that existed before the classical Muses. Davenant rejected inspiration in *Gondibert* for its radical political implications.[19] And when those two determined anti-revolutionaries, Butler and Dryden, allude to the Muses and inspiration, it is derisively, contemptuously: the stress is put on the badness of those poets who claim inspiration. The plea of inspiration becomes the insignia of incompetence. Butler writes in *Hudibras*:

> We should, as learned Poets use,
> Invoke th'assistance of some *Muse*:
> However Criticks count it sillier
> Then Juglers talking t'a Familiar.
> We think 'tis no great matter which:
> They'r all alike: yet we shall pitch
> On one that fits our purpose most,
> Whom therefore thus do we accost.
>
> Thou that with Ale, or viler Liquors,
> Didst inspire *Withers*, *Pryn*, and *Vickars*,
> And force them, though it were in spight
> Of nature and their stars, to write . . .

(I. i. 631–43)

The political associations are unmistakable: Withers, Prynne, Vickars: all anti-Royalist writers.[20] And the breath of inspiration that Dryden has Flecknoe bequeath to Shadwell in 'MacFlecknoe' is a fart:

> The Mantle fell to the young Prophet's part
> With double portion of his Father's art.

(216–7)[21]

Christopher Hill has pointed out that

Although after the restoration he wrote under a strict censorship and was himself deeply suspect, Milton still managed to convey many radical opinions in the later poems—using e.g. 'the parsimonious emmet' as a 'pattern of

---

[19] William Kerrigan, *The Prophetic Milton* (Charlottesville, 1974), pp. 70–82.

[20] On Withers see Christopher Hill, *Collected Essays* (Brighton, 1985), i. 133–56.

[21] *The Poems of John Dryden*, ed. James Kinsley (Oxford, 1958). See Michael Wilding, 'Allusion and Innuendo in MacFlecknoe', *Essays in Criticism*, 19 (1969), 355–70.

just equality' in a future republic—covering himself by an ambiguous 'perhaps'.[22]

The emmet is 'pattern of just equality perhaps / Hereafter' (vii. 487–8). Earlier Milton had asserted that Eden was communist, there was no private property, everything was shared except the marriage partner:

> Haile wedded Love, mysterious law, true source
> Of human offspring, sole propriety
> In Paradise of all things common else.
>
> (iv. 750–2)

There is no qualifying 'perhaps' here; the political message is slipped into a description, part erotic, part polemical, of Adam and Eve's sexuality. Sexual sharing on the Ranter model[23] is firmly rejected; the absence of private property is unambiguously asserted.

The assertions of equality and communal property and landholdings were expressed most cogently by Winstanley in the various Digger tracts. And their spirit is echoed elsewhere by Milton. After the execution of King Charles I in 1649, Milton wrote a pamphlet justifying the execution, *The Tenure of Kings and Magistrates*. Explaining the origin and development of the institution of monarchy, he wrote:

No man who knows ought, can be so stupid to deny that all men naturally were born free, being the image and resemblance of God himself, and were by privilege above all the creatures, born to command and not to obey . . .[24]

The same belief is expressed in the same year in the Diggers' manifesto, *The True Levellers' Standard Advanced: or, The State of Community opened, and Presented to the Sons of Men*. Their declaration, addressed 'to the powers of England and to all the powers of the world, shewing the cause why the common people of England have begun and give consent to dig up, manure and sow

[22] Christopher Hill, *The World Turned Upside Down* (Harmondsworth, 1975), p. 399.

[23] See Nigel Smith, ed., *A Collection of Ranter Writings of the Seventeenth Century* (London, 1983).

[24] *CPW* iii. 198–9. 'If political equality can be imputed to Milton at all, it arises from statements such as the following' (i.e. the passage quoted); Charles R. Geisst, *The Political Thought of John Milton* (London, 1984), p. 73.

corn upon George Hill in Surrey' is a powerful, moving document. It opens:

> In the beginning of time, the great creator Reason made the earth to be a common treasury, to preserve beasts, birds, fishes and man, the lord that was to govern this creation; for man had domination given to him, over the beasts, birds and fishes; but not one word was spoken in the beginning, that one branch of mankind should rule over another.[25]

This same stress, that man was given command over the animals, birds, fish, and so on, but not over other men, is repeated in *Paradise Lost*. Having seen the career of the tyrant Nimrod and the building of the tower of Babel in his vision of the future, Adam declaims,

> . . . fatherly displeas'd.
> O execrable son so to aspire
> Above his Brethren, to himself assuming
> Authority usurped, from God not given:
> He gave us only over Beast, Fish, Fowl
> Dominion absolute; that right we hold
> By his donation; but Man over men
> He made not Lord; such title to himself
> Reserving, human left from human free.

(xii. 63–71)

The stress on the individual human's freedom, the rejection of the right of any individual to rule another, is unambiguous, unavoidable. Milton here is reasserting the radical egalitarian sentiments of 1649. The spirit of his pamphlet justifying regicide, the spirit of the Diggers, is given voice again. As with the reassertion of the doctrine of the spirit available to all men, it is placed at the end of the poem: only the committed will read this far. But these radical doctrines are also placed at the end of the poem because they are the culmination of the poem's wisdom; these are the final message. The last two books of *Paradise Lost* are often neglected as uninteresting, as a routine run-through of the history of the world. C. S. Lewis writes: 'Such an untransmuted lump of futurity, coming in a position so momentous for the structural effect of the whole work, is inartistic'.[26] And indeed the position, the placing of this material in the conclusion,

[25] *Winstanley: The Law of Freedom and other Writings*, ed. Christopher Hill, p. 77. On the Diggers, see *supra*, p. 150–5.
[26] C. S. Lewis, *A Preface to Paradise Lost*, p. 129.

the climax of the poem, is momentous. It is here that Milton gives his statement about the contemporary world. Having set most of his epic in prehistory and Paradise, for his conclusion he relates firmly to the immediate present.

If it has been—and still is—a long and arduous process to remove the traditional image of Milton as 'august, solemn, proud, and (on the whole) unintelligent and uninteresting' (as Charles Williams characterized the received position in 1940)[27] and replace this with a sense of Milton the radical, how much harder is it to establish Milton the pacifist. Walter Raleigh's labelling *Paradise Lost* as 'a monument to dead ideas'[28] was a phrase that stuck—and it explains how Milton has been seen as one of the nation's glories, the Establishment poet. He had a good organ voice, and there were no troublesome ideas to worry about. But Milton the radical, Milton the pacifist—*that* Milton would have something to say to us today; that Milton would be politically and socially troubling. Let us then look at the pacifism.

After the failure of the Good Old Cause and the re-establishment of the Stuart monarchy, Christ's kingdom was no longer seen by most of the Puritan sects as a military, political objective of this world, but as a moral objective of the spirit.[29] At the end of *Paradise Lost* Michael offers Adam 'A paradise within thee, happier far' (xii. 587)—not a physical place but a set of moral precepts to prepare his soul for the kingdom of Heaven. In *Paradise Regained* Milton explores this new spiritual paradise, this quietist rejection of the world, of earthly kingdoms gained by military means.

He does not reject those earthly ambitions as totally ignoble. To do so would be utterly to condemn those twenty years of labouring for the republic. Instead, he rejects them as immature. And by an amazingly bold stroke he gives them to Christ as his childish ambitions. Christ in his maturity rejects them: but by presenting Christ as once having had those aims of using a military revolution to establish his kingdom on earth, Milton is able to exonerate the Puritans for having shared that delusion. There is no doubt that they

---

[27] Charles Williams, Introduction to *The English Poems of Milton* (London, 1940), quoted in Ricks, *Milton's Grand Style*, p. 5.

[28] Walter Raleigh, *Milton* (London, 1900), p. 88.

[29] Michael Fixler, *Milton and the Kingdoms of God* (London, 1964), p. 273. Christopher Hill, *The Century of Revolution* (Edinburgh, 1961), p. 170.

were *wrong*, but they were not *evil*: just as the angels were not *evil* for engaging in the war in heaven against the devil, simply strategically wrong. That is not the way to go about things. The angels, like the revolutionary Milton, learn by experience. Christ was able to learn by insight, without compromising the purity of his pacifism. As a child, Christ says:

> victorious deeds
> Flamed in my heart, heroic acts, one while
> To rescue Israel from the Roman yoke,
> Thence to subdue and quell o'er all the earth
> Brute violence and proud tyrannic power,
> Till truth were freed, and equity restored:
> Yet held it more humane, more heavenly first
> By winning words to conquer willing hearts,
> And make persuasion do the work of fear;
> At least to try, and teach the erring soul
> Not wilfully misdoing, but unaware
> Misled: the stubborn only to destroy.
>
> (i. 214–26)

The way the victorious deeds 'flamed' suggests the Satanic nature of this military solution—Satan the traditional military hero, Satan with his flames of Hell. But another Satanic association creeps in where it should not. Christ rejects 'brute violence and proud tyrannic power' (Satan was explicitly called a 'tyrant' in *Paradise Lost*) but his patience wears out with the stubborn—'the stubborn only to destroy'. 'Destroy' is Satan's word; 'only in destroying I find ease' (ix. 129), Satan confesses in *Paradise Lost*; and 'our destroyer' Adam calls him (iv. 749). In the Errata prefacing *Paradise Regained* we are told to replace 'destroy' by 'subdue' in this line.

My concern is not to speculate on what went wrong here. It is *just* possible that the printer, composing the line in his head, replaced the manuscript 'subdue' with his own 'destroy'; it is possible that the old righteous revolutionary Milton got carried away with a flare-up of military zeal and had Christ *destroy* the stubborn. But whatever the causes for the error, more important is the *correcting* of it. The correction shows Milton's anxiety to get the morality of Christian heroism right.

Thomas Newton in his edition of *Paradise Regain'd* (1766) stresses the importance of the emendation:

We cannot sufficiently condemn the negligence of the former editors and printers, who have not so much as corrected the Errata pointed out to them by Milton himself, but have carefully followed all the blunders of the first edition, and increased the number with new ones of their own. This passage affords an instance. In all the editions we read

> —the stubborn only to *destroy*;

and this being good sense, the mistake is not so easily detected: but in the first edition the reader is desired in the table of Errata for *destroy* to read *subdue*; and if we consider it, this is the more proper word, more suitable to the humane and heavenly character of the speaker: and besides it answers to the *subdue and quell* in ver. 218. *The son of man came not to destroy men's lives* etc. Luke IX. 56.[30]

And Newton comments on the passage as a whole, from Christ's 'Yet it held it more humane, more heavenly' (i. 221):

Here breathes the true spirit of toleration in these lines, and the sentiment is very fitly put into the mouth of him, who *came not to destroy men's lives but to save them*. The alliteration of the w's in this line, and the assonance of winning and willing have a very beautiful effect.

> By winning words to conquer willing hearts.

> —victorque volentes
> Per populos dat jura, viamque affectat Olympo.

Our author was always a declar'd enemy to persecution, and a friend to liberty of conscience. He rises above himself, whenever he speaks of the subject; and he must have felt it very strongly, to have express'd it so happily. For as Mr. Thyer justly remarks upon this passage, there is a peculiar softness and harmony in these lines, exactly suited to that gentle spirit of love that breathes in them: and that man must have an inquisitorial spirit indeed who does not feel the force of them.[31]

Christ's rejection of military means is one of the major themes of *Paradise Regained*. Indeed, that should be no surprise, for Christ's rejection of the role of military Messiah who would drive out the Romans and free the Jews from domination by foreign powers is central to the events of his life. But what I am concerned about here is why Milton should choose to write this poem celebrating Christ's pacifism—why he should stress that aspect of the New Testament story—what that means about his attitude to pacifism, what it means about his judgement on the Civil Wars, and how this relates to his

---

[30] Thomas Newton, ed., *Paradise Regain'd* (London, 1766), i. 24–5.
[31] Ibid., i. 23.

portrayal of that indubitably military hero Samson in the companion-poem *Samson Agonistes*, published in the same volume as *Paradise Regained* in 1671.

If we look back at the temptations of Christ in the New Testament Gospels of St Matthew (4: 1–11) and St Luke (4: 1–13) we notice something that the critics of the poem seem not to remark: that military glory and military conquest are not among Satan's temptations. Satan does offer the temptation of earthly rule: he shows Christ 'all the kingdoms of the world' and says 'All this power will I give thee, and the glory of them' (Luke 4: 5–6) but there is nothing to imply that this glory has to be achieved by military means. Milton puts that interpretation on the temptation.

In Book iii Satan taunts Christ with his lack of achievement, saying that at his age Alexander the Great, Scipio, and Pompey had all shown their great military prowess: 'Thy years are ripe, and over-ripe' (iii. 31). Satan, typically, is not strictly honest, in that Pompey was forty when he overthrew Mithridates, but his point about Alexander and Scipio holds. Christ does not bother to repudiate the details. Instead he tells Satan:

> They err who count it glorious to subdue
> By conquest far and wide, to overrun
> Large countries, and in field great battles win,
> Great cities by assault: what do these worthies,
> But rob and spoil, burn, slaughter, and enslave
> Peaceable nations, neighbouring, or remote,
> Made captive, yet deserving freedom more
> Than those their conquerors, who leave behind
> Nothing but ruin whereso'er they rove,
> And all the flourishing works of peace destroy,
> Then swell with pride, and must be titled gods,
> Great benefactors of mankind, deliverers,
> Worshipped with temple, priest, and sacrifice;
> One is the son of Jove, of Mars the other,
> Till conqueror Death discover them scarce men,
> Rolling in brutish vices, and deformed,
> Violent or shameful death their due reward.
> But if there be in glory aught of good,
> It may by means far different be attained
> Without ambition, war, or violence;
> By deeds of peace, by wisdom eminent,
> By patience, temperance . . .

>   (iii. 71–92)

When Satan goes on to show Christ the glories of a huge battle, Christ replies, unimpressed:

> that cumbersome
> Luggage of war there shown me, argument
> Of human weakness rather than of strength.

(iii. 400–2)

The indictment of war reminds us, with some deliberate verbal echoes, of the indictment of war in *Paradise Lost*, when Michael comments on the episode of Giants in his concluding dialogues with Adam (xi. 688–97). It relates to Milton's continuing pacifist beliefs: but it has no source in the New Testament temptations of Christ. Milton decides to interpret the earthly 'glory' that Satan offers Christ, as the glory not of *achieved* rule, but the glory of the military *achievement* of rule.

Milton's emendation of 'subdue' for 'destroy' emphasizes both the pacifist note, the repudiation of force that is the theme of his major poetry; and also his poetic method of characterization by language. Certain characters, certain moral positions, have a language that characterizes them and is specifically and solely applied to them. 'Destroy' is Satan's word and applies only to his ethic.

With these two things in mind — pacifism and verbal characterization — let us look at the climax of *Samson Agonistes*, the poem published alongside *Paradise Regained*.

Manoah asks the Messenger how Samson died:

> How died he? death to life is crown or shame.
> All by him fell thou say'st, by whom fell he,
> What glorious hand gave Samson his death's wound?
> *Messenger:* Unwounded of his enemies he fell.
> *Manoah:* Wearied with slaughter then or how? explain.
> *Messenger:* By his own hands.
> *Manoah:*   Self-violence? what cause
> Brought him so soon at variance with himself
> Among his foes?
> *Messenger:*   Inevitable cause
> At once both to destroy and be destroyed;
> The edifice where all were met to see him
> Upon their heads and on his own he pulled.

(1579–89)

The Messenger's statement 'inevitable cause / At once both to destroy and be destroyed' is not simply a pragmatic observation on what happens when you pull the roof down. It carries a moral resonance too: if you choose to destroy you will destroy yourself. For 'destroy' is Satan's word; and Satan's fate is to 'heap on himself damnation, while he sought / Evil to others' (i. 215–16); Satanic systems rebound. 'Revenge, at first though sweet, / Bitter ere long back on it self recoils' (ix. 171–2). No matter what the cause—and here the liberation of a people can be seen as a just cause and Samson seen as a liberation-fighter—the use of the Satanic tactic of destruction destroys the destroyer, morally as well as physically. And the word is repeated; the chorus call Samson the *destroyer* of the Philistines, it is their *destruction* he achieves (1678, 1681).

Destroy is not the only Satanic word offering a moral evaluation here. The *glory* that Satan tempts Christ with in the Gospels is defined by Milton as military glory—which we have seen him place as Satanic in *Paradise Lost*—'the strife which thou call'st evil, but we style / The strife of glory' as Satan tells Michael (vi. 289–90). The chorus praise the *glorious* achievement of Samson, the *revenge* he exercised:

> O dearly-bought revenge, yet glorious!
> Living or dying thou has fulfilled
> The work for which thou wast foretold
> To Israel, and now li'st victorious
> Among the slain self-killed
> Not willingly, but tangled in the fold,
> Of dire necessity, whose law in death conjoined
> Thee with thy slaughtered foes in number more
> Than all thy life had slain before.

> (1660–8)

In view of Milton's previous definitions of 'glory' and the identification of 'revenge' as Satanic, it should not surprise us that the chorus's measurement of Samson's achievement should be so barbaric; they evaluate his success by indicating how many people he has killed in one go, 'more than all thy life had slain before'. They assess his *life* in terms of the numbers it has *slain*; and they use the word 'life', not 'years' or 'career' or any other possible noun: 'life had slain' is a telling collocation. The chorus, of course, as the prefatory dramatis personae indicates, is a chorus of *Danites*; they are fellow members of Samson's tribe. They are not impartial, objective commentators, but partisan supporters.

Samson's own death amidst the slaughter is explained as 'dire necessity'—and this is yet another Satanic concept expressed in Satanic vocabulary. Dennis Burden points out:

Lacking the sense of God's providence, the devils lack enlightenment when they consider the manner in which their world is disposed. In their view they are subject either to chance or to fate. There is either no system at all, or else they are constrained by the wrong sort of system. It is these two concepts of fate and chance that need to be identified as the ideological enemy in *Paradise Lost* (65).[32]

'Necessity' is one of Satan's words. After Satan has justified to himself destroying Adam and Eve, the poet comments:

> So spake the fiend, and with necessity,
> The tyrant's plea, excused his devilish deeds.
>
> (iv. 393–4)

Samson is clearly enough an old-style military hero. He achieves his victory with massive slaughter. Most of the critical discussion about the circumstances of his final massacre has revolved round the issue of whether this was suicide or not. That is the problem which worries Manoah, and worried theologians. But it is possible for us to see now that Milton's emphasis was on the nature of Samson's 'heroism'. Given our new understanding of the precision of Milton's vocabulary, and our rediscovery of the pacifist emphasis of his work, we can see that Samson is placed for us as the old-style pagan hero, the military warrior who uses the military means of Satan—as the key words 'destroy', 'glory', 'revenge', and 'necessity' establish.

In this reading *Samson Agonistes* emerges as a meaningful companion-piece to *Paradise Regained*. Samson is the old-fashioned, active, military hero who uses the old, pagan, military, heroic means to save his people. Christ is the new hero whose method is *patience and heroic martyrdom, suffering for truth's sake* instead of killing. Samson offers death, Christ offers life. Samson uses force and kills himself as well as his enemies; Christ abjures force and saves mankind; he takes on death for himself in order that others will be saved from death and brought into eternal life.[33]

---

[32] Denis H. Burden, *The Logical Epic* (London, 1967), p. 65.

[33] For a typological reading of the two poems, with Samson as a type of Christ, see William G. Madsen, *From Shadowy Types to Truth: Studies in Milton's Symbolism* (New Haven and London, 1968), pp. 181–202.

Samson had seen his role as the instrument of God who would save his people. He adopted a public role as his people's 'deliverer'. It is just such a role that Christ rejects. Satan taunts him for 'affecting private life, or more obscure / In savage wilderness' (iii. 22–3), but Christ has already made his statement that:

> he who reigns within himself, and rules
> Passions, desires, and fears, is more a king;
> Which every wise and virtuous man attains;
> And who attains not, ill aspires to rule
> Cities of men, or headstrong multitudes,
> Subject himself to anarchy within,
> Or lawless passions in him which he serves.
> But to guide nations in the way of truth
> By saving doctrine, and from error lead
> To know, and, knowing worship God aright,
> Is yet more kingly, this attracts the soul.
> Governs the inner man, the nobler part,
> That other o'er the body only reigns.
> And oft by force, which to a generous mind
> So reigning can be no sincere delight
> Besides to give a kingdom hath been thought
> Greater and nobler done, and to lay down
> Far more magnanimous, than to assume.
>
> (ii. 466–83)

Milton had made the same point in the *Second Defence*; that until the individual rejected the tyranny of emotions, desires, and ambitions, there could be no true freedom from political tyranny:

Unless you expel avarice, ambition, and luxury from your minds, yes, and extravagance from your families as well, you will find at home and within that tyrant who, you believed, was to be sought abroad and in the field— now even more stubborn. In fact, many tyrants, impossible to endure, will from day to day hatch out from your very vitals. Conquer them first. This is the warfare of peace, these are its victories, hard indeed, but bloodless, and far more noble than the gory victories of war. Unless you be victors here as well, that enemy and tyrant whom you have just now defeated in the field has either not been conquered at all or has been conquered in vain.[34]

The psychological and the political are interrelated, inseparable. The rejection of militarism, the literary rejection of the old heroic code

---

[34] *CPW* iv/1. 680–1.

as the fit subject for poetry, the moral rejection of force as a means
of change, the rejection of political and public aims in favour of the
individual, private, moral aims—all these combine in *Paradise
Regained*. The ending of the poem succinctly expresses them. Christ
'unobserved / Home to his mother's house private returned' (iv.
638-9). No pomp, no noise, no celebration: the emphatically *private*,
not public man—the humble cultivation of moral goodness, not
the public imposition by force of something on to others. The
ending of *Samson Agonistes* is there as a pointed contrast. Manoah
announces:

> Let us go find the body where it lies
> Soaked in his enemies' blood, and from the stream
> With lavers pure, and cleansing herbs wash off
> The clotted gore. I with what speed the while
> (Gaza is not in plight to say us nay)
> Will send for all my kindred, all my friends
> To fetch him hence and solemnly attend
> With silent obsequy and funeral train
> Home to his father's house.
>
> (1725-33)

Samson is carried dead back to his father's house with ceremony.
The living Christ walks alone and unobserved back to his mother's
house. The masculine military values, the maternal peace: death
against life. It is appropriate that we should leave the old hero dead,
for his values have been superseded by the new Christian values of
'patience and heroic martyrdom', that are alive, humble, modest,
private. With these two final poems, Milton established a pointed
contrast between the old heroic ambition of military glory, the old
idea of the Messiah as military deliverer, and the new values that
the Messiah actually brought. The public world of ceremony and
violence, the attempts to create a juster world by the Satanic ethos
of war has all been replaced by the quietist ethic of private moral
victories, the preparation of the individual soul for the eternal
Kingdom of Heaven.

For too long the work of Milton has suffered from a huge mys-
tification; it has been de-historicized, it has been distorted. The
rediscovery of Milton's radicalism requires not any discovery of new
evidence, but a rereading of the material we already have. Already
Christopher Hill's work has revealed Milton's close associations with

the various radical and revolutionary groups flourishing in the 1640s.[35] We need to explore the way in which the beliefs and commitments of that period are carried through into his great poetry. We need to examine, too, the contradictions that arose when he renounced the attempt to establish by military means a radical Kingdom of Heaven on earth, and turned instead to the private preparation of the soul for the paradise within. This was a shift that in effect led to a quietist acceptance of the political status quo: 'tyranny must be, / Though to the tyrant thereby no exuse' (xii. 95–6), Michael tells Adam. But is this tragic acceptance, or strategic realism? Is this the end, or a beginning? We might remember Dr Johnson's characterization of Milton's politics:

He hated monarchs in the state and prelates in the church; for he hated all whom he was required to obey. It is to be suspected that his predominant desire was to destroy rather than establish, and that he felt not so much the love of liberty as repugnance to authority.[36]

These anti-authoritarian attitudes remain with him till the end. Johnson recognized them; later critics ignored them. They are attitudes that need to be rediscovered; as do the positive aspects that Dr Johnson denied—the love of liberty, the desire to establish a new society. Then we will have come closer to understanding Milton's radicalism. 'Milton produced *Paradise Lost* for the same reason that a silkworm produces silk. It was an activity of *his* nature', Marx remarked in his *Theories of Surplus Value* (1905–10).[37] What is now being rediscovered is how radical Milton's nature was.

---

[35] Christopher Hill, *Milton and the English Revolution*. See also Bernard Sharratt, 'The Appropriation of Milton', in S. Bushrui, ed., *Essays and Studies 1982* (London, 1982), pp. 31–44. Z. S. Fink, 'The Political Implications of *Paradise Regained*', *JEGP* 40 (1941), 482–8, explores the presentation of Satan as 'dictator'.

[36] Samuel Johnson, *Lives of the English Poets*, ed. G. Birkbeck Hill (Oxford, 1905), i. 157.

[37] S. S. Prawer, *Karl Marx and World Literature* (Oxford, 1976), p. 310.

BIBLIOGRAPHY

ALLEN, DON CAMERON, *Image and Meaning: Metaphoric Tradition in Renaissance Poetry*, Baltimore, 1968.
—— *The Harmonious Vision: Studies in Milton's Poetry*, 2nd edn., Baltimore, 1970.
ALVAREZ, A., *The School of Donne*, London, 1961.
ASHLEY, MAURICE, *The Greatness of Oliver Cromwell*, New York, 1962.
AUBREY, JOHN, *Aubrey's Brief Lives*, ed. Oliver Lawson Dick, Harmondsworth, 1982.
AYLMER, G. E. (ed.), *The Levellers in the English Revolution*, London, 1975.
BAGEHOT, WALTER, *Literary Studies*, London, 1911.
BALDWIN, E. C., 'A Suggestion for a New Edition of Butler's *Hudibras*', *PMLA* 26 (1911), 528–48.
BAMBOROUGH, J. B., *The Little World of Man*, London, 1952.
BARKER, ARTHUR, 'The Pattern of Milton's "Nativity Ode" ', *UTQ* 10 (1941), 167–81.
—— *Milton and the Puritan Dilemma 1641–1660*, Toronto, 1942.
BARKER, FRANCIS, *et al.* (eds.), *1642: Literature and Power in the Seventeenth Century*, Colchester, 1981.
BARTHES, ROLAND, *The Pleasure of the Text*, New York, 1975.
BAUDELAIRE, CHARLES, *Intimate Journals*, trans. Christopher Isherwood, San Francisco, 1983.
BAXANDALL, LEE (ed.), *Radical Perspectives on the Arts*, Harmondsworth, 1972.
BAXTER, RICHARD, *The Autobiography of Richard Baxter*, abridged by J. M. Lloyd Thomas, ed. N. H. Keeble, London, 1974.
BENNETT, JOAN, *Sir Thomas Browne*, Cambridge, 1962.
—— *Five Metaphysical Poets*, London, 1964.
BENNETT, JOSEPHINE WATERS, 'Britain Among the Fortunate Isles', *SP* 53 (1956), 114–40.
BERKELEY, DAVID S., 'A Possible Biblical Allusion in "Lycidas" ', *NQ*, NS 8 (1961), 178.
BERGER, HARRY, JR., 'Marvell's "Upon Appleton House": An Interpretation', *Southern Review*, 1 (1965), 7–32.
BERGER, JOHN, *About Looking*, London, 1982.
—— *et al.*, *Ways of Seeing*, Harmondsworth, 1972.
BERKOWITZ, M. S., 'An Earl's Michaelmas in Wales', *Milton Quarterly*, 13 (1979), 122–5.
BERTHOFF, ANN EVANS, *The Resolved Soul: A Study of Marvell's Major Poems*, Princeton, 1970.
BLAKE, WILLIAM, *The Marriage of Heaven and Hell*, London, 1975, facsimile.

BOUCHARD, DONALD F., *Milton: A Structural Reading*, London, 1974.

BRADBROOK, M. C., and LLOYD THOMAS, M. G., *Andrew Marvell*, Cambridge, 1940.

BRAILSFORD, H. N., *The Levellers and the English Revolution* (1961), Nottingham, 1976.

BREASTED, BARBARA, 'Comus and the Castlehaven Scandal', *Milton Studies*, 3 (1971), 201–24.

BRETT, R. L. (ed.), *Andrew Marvell: Essays on the Tercentenary of His Death*, Oxford, 1979.

BROCKBANK, PHILIP, 'The Measure of *Comus*', *E&S*, NS 21 (1968), 46–61.

BROOKS, CLEANTH, *The Well Wrought Urn* (1947), London, 1968.

—— 'Literary Criticism', *English Institute Essays 1946*, New York, 1947, 127–58.

—— 'A Note on the Limits of "History" and the Limits of "Criticism" ', *Sewanee Review*, 61 (1953), 129–35.

—— *A Shaping Joy*, London, 1971.

—— and HARDY, JOHN E. (eds.), *Poems of Mr. John Milton: The 1645 Edition with Essays in Analysis*, New York, 1951.

BROOKS-DAVIES, DOUGLAS, 'Marvell's Political Mysticism: Hermes and the Druids at Appleton House', *Studies in Mystical Literature*, 1 (1980), 97–119.

—— *The Mercurian Monarch*, Manchester, 1983.

BROWN, CEDRIC, 'The Shepherd, the Musician, and the Word in Milton's Masque', *JEGP* 78 (1979), 522–44.

—— *John Milton's Aristocratic Entertainments*, Cambridge, 1985.

BROWNE, Sir THOMAS, *Sir Thomas Browne: The Major Works*, ed. C. A. Patrides, Harmondsworth, 1977.

—— *Religio Medici: A Facsimile of the First Edition*, ed. W. A. Greenhill, London, 1883.

—— *Religio Medici*, ed. Jean-Jacques Denonain, Cambridge, 1953.

—— *The Works of Sir Thomas Browne*, ed. Simon Wilkin, London, 1846.

BUCHAN, JOHN, *Oliver Cromwell*, London, 1934.

BURDEN, DENNIS H., *The Logical Epic*, London, 1967.

—— (ed.), *John Milton: Shorter Poems*, London, 1970.

BURNETT, ARCHIE, *Milton's Style: The Shorter Poems, Paradise Regained and Samson Agonistes*, London, 1981.

BURNS, NORMAN T., *Christian Mortalism from Tyndale to Milton*, Cambridge, Mass., 1972.

BUSH, DOUGLAS, *Paradise Lost in Our Time*, Ithaca, 1945.

—— *English Literature in the Earlier Seventeenth Century*, 2nd edn., Oxford, 1962.

—— 'Marvell's Horatian Ode', *Sewanee Review*, 60 (1952), 363–76.

BUTLER, SAMUEL, *Hudibras*, ed. Zachary Grey, 2 vols., Cambridge, 1744.

—— *Hudibras*, ed. John Wilders, Oxford, 1967.

—— *Poetical Works*, ed. G. Gilfillan, vol. ii, Edinburgh, 1854.

—— *Characters and Passages from Note-books*, ed. A. R. Waller, Cambridge, 1908.

BUTLER, SAMUEL, *Prose Observations*, ed. Hugh de Quehen, Oxford, 1979.

CAMPBELL, GORDON, 'Milton and the Lives of the Ancients', *JWCI* 47 (1984), 234–8.

CAREY, JOHN (ed.), *Andrew Marvell*, Harmondsworth, 1969.

—— *Milton*, London, 1969.

CHERNAIK, WARREN L., *The Poet's Time: Politics and Religion in the Work of Andrew Marvell*, Cambridge, 1983.

COHN, NORMAN, *The Pursuit of the Millenium*, New York, 1957.

COLIE, ROSALIE, *'My Echoing Song': Andrew Marvell's Poetry of Criticism*, Princeton, 1970.

COOLIDGE, JOHN S., 'Marvell and Horace', *MP* 63 (1965), 111–20.

COPE, JACKSON I., *The Metaphoric Structure of Paradise Lost*, Baton Rouge, 1955.

CORNS, THOMAS N., *The Development of Milton's Prose Style*, Oxford, 1982.

—— 'Milton's Quest for Respectability', *MLR* 77 (1982), 769–79.

—— 'Ideology in the Poemata (1645)', *Milton Studies*, 19 (1984), 195–203.

COX, JOHN D., 'Poetry and History in Milton's Country Masque', *ELH* 44 (1977), 622–40.

CRAZE, MICHAEL, *The Life and Lyrics of Andrew Marvell*, London, 1979.

CREASER, JOHN, 'The Popularity of Jonson's Tortoise', *RES*, NS 27 (1976), 38–46.

—— ' "The Present Aid of this Occasion": The Setting of *Comus*', in David Lindley (ed.), *The Court Masque*, Manchester, 1984.

—— 'Milton's *Comus*: The Irrelevance of the Castlehaven Scandal', *NQ*, NS 31 (1984), 307–17.

CUMMINGS, ROBERT, 'The Forest Sequence in Marvell's *Upon Appleton House*', *HLQ* 47 (1984), 179–210.

DARBISHIRE, HELEN (ed.), *The Early Lives of Milton*, London, 1965.

DAVISON, DENNIS, *The Poetry of Andrew Marvell*, London, 1964.

DE BEER, E. S., 'The Later Life of Samuel Butler', *RES* 4 (1928), 159–66.

DENONAIN, JEAN-JACQUES (ed.), *Religio Medici*, Cambridge, 1953.

DIEKHOFF, JOHN S. (ed.), *A Maske at Ludlow: Essays on Milton's Comus*, Cleveland, Ohio, 1968.

DI SALVO, JACKIE, *War of Titans: Blake's Critique of Milton and the Politics of Religion*, Pittsburgh, 1984.

DOBSON, AUSTIN, *Eighteenth Century Vignettes: Third Series*, London, 1923.

DODD, A. H., *Studies in Stuart Wales*, Cardiff, 1952.

DODDRIDGE, Sir JOHN, *The History of the Ancient and Moderne Estate of the Principality of Wales, Dutchy of Cornewall and Earldome of Chester*, London, 1630; facsimile, London and New York, 1973.

DONALDSON, IAN, 'Jonson's Tortoise', *RES*, NS 19 (1968), 162–6.

DONNO, ELIZABETH STORY (ed.), *Andrew Marvell: The Complete Poems*, Harmondsworth, 1972.

—— (ed.), *Andrew Marvell: The Critical Heritage*, London, 1978.

DRYDEN, JOHN, *The Poems of John Dryden*, ed. James Kinsley, 4 vols., Oxford, 1958.

DUNCAN-JONES, E. E., 'A Great Master of Words: Some Aspects of Marvell's Poems of Praise and Blame', *PBA* 61 (1975), 267–90.

DUNN, WILLIAM P., *Sir Thomas Browne*, Minneapolis, 1950.

DYSON, A. E., 'The Interpretation of *Comus*', *E&S*, NS 8 (1955), 89–114.

EAGLETON, TERRY, *Criticism and Ideology*, London, 1976.

—— *Literary Theory*, Oxford, 1983.

EL-GABALAWY, SAAD, 'Christian Communism in *Utopia*, *King Lear*, and *Comus*', *UTQ* 47 (1978), 228–38.

ELIOT, T. S., *Selected Essays*, London, 1961.

—— *On Poetry and Poets*, London, 1957.

EMPSON, WILLIAM, *Seven Types of Ambiguity*, London, 1930.

—— *Some Versions of Pastoral*, London, 1935.

—— *Milton's God*, 2nd edn., London, 1965.

ERICKSON, LEE, 'Marvell's "Upon Appleton House" and the Fairfax Family', *ELR* 9 (1979), 158–68.

FAIRFAX FAMILY,*The Fairfax Correspondence: Memoirs of the Reign of Charles I*, vol. i, ed. George W. Johnson, London, 1848.

FAIRFAX, THOMAS, Lord, *Short Memorials of Thomas Lord Fairfax written by Himself*, London, 1699.

—— Poems, Bodleian MS 40, transcription in *Transactions of the Connecticut Academy of Arts and Sciences*, 14 (1909), 237–90.

FINK, Z. S., 'The Political Implications of *Paradise Regained*', *JEGP* 40 (1941), 482–8.

FISH, STANLEY E., *Surprised by Sin: The Reader in Paradise Lost*, London, 1967.

—— 'What It's Like to Read L'Allegro and Il Penseroso', *Milton Studies*, 7 (1975), 77–99.

FIXLER, MICHAEL, *Milton and the Kingdoms of God*, London, 1964.

FOWLER, ALASTAIR, *Conceitful Thought*, Edinburgh, 1975.

—— *Kinds of Literature*, Oxford, 1982.

FOX, GEORGE, *Journal*, vol. i, Leeds, 1836.

FRASER, ANTONIA, *Cromwell*, New York, 1973.

—— *King Charles II*, London, 1979.

FRENCH, J. MILTON, *Life Records of John Milton*, 4 vols., New Brunswick, 1954.

FRIEDENREICH, KENNETH (ed.), *Tercentenary Essays in Honor of Andrew Marvell*, Hamden, Conn., 1977.

FRIEDMAN, DONALD M., *Marvell's Pastoral Art*, Berkeley, 1970.

GARDNER, HELEN, *A Reading of Paradise Lost*, Oxford, 1965.

GARRY, JANE, and SHAPIRO, FRED R., 'Earlier Uses of Terms Relating to English Folk-Dance', *NQ*, NS 31 (1984), 304.

GEISST, CHARLES R., *The Political Thought of John Milton*, London, 1984.

GIBB, M. A., *The Lord General: A Life of Thomas Fairfax*, London, 1938.

GOLDBERG, JONATHAN, 'The Politics of Renaissance Literature: A Review Essay', *ELH* 49 (1982), 514–42.

GOOCH, G. P., *English Democratic Ideas in the Seventeenth Century* (1898), New York, 1959.

GREENHILL, W. A. (ed.), *Religio Medici: A Facsimile of the First Edition*, London, 1883.

GREY, ZACHARY (ed.), *Hudibras*, 2 vols., Cambridge, 1744.

—— *Notes to Hudibras*, London, 1752.

GROSS, JOHN, *The Rise and Fall of the Man of Letters*, Harmondsworth, 1973.

GROVE, ROBIN, 'Marvell', *Melbourne Critical Review*, 6 (1963), 31–43.

GRUNDY, JOAN, 'Marvell's Grasshoppers', *NQ*, NS 4 (1957), 142.

GUILD, NICHOLAS, 'The Context of Marvell's Early "Royalist" Poems', *SEL* 20 (1980), 125–36.

HALL, JOSEPH, *A Humble Remonstrance to the High Court of Parliament By a dutifull Sonne of the Church*, facsimile, Amsterdam, 1970.

HALLER, WILLIAM, *The Rise of Puritanism* (1938), Philadelphia, 1972.

—— *Liberty and Reformation in the Puritan Revolution*, New York, 1955.

—— and DAVIES, GODFREY (eds.), *The Leveller Tracts 1647–1653*, New York, 1944.

HAMILTON, K. G., *Paradise Lost: A Humanist Approach*, St Lucia, 1981.

HANFORD, JAMES HOLLY, *John Milton, Poet and Humanist*, Cleveland, 1966.

HARDING, DAVIS P., *The Club of Hercules: Studies in the Classical Background of 'Paradise Lost'*, Urbana, 1962.

HAZLITT, WILLIAM, *The Complete Works of William Hazlitt*, ed. P. P. Howe, 21 vols., London, 1930–4, vol. vi, London, 1931.

—— *Lectures on the English Poets*, London, 1911.

HERMES TRISMEGISTUS, *Hermetica*, ed. Walter Scott, 4 vols., Cambridge, 1924.

HERRICK, ROBERT, *The Poems of Robert Herrick*, ed. L. C. Martin, Oxford, 1965.

HIBBARD, G. R., 'The Country House Poem of the Seventeenth Century', *JWCI* 19 (1956), 159–74.

HILL, CHRISTOPHER, *Antichrist in Seventeenth Century England*, London, 1971.

—— *Change and Continuity in Seventeenth Century England*, London, 1974.

—— *The Century of Revolution, 1603–1714*, Edinburgh, 1961.

—— *The Collected Essays of Christopher Hill*, vol. i: *Writing and Revolution in Seventeenth Century England*, Brighton, 1985.

—— *God's Englishman: Oliver Cromwell and the English Revolution*, Harmondsworth, 1972.

—— *Milton and the English Revolution*, London, 1977.

—— *Puritanism and Revolution*, London, 1958.

—— 'Seventeenth-century English radicals and Ireland', in *Radicals, Rebels and Establishments*, ed. Patrick J. Cornish, *Historical Studies* (Belfast), 15 (1985), 33–49.

—— *Society and Puritanism in Pre-Revolutionary England*, London, 1969.

HILL, CHRISTOPHER, *The World Turned Upside Down*, Harmondsworth, 1975.

HILL, JOHN SPENCER, *John Milton: Poet, Priest and Prophet*, London, 1979.

HOBBS, JOHN C., 'John Milton's Shrewsbury Connections', *Transactions of the Shropshire Archaeological Society*, 57 (1961), 26–30.

HODGE, BOB, 'Satan and the Revolution of the Saints', *Literature and History*, 7 (1978).

HODGE, R. I. V., *Foreshortened Time: Andrew Marvell and Seventeenth Century Revolutions*, Cambridge, 1978.

HONE, RALPH E., 'New Light on the Milton–Phillips Family Relationships', *HLQ* 22 (1958), 63–75.

HUGHES, MERRITT Y., *Ten Perspectives on Milton*, New Haven, 1965.

HUNT, JOHN DIXON, *Andrew Marvell: His Life and Writings*, London, 1978.

HUNTER, WILLIAM B., Jr., 'The Liturgical Context of *Comus*', *ELN* 10 (1972), 11–15.

HUNTLEY, F. L., *Sir Thomas Browne*, Ann Arbor, 1962.

HUTCHINSON, LUCY, *Memoirs of the Life of Colonel Hutchinson*, ed. C. H. Firth, London, 1906.

HYMAN, LAWRENCE, 'Politics and Poetry in Andrew Marvell', *PMLA* 73 (1958), 475–9.

—— *Andrew Marvell*, New York, 1964.

JACK, IAN, *Augustan Satire*, Oxford, 1952.

JAMESON, FREDERIC, 'Religion and Ideology', in *1642: Literature and Power in the Seventeenth Century*, ed. Francis Barker *et al.*, Colchester, 1981.

—— *Fables of Aggression*, Berkeley, 1979.

JAYNE, SEARS, 'The Subject of Milton's Ludlow Mask', *PMLA* 74 (1959), 533–43.

JOHNSON, GEORGE W. (ed.), *The Fairfax Correspondence: Memoirs of the Reign of Charles I*, vol. i, London, 1848.

JOHNSON, SAMUEL, *Lives of the English Poets*, ed. G. Birkbeck Hill, vol. i, Oxford, 1905.

JONES, GARETH, *The Gentry and the Elizabethan State* (A New History of Wales), Swansea, 1977.

JONSON, BEN, *The Complete Plays*, ed. G. A. Wilkes, 4 vols., Oxford, 1982.

—— *Ben Jonson: The Complete Masques*, ed. S. Orgel, New Haven, 1969.

JORDAN, W. K., *The Development of Religious Toleration in England*, vol. ii, Cambridge, Mass., 1936.

JOSE, NICHOLAS, '*Samson Agonistes*: The Play Turned Upside Down', *EIC* 30 (1980), 124–50.

KEAST, W. R. (ed.), *Seventeenth Century English Poetry*, New York, 1962.

KELLIHER, HILTON, *Andrew Marvell Poet and Politician 1621–78*, London, 1978.

KERMODE, FRANK (ed.), *The Living Milton*, London, 1960.

—— (ed.), *The Metaphysical Poets*, Greenwich Conn., 1969.

KERMODE, FRANK (ed.), *The Selected Poetry of Andrew Marvell*, New York, 1967.

KERRIGAN, WILLIAM, *The Prophetic Milton*, Charlottesville, 1974.

KEYNES, GEOFFREY, *A Bibliography of Sir Thomas Browne, Kt. M.D.*, Cambridge, 1924.

KING, BRUCE, *Marvell's Allegorical Poetry*, New York, 1977.

KNIGHT, G. WILSON, *Chariot of Wrath*, London, 1942.

LACEY, DOUGLAS R., *Dissent and Parliamentary Politics in England 1661–89*, New Brunswick, 1969.

LEAVIS, F. R., *The Common Pursuit*, London, 1952.

—— *Revaluation*, London, 1936.

LEGOUIS, PIERRE, *André Marvell: poète, puritain, patriote, 1621–78*, Paris, 1928.

—— *Andrew Marvell: Poet, Puritan, Patriot*, Oxford, 1965.

LEISHMAN, J. B., *The Art of Marvell's Poetry*, London, 1972.

—— *Milton's Minor Poems*, London, 1969.

LENTRICCHIA, FRANK, *After the New Criticism*, London, 1980.

LERNER, LAURENCE, 'Farewell, Rewards and Fairies: An Essay on *Comus*', *JEGP* 70 (1971), 617–31.

LERNER, L. D., 'An Horatian Ode', in *Interpretations*, ed. John Wain, London, 1955, 59–74.

LEWALSKI, BARBARA, *Milton's Brief Epic: The Genre, Meaning and Art of Paradise Regained*. Providence, 1966.

LEWIS, C. S., *A Preface to Paradise Lost*, London, 1960.

LEWIS, DAVID, 'The Court of the President and Council of Wales and the Marches from 1478 to 1575', *Y Cymmrodor*, 12 (1897), 1–64.

LINDLEY, DAVID (ed.), *The Court Masque*, Manchester, 1984.

LINDSAY, JACK, *John Bunyan: Maker of Myths*, London, 1937.

—— *William Morris*, London, 1975.

LLOYD, MICHAEL, ' "Comus" and Plutarch's Daemons', *NQ* 205 (1960), 421–3.

LORD, G. DE F. (ed.), *Andrew Marvell: Complete Poetry*, New York, 1968.

—— (ed.), *Andrew Marvell: A Collection of Critical Essays*, Englewood Cliffs, 1968.

—— 'From Contemplation to Action: Marvell's Poetic Career', *PQ* 46 (1967), 207–24.

LOVE, HAROLD (ed.), *Restoration Literature: Critical Approaches*, London, 1972.

LOVELACE, RICHARD, *The Poems of Richard Lovelace*, ed. C. H. Wilkinson, Oxford, 1953.

MacCAFFREY, ISABEL G., *Paradise Lost as 'Myth'*, Cambridge, Mass., 1959.

McGAW, WILLIAM D., 'Marvell's "Salmon-Fishers"—A Contemporary Joke', *ELN* 13 (1976), 177–80.

MACHEREY, PIERRE, *A Theory of Literary Production*, London, 1978.

McKEON, MICHAEL, 'Pastoralism, Puritanism, Imperialism, Scientism: Andrew Marvell and the Problem of Mediation', *Yearbook of English Studies*, 13 (1983), 46–65.

MADELAINE, R. E. R., 'Parasites and "Politicians": Some Comic Stage Images in *Volpone*', *Aumla*, 58 (1982), 170–7.

MADSEN, WILLIAM G., *From Shadowy Types to Truth: Studies in Milton's Symbolism*, New Haven, 1968.

MAJOR, JOHN M., '*Comus* and *The Tempest*', *Shakespeare Quarterly*, 10 (1959), 177–83.

MANNING, BRIAN, *The English People and the English Revolution*, Harmondsworth, 1978.

MARKHAM, CLEMENTS R., *The Fighting Veres*, London, 1888.

—— *A Life of the Great Lord Fairfax*, London, 1870.

MARTZ, LOUIS L., *The Paradise Within*, New Haven, 1964.

MARVELL, ANDREW, *Complete Poetry*, ed. G. deF. Lord, New York, 1968.

—— *The Poems and Letters of Andrew Marvell*, ed. H. M. Margoliouth, rev. Pierre Legouis with Elsie Duncan-Jones, 2 vols., Oxford, 1971.

—— *The Complete Poems*, ed. Elizabeth Story Donno, Harmondsworth, 1972.

MARX, KARL, *A Contribution to a Critique of Political Economy*, London, 1971.

MASSON, DAVID, *A Life of John Milton*, 7 vols., London, 1859–94, vol. i rev., London, 1881.

MAZZEO, JOSEPH ANTHONY, *Renaissance and Seventeenth Century Studies*, New York, 1964.

—— (ed.), *Reason and Imagination*, New York, 1962.

—— 'Cromwell as Machiavellian Prince in Marvell's "An Horatian Ode" ', *Journal of the History of Ideas*, 21 (1960), 1–17.

MILNER, ANDREW, *John Milton and the English Revolution*, London, 1981.

MILTON, JOHN, *The Poems of John Milton*, ed. John Carey and Alastair Fowler, London, 1968.

—— *The Complete Prose Works of John Milton*, ed. Don M. Wolfe *et al.*, 8 vols., New Haven, 1953–82.

—— *Milton: Private Correspondence and Academic Exercises*, eds., Phyllis B. and E. M. W. Tillyard, Cambridge, 1932.

—— *John Milton: Shorter Poems*, ed. Dennis H. Burden, London, 1970.

—— *Paradise Lost and Paradise Regained*, ed. Christopher Ricks, New York, 1968.

—— *Paradise Regain'd. A Poem, in Four Books. To which is Added Samson Agonistes; and Poems Upon Several Occasions*, 2 vols., ed. Thomas Newton, London, 1766.

MINER, EARL, *The Metaphysical Mode from Donne to Cowley*, Princeton, 1969.

—— *The Cavalier Mode from Jonson to Cotton*, Princeton, 1971.

—— *The Restoration Mode from Milton to Dryden*, Princeton, 1974.

MORRILL, J. S., *The Revolt of the Provinces: Conservatives and Radicals in the English Civil War 1630–1650*, London, 1976.

MORTON, A. L. (ed.), *Freedom in Arms: A Selection of Leveller Writings*, London, 1975.

NEWTON, J. M., 'What do we know about Andrew Marvell?', *Cambridge Quarterly*, 4 (1973), 125–35.

NEWTON, THOMAS (ed.), *Paradise Regain'd. A Poem, In Four Books. To which is Added Samson Agonistes; and Poems upon Several Occasions*, 2 vols., London, 1766.

NORBROOK, DAVID, *Poetry and Politics in the English Renaissance*, London, 1984.

—— 'The Reformation of the Masque', in *The Court Masque*, ed. David Lindley, Manchester, 1984, 94–110.

PARKER, WILLIAM RILEY, *Milton*, 2 vols., Oxford, 1968.

PATRIDES, C. A. (ed.), *Approaches to Marvell*, London, 1978.

—— (ed.), *Approaches to 'Paradise Lost'*, London, 1968.

—— (ed.), *Approaches to Sir Thomas Browne*, Columbus, 1982.

—— ' "The Beast with Many Heads": Renaissance Views on the Multitude', *Shakespeare Quarterly*, 16 (1965), 241–6.

—— (ed.), *Sir Thomas Browne: The Major Works*, Harmondsworth, 1977.

PATTERSON, ANNABEL M., *Marvell and the Civic Crown*, Princeton, 1978.

PATTISON, MARK, *Milton*, London, 1879.

PECHEUX, MOTHER M., 'The Dread Voice in *Lycidas*', *Milton Studies*, 9 (1976), 221–41.

PETER, JOHN, *A Critique of Paradise Lost*, London, 1960.

PETERGORSKY, DAVID W., *Left-wing Democracy in the English Revolution*, London, 1940.

POUND, EZRA, *The Literary Essays of Ezra Pound*, ed. T. S. Eliot, London, 1954.

PRALL, STUART (ed.), *The Puritan Revolution: A Documentary History*, New York, 1968.

PRAWER, S. S., *Karl Marx and World Literature*, Oxford, 1976.

QUINTANA, RICARDO, 'The Butler–Oxenden Correspondence', *MLN* 48 (1933), 1–11, 486.

RADZINOWICZ, MARY ANN, *Toward 'Samson Agonistes'*, Princeton, 1978.

RAJAN, BALACHANDRA, *The Lofty Rhyme*, London, 1970.

RALEIGH, WALTER, *Milton*, London, 1900.

REBHOLZ, RONALD A., *The Life of Fulke Greville*, Oxford, 1971.

REILEIN, DEAN A., 'Milton's Comus and Sabrina's Compliment', *Milton Quarterly*, 5 (1971), 42–3.

RICHARDS, JUDITH, 'Literary Criticism and the Historian: Towards Reconstructing Marvell's Meaning in "An Horatian Ode" ', *Literature and History*, 7 (1981), 25–47.

RICHMOND, HUGH, *The Christian Revolutionary: John Milton*, Berkeley, 1974.

RICKS, CHRISTOPHER, *Milton's Grand Style*, Oxford, 1963.

—— (ed.), *Paradise Lost and Paradise Regained*, New York, 1968.

—— (ed.), *English Poetry and Prose, 1540–1674*, London, 1970.

ROBSON, W. W., *Critical Essays*, London, 1966.

RØSTVIG, MAREN SOFIE, *The Happy Man*, 2nd edn., Oslo, 1962.

RUBIN, ISAAC, *A History of Economic Thought*, London, 1979.

SAURAT, DENIS, *Milton: Man and Thinker*, New York, 1925.

SAVAGE, J. B., '*Comus* and Its Traditions', *ELR* 5 (1975), 58–80.

SCHOENBAUM, S., *William Shakespeare: A Documentary Life*, Oxford, 1975.

SEATON, ETHEL, '*Comus* and Shakespeare', *E&S* 31 (1945), 68–80.

SELDEN, RAMAN, 'Historical Thought and Marvell's Horatian Ode', *Durham University Journal*, 34 (1972–3), 41–3.

SHAKESPEARE, WILLIAM, *Richard II* (Arden Shakespeare), ed. Peter Ure, Cambridge, Mass., 1956.

SHARRATT, BERNARD, 'The Appropriation of Milton', *E&S* 35 (1982), 30–44.

SHAWCROSS, J. T. (ed.), *Milton: The Critical Heritage*, London, 1970.

—— (ed.), *Milton 1732–1801: The Critical Heritage*, London, 1972.

SHELLEY, PERCY BYSSHE, *Shelley's Prose*, ed. David Lee Clark, Albuquerque, 1966.

SIDNEY, Sir PHILIP, *A Defence of Poetry*, ed. Jan van Dorsten, London, 1966.

SIEMON, J. E., 'Art and Argument in Marvell's "Horatian Ode upon Cromwell's Return from Ireland" ', *Neuphilologische Mitteilungen*, 73 (1972), 823–35.

SKEEL, CAROLINE A. J., *The Council in the Marches of Wales*, London, 1904.

—— 'Social and Economic Conditions in Wales and the Marches in the Early Seventeenth Century, as illustrated by Harl. MS 4220', *Transactions of the Society of Cymmrodorion* (1916–17), 119–44.

—— 'The St. Asaph Cathedral Library MS of the Instructions to the Earl of Bridgewater, 1633', *Archaeologia Cambrensis*, 6th ser., 17 (1917), 177–234.

SLOANE, CECILE A., 'Imagery of Conflict in *Religio Medici*', *ELN* 8 (1971), 260–2.

SMITH, DONAL, 'The Political Beliefs of Andrew Marvell', *UTQ* 36 (1966), 55–67.

SMITH, NIGEL (ed.), *A Collection of Ranter Writings from the Seventeenth Century*, London, 1983.

SOMERVILE, WILLIAM, *Occasional Poems, Translations, Fables, Tables, &c.*, London, 1717.

SOUTHALL, RAYMOND, *Literature and the Rise of Capitalism*, London, 1973.

SPENCER, T. J. B., '*Paradise Lost*: The Anti-Epic', in *Approaches to Paradise Lost*, ed. C. A. Patrides, London, 1968, 81–98.

SPROTT, S. E. (ed.), *John Milton, 'A Maske': The Earlier Versions*, Toronto, 1973.

STAVELY, KEITH W., *The Politics of Milton's Prose Style*, New Haven, 1975.

STEAD, C. K., 'The Actor and the Man of Action: Marvell's Horatian Ode', *Critical Survey*, 3 (1967), 145–50.

STEADMAN, JOHN M. *Milton and the Renaissance Hero*, Oxford, 1967.

STEIN, ARNOLD, *Answerable Style*, Minneapolis, 1953.

STONE, LAWRENCE, *The Causes of the English Revolution 1529-1642*, London, 1972.

—— *Social Change and Revolution in England 1540-1640*, London, 1965.

SUMMERS, JOSEPH H. (ed.), *The Lyric and Dramatic Milton*, New York, 1965.

SUMMERS, MONTAGUE, *Witchcraft and Black Magic*, London, 1974.

SYFRET, R. H., 'Marvell's "Horatian Ode" ', *RES* 12 (1961), 160-72.

TAAFE, JAMES G., 'Michaelmas, the "Lawless Hour," and the Occasion of Milton's *Comus*', *ELN* 6 (1969), 257-62.

TAYLER, E. W., *Nature and Art in Renaissance Literature*, New York, 1964.

—— *Milton's Poetry: Its Development in Time*, Pittsburgh, 1979.

TAYLOR, GEORGE COFFIN, 'Shakespeare and Milton Again', *SP* 23 (1926), 189-99.

THALER, ALWIN, *Shakespeare's Silences*, Cambridge, Mass., 1929.

—— 'Shakespeare and Milton Once More', *SAMLA Studies in Milton*, Miami, 1953, 80-99.

THOMAS, D. LLEUFER, 'Further Notes on the Court of the Marches', *Y Cymmrodor*, 13 (1900), 97-163.

THOMPSON, E. P., 'Time, Work Discipline, and Industrial Capitalism', *Past and Present*, 38 (1967), 57-97.

TILLYARD, E. M. W., *Milton*, London, 1930.

—— *Myth and the English Mind*, New York, 1962.

TILLYARD, PHYLLIS B., and TILLYARD, E. M. W. (eds.), *Milton: Private Correspondence and Academic Exercises*, Cambridge, 1932.

TOLAND, JOHN, *The Life of John Milton* in *The Early Lives of Milton*, ed. Helen Darbishire, London, 1965.

TOLIVER, HAROLD E., *Marvell's Ironic Vision*, New Haven, 1965.

TURNER, JAMES, 'Marvell's Warlike Studies', *EIC* 28 (1978), 288-301.

—— *The Politics of Landscape*, Oxford, 1979.

TUVE, ROSEMOND, *Images and Themes in Five Poems by Milton*, Cambridge, Mass., 1957.

UNDERDOWN, DAVID, *Pride's Purge: Politics in the Puritan Revolution*, Oxford, 1971.

—— *Royalist Conspiracy in England 1649-60*, New Haven, 1960.

URE, PETER (ed.), *Richard II* (Arden Shakespeare), Cambridge, Mass., 1956.

WAIN, JOHN (ed.), *Interpretations*, London, 1955.

WALDOCK, A. J. A., *Paradise Lost and Its Critics*, London, 1961.

WALLACE, JOHN M., *Destiny His Choice: The Loyalism of Andrew Marvell*, Cambridge, 1968.

WALLERSTEIN, RUTH, *Studies in Seventeenth-Century Poetic*, Madison, 1950.

WALTON, IZAAK, *Lives of John Donne, Sir Henry Wotton, Richard Hooker, George Herbert and Robert Sanderson*, London, 1973.

WALTON, IZAAK and COTTON, CHARLES, *The Compleat Angler*, ed. John Buxton, Oxford, 1982.

WEDGWOOD, C. V., *Poetry and Politics Under the Stuarts*, London, 1960.

WILCHER, ROBERT, *Andrew Marvell*, Cambridge, 1985.

WILDING, MICHAEL (ed.), *Marvell: Modern Judgements*, London, 1969.

—— *Milton's 'Paradise Lost'*, Sydney, 1969.

—— *Political Fictions*, London, 1980.

WILKES, G. A., *The Thesis of 'Paradise Lost'*, Melbourne, 1961.

WILKIN, SIMON (ed.), *The Works of Sir Thomas Browne*, London, 1846.

WILLEY, BASIL, *The Seventeenth Century Background*, London, 1934.

WILLIAMS, DAVID, *A History of Modern Wales*, 2nd edn., London, 1977.

WILLIAMS, PENRY, 'The Activity of the Council in the Marches Under the Early Stuarts', *Welsh Historical Review*, 1 (1961), 133–60.

—— *The Council in the Marches of Wales Under Elizabeth I*, Cardiff, 1958.

WILLIAMS, RAYMOND, *The Country and the City*, St Albans, 1975.

WILLIAMSON, GEORGE, *Milton and Others*, London, 1965.

WILLIS BUND, J. W., *The Civil War in Worcestershire 1642–1646* (1905), Gloucester, 1979.

WILSON, A. J. N., 'Andrew Marvell, "An Horatian Ode upon Cromwell's Return from Ireland": The Thread of the Poem and its Use of Classical Allusion', *CQ* 11 (1969), 325–41.

WILSON, A. N., *The Life of John Milton*, Oxford, 1983.

WILSON, JOHN, *Fairfax*, London, 1985.

WINSTANLEY, GERRARD, *The Law of Freedom and Other Writings*, ed. Christopher Hill, Harmondsworth, 1973.

WOLFE, DON M. (ed.), *Leveller Manifestoes of the Puritan Revolution*, New York, 1944.

—— *Milton in the Puritan Revolution*, London, 1941.

WOODHOUSE, A. S. P., *The Heavenly Muse: A Preface to Milton*, ed. Hugh MacCallum, Toronto, 1972.

—— and BUSH, DOUGLAS (eds.), *A Variorum Commentary on the Poems of John Milton*, vol. i/3, New York, 1972.

WORDEN, BLAIR, *The Rump Parliament 1648–53*, Cambridge, 1977.

WRIGHT B. A., *Milton's Paradise Lost*, London, 1962.

YATES, FRANCIS, *The Occult Philosophy in the Elizabethan Age*, London, 1983.

ZAGORIN, PEREZ, *The Court and the Country: The Beginning of the English Revolution*, New York, 1970.

INDEX